Re Stark

DATA
COMMUNICATIONS:
A Users Guide

DATA
COMMUNICATIONS:
A Users Guide

Kenneth Sherman

Reston Publishing Company, Inc.
A Prentice-Hall Company
Reston, Virginia

DEDICATED TO

Gayle, Mark, and Samantha

Library of Congress Cataloging in Publication Data

Sherman, Kenneth.
  Data Communications: A Users Guide

  Includes index.
  1. Computer networks.   2. Data transmission
system.   I. Title.
TK5105.5.S43   001.64'404   80-17887
ISBN 0-8359-1227-2

© 1981 by Reston Publishing Company, Inc.
A Prentice-Hall Company
Reston, Virginia 22090

10   9   8   7   6

Printed in the United States of America

CONTENTS

Chapter 15   264
Communications System Transactions and Applications

Chapter 16   282
System Considerations to Evaluate

Chapter 17   312
System Implementation and Support

Glossary of Terms

Index

ILLUSTRATIONS
AND TABLES

Illustrations

Tables

ACKNOWLEDGMENTS

As with almost all efforts of the magnitude which is required to generate the quantity of material for a textbook, the primary requirement is the incentive not only to start, but to finish the initial text generation. In this regard I would like to thank the two people who were most responsible for getting this book off the ground and providing the necessary impetus and support while it was being generated. They are Ad Creemers and Jack Godwin. Their comments and suggestions provided an invaluable input to this text.

Along with the development of any project there must be support personnel. In this case almost the entire secretarial effort was provided by my "Girl Friday" Joyce Martin, without whose extra hours of typing at night and on the weekends, this book could not have been done on time.

Another area of support which is mandatory is the technical editing. In this area I had the help of two close associates. The first, Ben McCandlass provided his sage advice, especially in those areas where software functions were involved, and it is with a deep feeling of sadness and regret that Ben will not be able to see the fruits of his labor. I also lost a good friend. The second editor to whom I also owe a great deal is Rick Watkins. Rick is much better at the bit and byte level than I am and is not afraid to ask embarrassing questions if they apply. His input helped to maintain the integrity of the material.

Last but not least I owe a debt of gratitude to the many hundreds of students whom I have had in my classes over the past four years. In a subject which changes as fast as Data Communications there is no way for any individual to stay current with all of the developments which are occurring. By providing a dynamic feedback in almost every one of my classes, and keeping me informed of the kinds of things they were doing and the problems they were running into, I was able to stay more current on what was really happening in the user environment, which is to me, a much better way of learning about all facets of the subject, as opposed to reading vendor literature, magazines, periodicals, etc. In many instances I felt that I was getting more information from the students than I was giving them. I hope this book will give them back information in some of the other areas that they may not be familiar with.

K. S.

INTRODUCTION

In just about every technical subject there are literally hundreds of books available to tell you what you want to know about that subject, and in almost every case the material presented is derived from the author's special area of expertise. This experience may be at a management level, at a system design level, or at an engineering or programming level, but it has been my experience that the books fall generally into two categories. The first of these categories is detailed academic or tutorial technical type of text where the material is presented as if it was being taught at a college level course environment. The second level is at the managerial or system level which is very much oriented towards specific management decision-making environments. For the most part, the people who have to use these various systems are left to try and figure out how to relate the material they read to the particular job which they have in hand.

In conjunction with the two standard approaches, it also seems that by far the biggest problem in all of Data Communications is the ability to communicate at all. In over 23 years I have found that the hardest problem I have run into was the fact that even though the words were in the same language, the meanings of those words varied over a very wide range. The same people use different words to mean the same things, while at the same time they use the same words to mean different things. It was not an uncommon experience in the working environment to have a group of eight or ten people meet for three or four days, discuss a communications-oriented problem, agree on what had to be done, document what they had agreed to, sign off on the agreement, and then when they tried to implement the agreement, found there were entirely different interpretations of what the agreements actually were by more than half of the original parties to the agreement. The basic cause of this problem is obviously a lack of baseline definitions for the terminology which they were using. It is a sad but true fact that for the most part there are no real standard definitions for many of the terms used commonly in Data Communications, and therefore present in each group of people reading the same text material, there may be a wide variance of interpretation in what was actually meant by the writer. It is for this reason that I tried very hard in this book to provide the basic definition of terminology as to "how I was using the term" when a term was being used. The definition may not be accepted by all the readers because they may have either different opinions or experiences, but at least they will know what I am trying to say when I use a particular term.

In line with this method of terminology definition I have also tried to put together the material in this text for the people who are going to use a Data Communications System, and tried to put together the descriptions and diagrams in a manner which is neither academic nor management oriented, but at a level where anyone, regardless of experience, can relate what they are doing to the Data Communications environment. If they put all the material into context they may not be experts in the subject, but they should be able to ask intelligent questions and have a very good idea what the responses mean relative to the job which must be performed.

The material for this text has come primarily from the notes and lectures which I use in my public seminars. As such, it is drawn from a wide variety of user sources and very rarely from existing texts and periodicals which were used primarily as validations for the other sources. Because the creation of this material took place over a four-year period, it is not possible to list all of the references, and since much of the input has come from my associate instructors who did not keep lists of references either, there is no applicable bibliography for this text. In reality, it is a summation of a wide variety of experiences from a wide variety of people whose predominant efforts in a Data Communications environment have been oriented towards the user's point of view—not academic, not necessarily managerial, and not necessarily from the technical system point of view, but from the overall user's point of view in which the Data Communications environment is just one of the many pieces.

It was my original intent when generating the material for this text to present it in a logical sequence which could be understood by both the novice and the experienced user. The primary intent is to put the subject into perspective so that the reader will not be afraid to ask questions because of a fear of being embarrassed and at the same time give him a greater level of confidence that the responses will be understood. In turn this should enable the user to contribute more significantly to the growth and success of the organization he is involved with. Because after all, that is where your paycheck comes from, and if your organization does well you should do well also.

Kenneth Sherman

chapter

1

BACKGROUND OF DATA COMMUNICATIONS AND TERMINOLOGY

Prior to actually discussing the detailed components which make up the subject in any source of study, it is customary to review the background material as well as the terminology which is involved in the subject so that the reader will be better able to put the various segments of the subject into context and have a better understanding of the integrated use that results when the individual segments are put together.

In the subject of data communications there is a long history of different techniques which were used to move information from one point to another. For purposes of this text, however, the descriptions will be limited to electronic communications and the sequences of equipments and systems which evolved into the present-day data communications environment.

A.

Background

The function of communicating has been studied for many years, but only within the last 150 years or so has the capability for electronic communication been available, and only within the last 40 years has a detailed analysis of the theory of communications been made. A pioneer in communications was Claude E. Shannon who wrote a paper titled "A Mathematical Theory of Communication" which laid the groundwork for much of the present theory on communications and also identified many of the problems which would be involved, along with the concepts which could be used for the solving of those problems.

The minimum components within any communication process are a transmission source, a transmission receiver, and a medium through which the information is to be transmitted. On an elementary level this may be typified by one person talking to another. The person who is doing the talking is the transmitter, the one who is listening is the receiver, while the air is the medium for moving the information. The information moves through the medium because the molecules of air strike each other from the transmitter to the receiver, and then the receiver's ear, which is sensitive to those vibrations, is able to receive the message. The same holds true for transmission of information via the written word. The author, who is the transmitter, writes the information. The reader is the receiver, and the medium is the document which is being read. Many examples like these can be shown, but the important concept to recognize is the fact that in order to have communications the transmitter must not only be able to generate the information and the receiver be able to detect the information, but the medium used must be compatible to both ends and be in a form that does not alter or modify the transmitted information so that the receiver can reliably detect what the transmitter was sending as information.

Since most communications are transmitted through a medium which may distort the transmission there must be some means of providing a method for the receiver to obtain a retransmission in the event the initial transmission is not recognizable. When two people are talking to each other it is easy for the receiver to ask the transmitter to repeat what was said, but in the case of a written document it is virtually impossible to get back to the author for clarification. What we really have here is in the first case a two-way transmission while in the latter case, only a one-way transmission.

Figure 1-1.   Simple Telegraph System

Data communications can be looked at in exactly the same way. There is transmission equipment, receiving equipment, and a facility (the medium) which carries the information from one to the other. In most cases the medium is provided by the telephone company and, as reliable as it is, can cause errors or distortions to occur to the transmission, whether it is voice or data. This text will deal primarily with the data communications capabilities, but because the facilities used were initially designed for voice transmission, some of the voice characteristics will also be discussed.

The earliest and simplest of all electronic data communications was the telegraph system. The telegraph system basically included a closed circuit which had an electrical source, a switch which could be opened and closed, and a sensing unit which was either a light or some other kind of indicator. This is shown in Fig. 1-1.

This configuration allows for the transmission of information in one direction only, because the switch which allows current to flow in the line (and therefore light the light) can be opened and closed at only one location, while the light is at the other location.

Since it is usually desirable to be able to transmit information in two directions, there are alternative telegraph configurations which will allow either the transmission of information one way at a time or both ways at the same time. These are shown in Figs. 1-2 and 1-3.

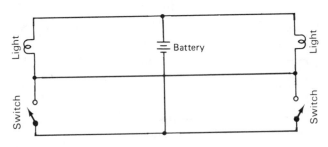

Figure 1-2.   Half-Duplex Telegraph (one way at a time)

Figure 1-2 allows the transmitter at either end to transmit; but since that would provide for the lighting of the light at both locations, only one end can transmit at a time. This is called a half-duplex transmission, because only one transmitter can be active at any one time.

Figure 1-3 shows a configuration where each end can transmit to the other end at the same time. Note that there are two independent power sources and two independent transmission paths. This mode of transmission is known as full duplex because both ends can transmit at the same time, and the receiver at the opposite end will not have any interference or distortion due to its own transmissions.

Since the telegraph mode of communications involved the closing of a circuit and the current from a power source flowing through that circuit, this mode of communication eventually evolved into what is known as the *Current Loop* interface where a specific current level (20 milliamps or 60 milliamps) was used as a standard for devices which eventually evolved into such equipments as teletypes (TTY).

The telegraph required a human interface at each end to recognize the information when it was transmitted because there was no means of storing the information while being transmitted. Teletype equipment, which could store information on paper tapes, was derived from the invention by E. Baudot in France of what was known as the *Baudot Distributor*. The Baudot Distributor allowed for the segmentation of a predefined character into five unique electrical signals which could be used to identify those characters at the other end of the line and either print the representative character or punch a series of holes in paper tape; thus the receiving location would not have to have a human in attendance. This was significantly different from the telegraph, which required the sequential transmission of dots and dashes that could not be stored on a permanent medium while being transmitted.

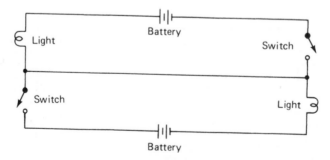

Figure 1-3. Full-Duplex Telegraph (both ways at the same time)

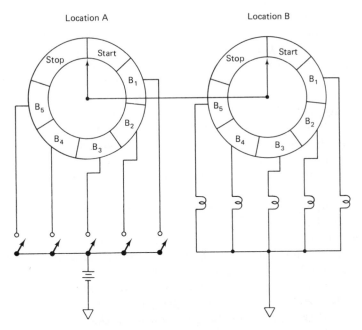

Figure 1-4. Baudot Distributor

Once the storage capability existed, the sequential transmission of information could be made from either a mechanically or an electrically stored medium at a faster transmission rate than a human operator could physically generate the information at some type of entry device. In actuality the initial teletypes transmitted information at a rate of 10 characters per second. This rate was determined by the physical limitations of the "distributor," which was a mechanical ring with a commutator that rotated 10 times per second. An example of this commutator is shown in Fig. 1-4.

What the distributor configuration provided was the opening and closing of a circuit at a relatively fast rate which allowed current to flow or not flow in a transmission line. This current could then be detected by a similar distributor at the other end, and the existence or absence of current on the line could be directly related to a specific element of information which was known as a *bit*. A bit is a contraction of the term *binary digit*, which identified the existence of two possible states of information (current flow/no current flow). The *zero* or noncurrent flow is also known as a *blank* or *space*, while the current flow state is called either a *mark* or a *1* bit.

Baudot developed a code whereby five consecutive bits of information represent a particular alpha or numeric character, and this was known as *Baudot code.* (Codes will be described in Chap. 6 of this text.) Operation of the distributor required the receiver to know when the transmitter started transmitting, and therefore each set of five information bits was preceded by a special bit called a *start bit* and succeeded by, in the case of Baudot, a *stop bit* which is 1½ bit times long (actually 1.42 bit times long). These start and stop bits allowed the receiver to recognize when to start its rotational sequence and gave it time to come to a complete stop so that it would then be able to start at the appropriate time for the next character. This was called *asynchronous transmission,* which will be described in Chap. 5 of this text.

For many years there were separate communication lines which were used for telegraph and teletype transmissions only. This was because of the on/off nature of the current which in effect was digital type transmission and, at the time, not compatible with the facilities which existed for voice communications.

As the requirements for both voice and data communications grew, it became more and more impractical to provide a circuit which could go all the way from the transmitter to the receiver because of the degradation caused by the line itself, and in addition, it became more and more desirable for different transmitters and receivers to communicate with each other and at different points in time. This evolved into the requirement for establishment of a communications common carrier. A communications common carrier is a company whose business it is to supply communications facilities to public users. The different telephone companies are examples of these common carriers.

Because of the proliferation of the facilities and carriers, the U.S. government established the Federal Communications Commission in 1934 to regulate the facilities and services offered by the common carriers. This was done so that standards could be established for all users, making it possible for any one user to communicate through any of the common carriers to any other user anywhere within the United States.

At this point we have to take a look at the difference between the teletype kind of transmission and the voice transmission. Since teletype transmission consisted of the existence or absence of a current on a line, there was very little need for providing anything other than a conducting path for the current to flow. On the other hand, voice communications required a totally different kind of capability. The human voice is made up of frequencies with the most energy in approximately the 200 to 4000 Hertz range. This meant that whatever medium was used to transmit voice information, at least those frequencies must be supported. Due to the preponderance of voice frequencies in the middle range, it was eventually decided to establish as a standard a frequency range 300 to 3300 Hertz (cycles per second) which would be used for all voice communications on common carrier facilities. Even though the entire bandwidth to be provided was actually 4200 Hertz, the usable portion for voice would be between 300 and 3300. The range between 0 and 300 Hertz would be used, when applicable, for data transmission at rates of up to 150 bits per second, while the range of 3300 Hertz to 4200 Hertz would be used by the common carriers for signaling purposes to establish the circuits during dialing conditions, so that when the circuit was completed voice transmission could take place on the 300 to 3300 Hertz bandwidth.

The frequency spectrum mode of transmission (voice), not being compatible with the loop current mode of transmission, meant that normally two separate types of facilities would have to be maintained. Because of the desirability of communicating between teletype and teletype-like terminals using the facilities of the voice grade network, it became necessary to establish an interface which could be used by the teletype kind of equipment to interface with the voice grade facilities. The result of this requirement was the establishment of the RS-232 interface which allowed for the change of the current loop type interface into a voltage type of interface, which could then be converted through modulation equipment to the frequency range that could be supported on voice grade facilities. The voltage interface therefore opened up the entire voice grade network to use by digital type terminal and computer equipments. Except for the current growth of digital transmission networks, data communications is still almost totally dependent on the voice grade network for transmission of information.

As the data communications traffic increased, it also became necessary to establish some type of network for movement of information between multiple points which could not be predetermined utilizing the existing voice grade network capabilities. This involved the specific addressing of traffic between one terminal and another terminal where information had to be routed through a central point. A representative configuration of these types of connections is shown in Fig. 1-5 and was known as a *torn tape center*, typically utilizing teletypes. It consisted of the transmission of information from paper tape on one of multiple teletypes on a particular line to a teletype machine located at a central site. An operator would physically read

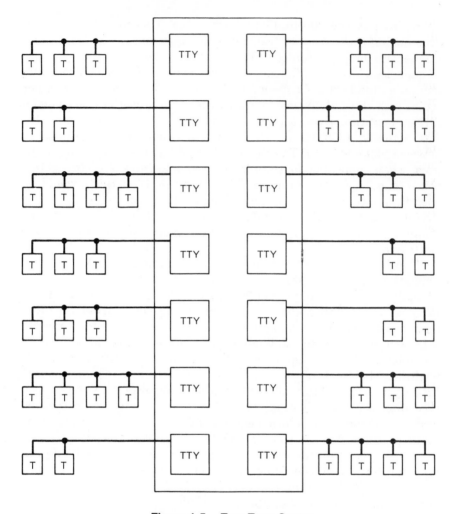

Figure 1-5.   Torn Tape Center

the tape, tear it off of the teletype it was received on, physically walk
over to the line on which the addressed teletype was resident, and
then transmit the message from the central-site teletype on the
outgoing line to the addressed terminal. This mode of communication
lasted for many years and in some places is still used today.
Operators are required to recognize the punched paper tape information and then establish the operating process whereby the information is to be transmitted to the final sites addressed. In effect, this

consists of what is known as *store-and-forward* communications, which graphically illustrates the problems encountered in almost every single area of data communications routing and handling.

Some of the most obvious of the problems which can be seen in a torn tape center are the conditions which arise when an addressed terminal is unavailable, the line is unavailable, or there are messages which were received previously but have not been transmitted out on that same line yet. It is relatively easy for the operator to establish a queueing situation and even a priority transmission situation, but the conversion of those types of functions to an automated mode is an extremely complex and comprehensive process. The entire queue management, buffer management, routing, priority, and validation processed must be automated in a software process so that all combinations and permutations of potential conditions which may occur are recognized and handled in the software.

If a single condition which is not planned for occurs on the line, then the program will in all likelihood malfunction or even abort. It is for these reasons that the most sensitive interfaces in all networks are those which involve the movement of data between points. This is over and above the problems which exist due to the inherent degradations that exist on a communication line all by itself.

Another area which is important to recognize in the communications environment is that when data processing itself started to evolve, the potential interfaces with communication equipments were not considered. It wasn't until the late 1940s and early 1950s that the data processing evolution got to the point where it seemed to be desirable to connect remote terminals to computer processing sites using data communications techniques.

Since Baudot code, which had no error-checking capability (no parity), was still used with teletypes, it was not a code that could be utilized to move information from one machine to another because there was no way for the machines to tell if there was an error in that information. It was not until 1963 that a standardized code was developed that was highly suited for information transmission. This was the ASCII code which was an 8-level code containing both a parity capability and 7 bits for information, which meant that all of the possible combinations of alphas, numerics, and controls could be identified with a unique bit configuration. ASCII was upgraded in 1967 with respect to the control characters identified, and this is the predominant code which is used today as a worldwide standard. At the same time ASCII was being developed, a new teletype was developed which could utilize the 8-level code (Model 33). Other 8-level code terminals followed shortly thereafter.

What also occurred in the same relative time frame was the integration of the communications type terminals with the data processing machines; but since the data-processing-oriented personnel were more interested in performing numerical functions and applications, they totally ignored the communications interface. For that reason it was left up to the designers of communications equipment such as front ends, store and forward message switches, concentrators, etc., to design interfaces, mostly in an emulation mode which would take the communication type inputs and convert them to a form which the data processing machines could interface with. The end result was that, for a long time, the only progress which was made in the area of communications interfaces was made by the manufacturers and vendors of communications equipments. It was not until the mid-1960s that the requirement was so overwhelming that manufacturers and vendors of data processing equipments turned their energy toward developing better communications interfaces.

The situation which exists today, therefore, is one where the vendors of data processing machines are developing software packages which will permit movement of data between different points in a network under individual or centralized control, while at the same time the vendors of communications equipments are developing faster and more reliable equipments to operate over the existing communication facilities. Added on top of both these areas of progress, we have the new technology of digital transmission and satellite communications which are being addressed by both parties. What has continued to develop is an integrated system where data can be processed at multiple points within a network, and if the capability does not exist to process the information at one location, it can be moved quickly and easily to another location where it can be processed. This is the concept of distributed network design.

One other major function which is being developed by the vendors of communication equipment is the capability for performing on-line/real-time monitoring and analysis of communication facilities, so that when there are problems anywhere in the network, they can be analyzed from a centralized location and within a relatively short period of time (like 10 minutes). Better than 90 percent of the problems which occur can be isolated so that the appropriate maintenance personnel can be called out to fix the problem.

With the development of new products and services coming at such a fast rate, there still is one very significant area which must be addressed by all personnel involved with data communications networks. That is the question of terminology. It has often been said that one of the biggest problems involved with communications is "communicating." Different people may use the same term to mean different things and at the same time use different terms to mean the same thing. If for no other reason than being able to understand what the other person is saying, it is therefore necessary to establish a baseline reference of terminology which can then be used by all parties to discuss, analyze, and then decide on a specific course of action. Everyone involved in the decision-making process will then be fully aware of what the others are talking about and know that all are agreeing to the same course of action, and that course of action will mean the same thing to all of the parties. A baseline for starting this kind of dialogue is depicted in Appendix I of this text.

QUESTIONS

1. What are the three minimum components which make up a communications process? Give two common examples of this process.
2. For the simple telegraph system draw a diagram for each of the following cases.
   a. Transmit one direction only (simplex).
   b. Transmit both directions, but only one way at a time (half duplex).
   c. Transmit both directions at the same time (full duplex).
3. Draw a diagram of a Baudot Distributor and describe the functions of the segments which make it up.
4. What is the frequency bandwidth of a voice grade line? How much is actually used for voice transmission?
5. What is the primary code used for data transmission today? What are the two primary features which make it efficient for use in a communications environment?
6. What is the single most significant problem in communications?

chapter

2

COMMON CARRIERS

With respect to communications, both voice and data, the organizations which provide the overwhelming majority of hardware, services, and facilities are the *common carriers*. The common carriers are under the jurisdiction of the Federal Communications Commission when dealing with interstate traffic and the State Public Utilities Commission when dealing with intrastate traffic. These regulatory agencies establish the standards, rules, tariffs, etc. which determine what the carriers can offer and how much they can charge for those offerings. The common carriers on the other hand must maintain a capability which meets a specific set of standards such that they can all interface with each other and therefore provide the capability for end users to obtain services, connections, interfacing hardware, etc. between any two points within the United States. After interfacing with the International Record Carriers, who do the same thing for international traffic, the end users can then communicate anywhere around the world.

A.

Telephone Companies/Specialized Carriers/VANs

There are many different common carriers, of which the largest by far is the American Telephone and Telegraph Company (AT&T). AT&T constitutes more than 80 percent of the common carrier capability in the United States. It operates in all of the contiguous forty-eight states either through total ownership of the local telephone company or through a working relationship with the local telephone company. Any telephone company in which AT&T has an interest is part of the Bell System. The Bell System is comprised of approximately 23 different operating companies, of which the Southwest Bell Telephone Company is the largest. After AT&T, the second largest telephone company is General Telephone and Electronics, which provides approximately 10 percent of the common carrier capabilities in the U.S.

The remaining telephone companies, and there are approximately 2000 of them, come in all different sizes, some as small as one hundred telephones operated by a single family. Most of these non-Bell telephone companies are members of the United States Independent Telephone Association (USITA), which supports and helps them in regulatory proceedings and provides business assistance which they could not otherwise get.

Any time a user has a requirement for common carrier services which involve more than one state, it is the responsibility of AT&T long lines department to provide the total capability. This is done by interfacing all of the involved telephone companies, regardless of size, so that the user only has to interface with a single organization, that being AT&T Long Lines. When there is more than one carrier involved within a particular state, the telephone company which handles the primary end of the service is usually the one which is responsible for integrating the service of all the telephone companies which are involved in providing the service within that state.

The oldest of the common carriers is Western Union International. The primary services offered by Western Union International are public telegraph and money order, public switched-teletype services (both Telex and TWX), computer-switched teletype and data terminal services, and a wide variety of communication facilities primarily dealing with dedicated network facilities.

Western Union International is also one of the International Record Carriers (IRC) which are tariffed to provide communications on an international basis. The three largest IRCs are International Telephone and Telegraph World Communications, Radio Corporation of American Global Communications, and Western Union International (which is now owned by Xerox). These carriers are allowed to operate between the United States and other countries from specified "gateway" cities only. Some of these gateway cities are New York, Washington, Miami, New Orleans, Los Angeles, and San Francisco. There are a few other smaller IRCs, and with the expansion of packet type services in the future, if existing IRCs do not handle that service, in all probability a new IRC will be established which will specialize in packet capabilities. (Packet transmission will be described in Chap. 15.) The services provided by IRCs cover the full range of telephone, telegraph, international Telex, radiogram and different types of data transmissions at a wide variety of speeds in the international market.

One of the long-term results of the problems which have arisen due to the interfacing of different common carriers for different services has been the emergence of a new group of carriers who are known as *specialized common carriers*. Because the transmission of data over facilities which were built primarily for voice commmunication has presented many problems to the user over the years and because of the new laws involving the interconnection of noncarrier-built telephone and special data facilities, several independent operators have applied for and have been granted common carrier status. The primary offerings of most of these carriers are the facilities and services which are more tailored to the requirements of organizations who must transmit high volumes of data.

There are two different groups that make up the specialized common carriers. They are the carriers who build and/or lease facilities and in turn sublease those services to the end user, and then there are the specialized common carriers who build and/or lease facilities, add some type of service to those facilities to increase the value of it, and then sublease the entire service to the end user. The latter type of organization is called a *Value-Added Network Carrier* (VAN) and is most often the organizations who offer time-sharing services.

The majority of the specialized common carriers (SCCs) offer a service which is primarily leased line facilities on an interstate basis. The SCC will interconnect with the local telephone company at each end of the leased line in order to provide a local loop which will then connect the end users to each other. In many cases the techniques which these SCCs use is the same as the Bell System, and in some cases the services provided may be in reality excess capacity on facilities which the company uses for its own in-house communications. Many companies such as Southern Pacific Communications Company, New York Penn Microwave Corporation, and Microwave Communications of America have facilities which they originally built for their own in-house use and when the in-house use did not require the full capabilities of the existing network, these companies applied for and were granted tariffs to sell or lease services utilizing that excess capacity and must therefore be defined as common carriers. As a common carrier they are required to meet the same regulatory standards as the telephone companies but are allowed to file for different tariffs, which means mostly a different pricing structure. If the technical standards which they are designed to meet are different from those which are provided by the telephone companies, this must be spelled out in the tariff, but in any case they must be compatible with the standard telephone company interfaces at the connection point to those telephone companies from their own dedicated network segments.

In the case of the VANs the oldest of them are the time-sharing houses such as Tymshare, University Computing Company, Boeing Computer Services, National CSS, and others. The value added on the network was to provide computing capability and data base storage on a time shared basis utilizing a common carrier network. Because the time-share operator was performing computations on data being transmitted from a remote location over a common carrier network, the operation was determined to be a data processing operation and not a communications function; therefore the time-share houses were not required to obtain common carrier status. If, however, the computer to which the terminals were connected were performing switching type functions only, the organization would become subject to regulations as a common carrier. It is interesting to note that some of the VANs also provide switching services and are at present involved in legal maneuvering with the FCC because they provide a combination of value-added functions and switching, which means they are therefore in the gray area of whether they should be tariffed or not. For those services where there is a question, it may be provided; but a portion of the revenue must be kept in an escrow type account so that if it is eventually ruled against them, the VANs will have to refund some portion of the revenue back to the users who paid for the unauthorized service. With the rate of progress to date it may be many years before this question is finally resolved.

To compound the confusion of carrier types a new type of value-added network operator has come into being in the last few years. These are the packet network operators, with the two largest of these being Telenet (owned by GT&E) and Tymnet (a division of Tymshare). In addition, not only have other companies decided to get into the packet business, but AT&T has announced a packet service which is expected to begin in the mid-1980s time frame. IT&T is one of the organizations in the process of installing a packet network. Initially it will be between New York and Houston, which will serve the southeastern United States. What makes these packet operators unique is the fact that they will use specially dedicated facilities to move information via what are known as *packets*. These packets are specific length segments of a message which are moved through the network as individual entities and then reassembled at the final destination for output to the receiving end of the user's connection. The user has a connection to the packet operator at each end of the packet network, and it is the responsibility of the packet operator to move the information between those ends where the user will receive a message at each receiving location as if it were received on a direct connection from the transmitting end. Because that is a common user type of network, the packet operators are required to file tariffs with respect to interfaces, services, and facilities. In almost all cases, however, the rates which are charged are based on volume of data and not distance. Packet will be discussed further in Chap. 15.

B.

Types of Service

The common carriers provide hardware, physical facilities such as communication lines, and transmission services. The services which are offered by the common carriers fall into three separate categories. They are voice, data, and others such as facsimile, television, and radio. The services are provided over either a private line which the user contracts for on a monthly basis or a dial-up line which uses the common carrier circuit switching facilities to establish a circuit every time the user wants to communicate between specific transmitting and receiving locations. The service may be offered with equipment leased from common carrier or third party leased equipments, or user-owned equipments, except that when a user provides his own interface equipments, either a special interface device called a *connecting arrangement* must be provided by the phone company or the user's device must be certificated. Certification was a recent FCC ruling which stated that if the user's equipment meets the interface requirements for connection to a voice grade line then it can be connected directly to that line. Both data and voice capabilities can be utilized over either the dedicated or dial-up facilities. The dial-up facilities are known as *Direct Distance Dial* (DDD) facilities. These dedicated and dial network facilities are by far the most common services offered by the common carriers.

Another widely used service which can be used for either voice, data, or both, is Wide Area Telephone Service (WATS). WATS is a bulk type of service where the user pays a fixed rate for a specified maximum amount of calls on a line with a specified maximum time utilization on a monthly basis. All calls made on a WATS line are specifically logged as far as quantity and length so that the user can see the specific utilization of that line. The maximum quantity at this time is 240 hours of utilization per month, which is called Business Day WATS. Any utilization over the 240 hours is billed as overtime charges. At the same time there is a limitation of 14,400 calls which have to be made on a monthly basis. This averages out to a message length of one minute per call for 240 hours. The reason for this limitation is the fact that when users started making computer to computer calls the average length of call was between ten and twenty seconds, and in each case, the call was routed over the DDD facilities, utilizing all of the switching network. In order to prevent this heavy load being generated from computerized calling, the telephone company put a maximum of 14,400 calls per business date month, over which there is a heavy overtime charge per call. WATS is also tariffed on a more limited basis such as a specific quantity of hours per month.

WATS comes in two forms. There is outbound WATS, which has a geographic limitation on the distance a call can be made. There are five "bands" of WATS for which band 5 covers the entire continental United States. Band 1 is usually the states which are contiguous to the state in which you are located. Band 2 is the states which are contiguous to the Band 1 states. Bands 3, 4, and 5 eventually cover all of the states. In order to determine which band classification is applicable in a particular environment, the user should contact his local telephone company who can provide the necessary identification of which remote cities are in which WATS bands for each specific user location from where calls will be made.

The second type of WATS line is known as inbound WATS and is sometimes called an 800 number. When a caller dials an 800 number the call is charged to the receiving party, and this service is normally utilized when the caller will be providing some business function in return for which he doesn't pay for the call. It should be noted that all WATS described here are interstate WATS. There are also intrastate

WATS but these are regulated by the State Public Utilities Commission and are very much different in rates than the interstate WATS. It is for this reason that most inbound WATS lines usually specify an 800 number to be called and then say, "for state X" dial a different 800 number. The state in which the different number must be dialed is the state that the WATS calls are being directed to, so for that state the residents must call a different 800 number since their call will be an intrastate WATS call.

There is also a measured WATS service where there is a flat rate for a specified amount of time which the user has contracted for, and if the calling time exceeds that number, the user will be charged with overtime rates.

Data transmission can take place on any voice grade facility for those companies who already have WATS lines, and if those lines are not utilized for voice to their full availability, they can be used very efficiently for data communications, getting what is, in effect, free transmission time. Along with this combined capability is the availability of hardware devices which can monitor and measure WATS utilization. These devices will identify the calling extension, called location, and duration of call on any WATS line so that the communications manager can determine whether an effective utilization of his facilities is being made. Based on this information, if there are times of the day when it would be desirable to set aside specific periods for either voice or data communications, the WATS facility could be utilized to its maximum benefit.

Another extensively used service is what is known as *Foreign Exchange Service* (FEX). A foreign exchange service is in reality a leased line which allows a user in one exchange area to make a local call to an exchange area which would be a toll call under normal circumstances. The way this service is implemented is that a leased line is provided from the local exchange to the foreign exchange and is paid for at regular leased line rates on a monthly basis. Depending on the specific service desired, callers at only one end or at either end are then able to initiate calls as if they were at the foreign exchange location. Many companies have extensive foreign exchange networks where they can make calls across the country on this type of service by dialing an access code in their local area which connects them to the specific foreign exchange line for the city they want to talk to. Because regular voice grade facilities are involved here too, either voice or data can be transmitted as desired.

The existing tariff for long distance calling is called the *HiLo rate*. This means that AT&T has identified certain cities as being high density calling areas. A HiLo rate is one which establishes a specific rate (lower) for calls between two high density cities or locations, while at the same time specifying a higher cost for calls which are made between a high density and low density or two low density cities. This specific tariff has been ruled discriminatory by the FCC, and AT&T is in the process of developing a new tariff schedule. The proposed tariff is called *Multischedule Private Line* (MPL). Until the MPL rate is finalized the HiLo rates will remain in effect, but it should be noted that the MPL rates, which appear to be higher, when implemented will mean all long distance dialing costs will be changed and the user must determine on a network by network basis what his monthly cost will be.

Another service which is provided by the common carriers is called a *tie line*. A tie line is a leased line which connects two specific branch exchanges so that if a phone connected to the tie line is picked up at any one of the locations, the instruments at the other locations will ring immediately without the necessity for dialing. This type of service is normally used for voice communications because if data was to be transmitted there would be a predetermined connection at each end and a ringing would not be required.

There are other specialized services provided, mostly at user's facilities, and these are determined individually by the capability of the local Private Branch Exchange (PBX) or Private Automatic Branch Exchange (PABX) and involve mostly in-house services. Any questions regarding the capability of these services should be referred either to the local telephone company or the third party vendor to determine what specifically will be provided and what the costs for those services are.

C.

Regulatory Agencies

The common carriers are regulated by two different agencies. For services which are provided between two or more states the common carrier is regulated by the Federal Communications Commission (FCC), while on services which are provided within a single state's boundaries the common carrier is regulated by the Public Utilities Commission (PUC) of that state. The FCC was formed as part of the Communications Act of 1934 to regulate all interstate communications and also has jurisdiction over international communications with respect to the interface in the United States.

The common carrier is accountable to the regulatory agency for specific geographic areas of operation, for specified services, for uniform policies applied to all users, and for establishing a maximum fixed return on investment. The geographic areas of operation are sometimes called "franchised monopolies" when referring to the local telephone company. The value of these controlled monopolies is that they prevent duplication of services in high density areas and at the same time prevent absence of service in the other areas. The natural problems of this type of system are the lack of competition and potential lack of choice of services, but this is exactly what the regulatory agency has been given the charter to monitor and control in the public interest, while at the same time allowing the carrier to earn a reasonable profit.

The document that a common carrier submits to the regulatory agency for permission to offer a service to the user is called a tariff. The tariff specifies the service to be offered, the rates to be charged, and the requirements to be imposed on both the carrier and the user. The tariff must be provided in sufficient detail for the regulatory agency and the using groups to identify clearly the equipment and/or services being offered, as well as the basis for which the rates will be established. The user's liabilities must be clearly understood especially concerning such things as penalties to be paid for maintenance or repair service eventually found to be the customer's fault. At the same time there are penalties established against the carrier for not maintaining the service to the standards specified in the tariff.

All tariffs which involve interstate service will be established by the FCC, while the tariffs for intrastate service will be established by the individual PUCs. For those cases where the dial-up facilities of the telephone company network are used, the terminal and local equipments will be tariffed on an intrastate basis and only the charge for the specific call itself will be on an interstate basis if the call crosses a state line when it is made.

With regard to uniform policies, the common carrier cannot show any discrimination to any user or group of users when offering services to the public. At the same time no preferential treatment can be given to any user or group of users. This means that rates must be uniformly applied even though it may actually cost the carrier more to provide the service to one particular user than to another, such as for local and remote geographic locations.

The money which a common carrier is allowed to make is regulated with regard to a specific rate of return on investment. The net profit allowed to the stockholders is controlled by the rates allowable for the various tariff services. The regulating agencies have the right to, and actually perform, audits of the financial records of the carriers, and all of the regulatory decisions are supposed to be based on the necessity and/or benefit to the using public. The common carrier rates are established via tariff submission to the regulatory body concerned with that particular tariff and are submitted at least thirty days prior to the date the new rate is supposed to take effect. Written testimony from expert witnesses in the area of both financial and technical expertise is submitted to the regulator and in turn distributed to potentially interested parties. This written testimony is required to justify and support the new rate for the service being offered and can be rebutted by written testimony of the user groups. There is a whole sequence of events which takes place during this phase, which is called the prehearing phase, and if a decision cannot be made in its final form, then the rate may be allowed to become effective but with an "accounting order" placed on the carrier which will require the deposit of any difference in revenues in an escrow account and eventually be returned to the users in the event that the new rate is not approved.

Finally, a rate hearing is held and all testimony of all witnesses, both for and against the common carrier, is heard along with cross examination by opposing parties. If approved, the new rate becomes law by issuance of a regulatory order. This is usually where the procedure ends, but either side can appeal through the appropriate courts. This has been happening more frequently in recent years and in many cases rates have been held up for years before finalization.

As a result of some Congressional action initiated in 1978, a new Communications Reform Act is in the process of being drafted which may radically change the present mode of regulation and tariffing. The new Communications Reform Act (CRA) proposes the elimination of the FCC and its replacement with an organization of more limited powers and the allowance of the telephone companies to perform some data processing type functions such as message switching. Since Congressional action in this area is normally a lengthy procedure, it is quite possible that the CRA will take years to pass; but it should be noted by the user that the long-range prognosis seems to be that the telephone companies will get more into the data processing business than they are today.

D.

Tariffs

As was stated in the previous sections, the tariffs are the documents which identify the services to be provided, the charges for those services, and the liabilities of both the common carrier and the user. Each tariff has a separate identifying number which specifies in detail all of the attributes of that particular service. The most common of the tariffs are FCC260, which specifies the interstate private line voice grade facility services, and FCC259, which does the same thing for WATS. Every single service provided by every common carrier is covered in a specific tariff, either under the FCC for interstate service or the PUC for intrastate service. Copies of each of the tariffs can be obtained from AT&T Long Lines in New York City for the interstate tariffs and from the Public Utilities Commission of each state for that particular state.

E.

Interconnection/Certification

Interconnection has been defined as the ability to utilize communications equipment and services that are not provided by the local telephone company in conjunction with equipment or facilities that were provided by that telephone company. The term *interconnection* is generally used in connection with the specialized common carriers, although recently it has also been used in relation to specific end users who are buying compatible equipment from manufacturers other than the common carriers and then integrating those equipments into the networks which are obtained from the common carriers. It is economically advisable in many cases to purchase equipment, and since the telephone company only leases that equipment, it may be more desirable for users to connect equipments to the network which were not obtained from the common carrier.

Up until 1962 any noncarrier device which a user wanted to connect to the common carrier network had to have a device called a *data access arrangement* (DAA) which would provide an interface between the user's equipment and the common carrier network. In 1961 the famous "Carterphone" decision was handed down by the United States Supreme Court. Thomas Carter brought suit against the Public Telephone Companies to allow direct connection of his acoustically coupled Carterphone without a special interfacing device or DAA. This suit was ruled in favor of Carter and was considered to be the birth of interconnection.

The next step in the interconnection sequence was the filing for common carrier status by Microwave Communications Incorporated to supply specialized microwave communications services for trucking companies between the St. Louis and Chicago areas. After six years in the courts, MCI was allowed to compete for some of the specialized communications services in parallel with the already existing common carriers (AT&T and Western Union). While the MCI suit was being considered, the Carterphone situation was also referred back to the courts, and in June 1968 the courts ruled that equipment not owned by the telephone company could be connected legally to the public network, and the FCC ordered both AT&T and Western Union to rewrite their tariffs so that the interconnects would be allowed.

In 1969 AT&T filed a new tariff which showed a connecting arrangement black box which the common carriers were to supply which would enable the interconnection of "foreign" equipment to the public network without any degradation of service. At the same time MCI was granted a construction permit for building a segment of their network between Chicago and St. Louis. This first application was to provide a 2000 Hertz bandwidth service which was different from any of the existing carrier services at that time along that route and was therefore a special service. This in turn made MCI the first of the specialized common carriers.

Also during 1969 the FCC authorized informal technical hearings on the subject of interconnection, and they were held under the auspices of the National Academy of Sciences (NAS). The result of the NAS hearings was that the report submitted in 1970 said that there was a potential for harm or degradation to the public network by indiscriminate interconnection. The degree of degradation was not stated due to the lack of data, but a program of certification could be implemented which would allow for control of interconnection to the degree that no potential harm would occur to the public network. As a result, in May of 1971 the FCC issued a ruling on the definition of a common carrier. This ruling permitted the formation and operation of the specialized common carriers, which were subject to more lenient rules of technical and financial qualification. This ruling fostered the formation of a number of new and competing companies in the communications market, and in the same year additional construction permits were issued to MCI for routes between New York and Washington and New York and Chicago.

In 1973 the State Public Utilities Commission in New York approved a tariff for a telephone company to directly connect equipment not owned by the telephone company (Rochester Telephone Company) to the public network. The California PUC also proposed the direct connection of equipment not owned by the telephone company if it was certified by a registered engineer. In 1976 most of the states as well as AT&T had tariffs which provided for the connection of non-telephone-company-owned equipment directly to the public network as long as the equipment was certified. Certification means that the equipment has been tested by an independently registered engineering organization and has been found to meet all of the interface requirements established for connection to the public network. In effect this allows for the connection of foreign equipments directly to the public network as long as those foreign equipments meet the same requirements as telephone-company-owned equipments which will tie into that network. Most terminal and communication equipment vendors now provide specific certified equipments which can be purchased by the end user and then connected directly into the common carrier network.

QUESTIONS

1. What organization has jurisdiction over interstate communications services? Over intrastate communications services?
2. What organizations are tariffed to provide communications outside the United States? Name three of them.
3. What is the difference between specialized common carriers and value-added network carriers?
4. What are the primary services offered by common carriers?
5. Describe WATS services and a typical application where they may be used.
6. Describe a Foreign Exchange line and a typical application where it may be used.
7. What are the primary functions specified in a tariff?
8. What are two methods whereby "foreign equipment" can be connected to the telephone network?

3

COMMUNICATIONS MEDIA

A.

Elementary Communications Theory

The biggest reason for communications, whether voice or data, is to move information from one location to another. When the transmitter and the receiver are in the same physical location it is relatively easy to perform that function. When the transmitter and the receiver are removed from one another, or if we want to move extremely high volumes of information in a short period of time, then some form of machine-to-machine type communication is necessary.

Of the various types of methods which are available, the primary mode of machine-to-machine communication is via an electronically generated signal. The reason for use of electronics is the ease with which it can be generated, transmitted, detected, and the fact that it can be stored transiently or permanently and is amenable to high volumes of information transmitted within a short period of time.

The basic concept of communications theory is that a particular electronic signal can be modified so that at least two different states of that signal can be detected. The two states will represent a zero or one, mark or space, on or off, etc. As soon as two or more different states can be detected, the capability for moving information exists. Specific combinations of states, which are known as codes, can then represent any alpha, numeric, or control character, so that information can be transmitted in either a pure information form for machines to interact with or a representative form (the code) that allows a human to recognize the information. Since most forms of communication are initiated by humans, there must be an interface to convert the information from the human source to machine-readable format. This conversion process will then allow the information to be stored, transmitted, used by the communications devices or data processing devices, and ultimately, if necessary, return some kind of information which will be converted back to recognizable information for use by the human.

The primary mode of generating electronic signals for transmission on voice grade communication lines is what is known as a *sine wave*. The sine wave is a particular frequency (the amount of complete cycles per unit time) during which the signal starts from a zero level, goes positive at a decreasing rate for a period of time, reaches a peak, in a negative direction to the zero level then to an equivalent level in the negative direction, as it went in the positive direction, and then returns to the zero level at an increasing rate which point in time the signal begins a new cycle. The more cycles per unit time, the higher the frequency. A sine wave is shown in Fig. 3-1.

Most data processing functions take place with signals that are in a mark and space configuration which really looks like a square wave, which is the same as a sine wave except for the fact that it

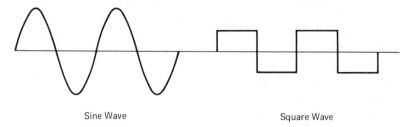

Sine Wave   Square Wave

Figure 3-1.   Sine   Wave

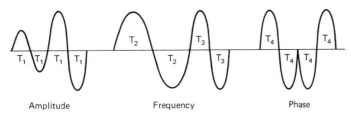

Amplitude   Frequency   Phase

Figure 3-2.   Sine Wave Changes

reaches its maximum value almost instantly, stays at that level for half of the cycle, goes to the full negative value almost immediately, and then stays at that value until the time for a new cycle to begin. Fig. 3-1 shows both a sine wave and a square wave.

In actuality however, the square wave is mathematically made up of many individual sine waves of which there are quite a few high frequency components. The high frequency components provide the squareness to the signal. The primary frequency is the frequency at which the square wave completes a single cycle, but in order to square the signal many high-frequency components have to be added for which the resultant figure is the square wave.

For communication purposes, especially over the voice networks which were designed for voice frequencies between 300 and 3300 Hz, the majority of the higher frequencies which are required to square the signal cannot be transmitted because of attenuation at those frequencies on the communications line. Therefore, it is mandatory that the frequencies used for communications purposes be totally contained within the 300 to 3300 Hz range. In order to accomplish this, techniques had to be developed which would permit detectable signal variations of the frequencies within the voice channel range. There are three ways in which a sine-wave signal can be changed so that information can be correlated with those individual changes. The three ways are: the amplitude or magnitude of the signal; frequency or the amounts of time the signal crosses the zero level per unit time; and phase, or the relative location where the signal crosses the zero level, referenced to the location the signal crossed the zero level on the previous cycle. An example of each one of these types of changes is shown in Fig. 3-2.

The actual manipulation of the sine waves which bear a specific relation to the digital information generated by a data processing machine is a process known as *modulation/demodulation,* which is fully described in Chap. 5. Modulation is the inherent capability of converting digital information (square waves) into the various frequencies which can be supported on a communications line so that information can be transmitted from one point to another electronically over those lines. Demodulation is the conversion of the manipulated sine waves back into digital form for data processing purposes.

Electronic transmission is not limited to voice grade lines only. It can also take place at much higher frequencies, but the basic techniques are the same. Changes of amplitude, frequency, and phase are the modes in which the information is transmitted, although, more recently, methods of transmitting *pulses,* which represent digital signals, have also been developed and are being implemented for high-speed digital type transmissions. Also, for purposes of extremely high transmission rates, an optical system is now being used, which is really the modulation of a "light" source. The basic technique still remains the same. Some "carrier" (in this case light) is being changed in a very specific manner so that the receiver can detect those changes and convert the changes into information which can be used by data processing machines and eventually by a human being.

No discussion of communications theory would be complete without some words on the problems which arise with that communication. Most of the problems are associated with what is known as *noise,* which distorts the signals being transmitted so that the changes describing the information cannot be recognized. When transmissions are not recognizable or are distorted to the point where they are recognized as something different from what was being sent, information is lost. Since noise exists in all communications type circuits, it is necessary to recognize the different types and to determine what their impact is on transmission. This is described in detail in Chap. 13.

B.

Communications Conductors

The primary media used for communications lines is, and has been for many years, heavily oriented toward wire conductors. Wire communications paths may be classified into four groups: open wire; twisted pair cable; coaxial cable; and the newest (emerging because of the economies of scale available)—fiber optic cable. Actually fiber optics is not really wire but is classified with wire communications due to the method of implementation.

Open-wire lines are still in use in various parts of the United States as well as in other parts of the world, principally in low density traffic areas. Wire sizes are measured several ways, the predominant method in the United States being the American Wire Gauge Standard (AWG). The range of open-wire sizes in widespread use is from 10 AWG (0.1019 inch diameter) to 19 AWG (0.0359 inch diameter). The composition of earlier open-wire lines was iron (steel) and was later changed to copper to overcome the corrosion caused by exposure to moisture. The wires were tied to glass insulators, which were in turn attached to wood cross arms and mounted on utility poles. The resistance to electric current flow of the open-wire line varies greatly with the weather conditions, and for this reason the twisted pair cable was adopted.

Twisted pair cable is composed of copper conductors, insulated by either paper or plastic and twisted into pairs. These pairs are further twisted into groups called units, and then units are twisted into the finished cable. The cable is covered by lead or plastic and either suspended from aerial cross arms or buried by one of three types of construction. The three types of twisted pair buried-cable laying are: direct burial, ducted runs between access vaults, and utility tunnels. The construction technique specifically used depends on the frequency of required access to the circuits inside the cable, i.e., infrequently accessed requires direct burial, very frequently accessed and large numbers of cables needed requires cable tunnels. Twisting of the cable pairs and then units is done with a different pitch for adjacent pairs or units so that noise interference, called *crosstalk,* will be minimized. Wire sizes commonly used for twisted pairs range from 19 AWG to 26 AWG.

At transmission frequencies above 1 megahertz, electrical interference in the form of crosstalk between adjacent circuits is the predominant design criteria. Attempts to overcome this impairment in twisted pair cables led to the development of coaxial cables. Grounded shields were placed around single copper conductors and, later, pairs of conductors to shield against the noise caused by adjacent pairs. Various kinds of insulation material, including paper and plastics, are used between the conductors and the shield. In order to carry higher frequencies, representing greater bandwidth or more information-carrying capability, the coaxial cable was constructed with air as the insulator between the current-carrying conductor and the shield. Thin insulating discs support the inner conductor and keep it away from the shield. Up to twenty of these coaxial pairs are twisted into a cable which is buried in similar fashion to the twisted pair cable.

Recent developments in laser technology have led to construction of thin plastic fibers which can carry information at frequencies into the visible light spectrum. This technology is still quite new but shows promise of very efficient and economical buried cable systems in the future. The optical fibers are covered to prevent loss of light along the line and joined with connectors which have a very low light loss. Typical losses being experienced at these junctions are in the order of ½ dB today.

Communications lines are also being constructed using radio signals between a transmitter and receiver. The names of these systems are based on the radio frequency bands being used or the wavelength, i.e., *Very High Frequency* (VHF) and *Microwave*. Again, as in the case of the coaxial cable and fiber optics cable, the higher the frequency, the greater the bandwidth. The largest used systems today are radio paths operating in the 4 to 12 gigahertz (GHz) bands whose wavelengths are very short (micrometer length). 2, 6 & 12 GHz

There are three principal groups of radio systems used for communications lines—broadcast, beam, and satellite. Broadcast radio is limited in that every receiver picks up the signals and therefore each receiver must be tuned to a unique frequency, within the range of the transmitter. Microwave or beam radio has the advantage of being a narrow beam which can be separated in space to form several channels using the same frequency. Beam radio has serious limitations in the distance the signals can travel before they must be repeated due to loss of signal strength, the curvature of the earth, and most important, the noise introduced because of the moisture in the air surrounding the earth's surface. Normal beam radio repeater stations are placed about thirty miles apart on mountaintops, towers, or the tops of tall buildings. The radio beam is usually on the order of 5 degrees width and operates with up to about 12 watts of power. The power level is kept low to prevent interference with other beams on the same frequency, as is also true of the narrow beams.

Satellite microwave radio is employed to overcome the problem of the curvature of the earth. Earlier systems were orbiting receiver-transmitters whereby the antennas on the earth's surface were directed toward the satellite as it moved across the operating area, while newer systems used geosynchronously orbiting satellites which were placed in an orbit over the earth at the appropriate distance from the earth to maintain the orbit and move with a relative zero–surface speed as the earth rotates. This distance is approximately 22,300 miles and gives the effect of the repeater satellite being suspended in space over the operating area. Satellites used for domestic communications are positioned at three-degree intervals between 70 and 130 degrees west longitude. This yields an operating area over the entire, contiguous United States. By positioning the satellite between 90 and 130 degrees, Hawaii and Alaska are included in the operating area, and the power levels are higher than for

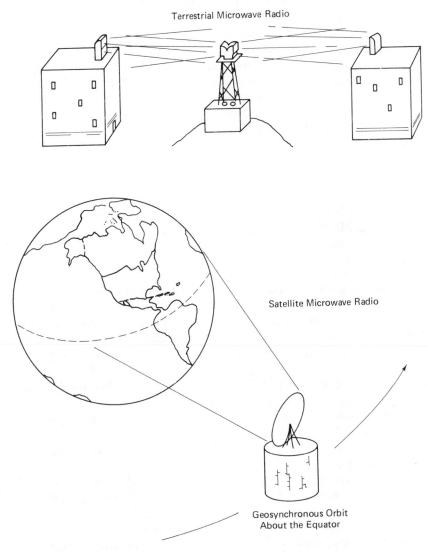

Figure 3-3. Terrestrial and Satellite Radio Systems

the terrestrial microwave systems to allow transmission over the greater distances. Since the area served is common, unique radio frequencies must be used, and this creates the requirement to divide the radio signal into many communications line channels. With satellites, the number of radio signal repeaters is reduced, relative to the terrestrial or beam radio, from several hundred to span the country to one, and in addition, the noise interference of the environment near the earth's surface is minimized due to the lesser total distance the signals travel through the environment by going away from and then returning to the surface. Figure 3-3 depicts terrestrial and satellite radio systems. One other media being used for communications is the waveguide which operates in the millimeter wavelength range. The bandwidth is extremely wide but due to the cost and critical mechanical construction requirements is only used in rare cases. One of the longest waveguide systems known is installed in England and runs the length of the island up into Scotland.

C.

Carrier Systems

The total bandwidth capacity of different communications media is usually much greater than is actually needed for an individual communications line, and therefore various carrier systems are used to increase media efficiencies. Carrier systems were first introduced in the telegraph industry and later used by the telephone company to divide the available bandwidth into specific channels. Frequency division multiplexing (FDM) is the technique most often used to build a carrier system. Teletypewriter or low-speed data channels are multiplexed into voice frequency (VF) channels which normally carry telephone conversations, and these VF channels are multiplexed into what are known as base groups, supergroups, mastergroups, and finally into jumbogroups.

Typical carrier systems for wire media handle from 4 to 10,800 VF channels, while radio systems handle from 600 to 1860 VF channels. Digital carrier systems typically handle data speeds from 1.544 million bits per second (Mbps) to 44.184 Mbps. Figures 3-4 and 3-5 show the Bell System hierarchy for combining voice grade channels at the various levels, while Fig. 3-6 shows the Bell System digital hierarchy for combining digital channels.

Carrier System	Facilities Media	Line Frequency Band	Voice Channels	Max. Mileage*
Voice Grade Channel	Wire or Cable (1 pair)	300-3300 Hz	1	–
C	Open Wire (1 pair)	4.6-30.7 KHz	1	500
J	Open Wire (1 pair)	36-143 KHz	12	800
N	Cable (2 pairs)	44-260 KHz	12	200
O	Open Wire (1 pair)	2-156 KHz	16	150
P	Open Wire	8-100 KHz	4	25
ON	Cable	36-268 KHz	24	200
ON/K	Cable	68-136 KHz	14	200
T1	MW Radio	10.7-11.7 GHZ	1200	200
K	Cable (2 pairs)	12-60 KHz	12-Basegroup	
L1	Coaxial Cable	60-2788 KHz	60-Supergroup	
L3	Coaxial Cable	312-8284 KHz	600-Mastergroup	
L4	Coaxial Cable	0.564-17.548 MHz	3600-Jumbogroup	
L5	Coaxial Cable	Under Development	10,800	
TD-2	MW Radio	3.7-4.2 GHz	600 Mastergroup	
TH	MW Radio	5.9-6.4 GHz	1860 3 Master 1 Supergroup	

MW – Microwave   * – No specific maximum mileage limitation

Figure 3-4. Telephone Carrier Systems

D.

Telephone Channel Composition

A typical communications path from a terminal to a computer at a remote processing center is composed of a line termination device at each end of the path, house cables which connect to the local tele-

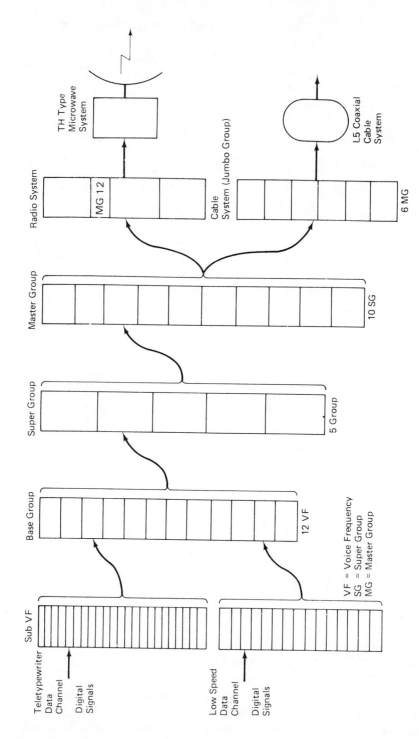

Figure 3-5. Telephone Voice Grade Carrier Hierarchy

34

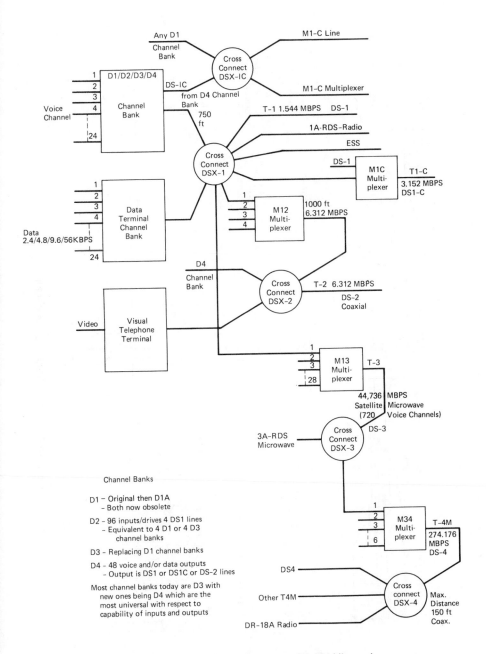

Figure 3-6. Telephone Company Digital Hierarchy

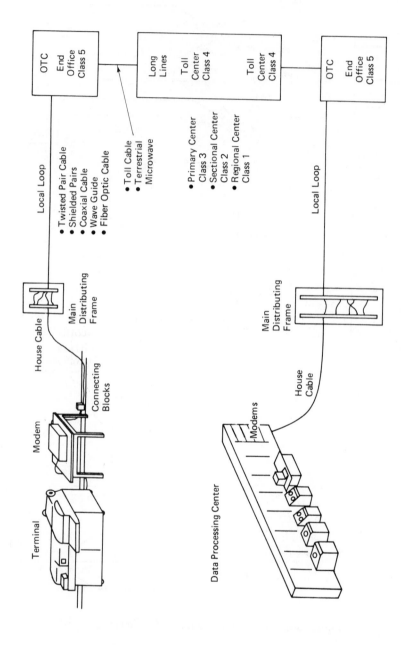

Figure 3-7. Data Channel Composition

phone company lines (local loops), local telephone company service offices (End Offices), trunk lines between serving offices, and possibly other telephone company or specialized common carrier offices.

Local loops and house cables are almost always wire conductors and trunks between local serving offices, while long haul offices are generally cable systems employing carrier systems of some type. If the distance is great inside a population center or the line is an intercity one, terrestrial microwave is generally used. The higher the density of the communications traffic, the more the need for a carrier system; therefore, individual communication lines are frequently carried over sophisticated, high-bandwidth carrier systems. Figure 3-7 shows the composition of a typical communications path used for data.

The line interface device on a data communications line is a modem (Data Set) for an analog line and is a Digital Service Unit (DSU) for a digital line. There will be numerous connecting blocks in both the terminal office location and data processing center. One such block, the main distributing frame (MDF) is considered to be the point of demarcation between the carrier-provided facility and the local wiring. Many larger installations have separate areas or rooms for modems, local switching machines, operational control areas, technical control areas, etc., and equip these areas with connecting blocks mounted into intermediate distribution frames (IDF).

QUESTIONS

1. What is the primary mode of machine-to-machine communication and what is the basic concept for information detection?
2. What are three ways to modify a sine wave so that identifiable differences can be recognized? What is this technique called?
3. Name four types of wire conductors.
4. Name three groups of radio systems used for communications. Draw a diagram of a typical configuration of each.
5. Name two other methods of transmitting electronic signals.
6. Draw a diagram of a typical telephone channel composition between a central site and a terminal location.

chapter

4

NETWORK TYPES

When discussing a network there are many definitions which come into a speaker's mind when he uses the term. Because of the different definitions used by the telephone company, vendors, and users, a very limited definition of a network will be used for this text. The network definition to be used here is *the configuration of common carrier facilities which is incorporated to connect the different geographic locations of the user's system.* The other definitions which relate to the mode under which information is transmitted such as packet, multiplex, satellite, etc., will be described separately under those particular headings. For purposes of this chapter the method of connecting the geographically separated points will be described.

Prior to describing the types of connections, there are two definitions which must be made as they apply to all of the different network configurations. They are *half duplex* (HDX) and *full duplex* (FDX). These definitions refer to the physical facilities which are provided to the user for connecting to a voice grade line. (Further definition of HDX and FDX relative to the movement of information will be made in Chap. 7). The term *half duplex* when used in referring to a circuit provided by the telephone company consists of a two-wire connection between two or more points. This is shown in Fig. 4-1. The two-wire connection consists of a signal lead over which the information is transmitted in either direction, while the other wire is a reference connection over which there are no signals transmitted. When drawing a network configuration the ground wire is usually not shown.

A full-duplex connection is a four-wire connection between two or more physical locations. The four wires actually consist of 2 two-wire pairs and are usually used for transmitting information in one direction on one pair while transmitting information in the other direction on the second pair of wires.

It is provided by the telephone carrier, except in special cases, on a leased basis only. When talking about a half-duplex circuit or a full-duplex circuit there is nothing more implied than a two-wire or a four-wire connection. There is such a circuit known as a simplex (SPX) circuit, which in reality is a two-wire circuit, but data moves only in one direction. Unless such a circuit is specifically requested and unidirectional amplifiers are installed, an SPX circuit is in reality the same as a half-duplex circuit (two wires). The full-duplex and simplex circuits are also shown in Fig. 4-1.

A.

Point to Point

A point-to-point circuit is the connection of a two-wire or four-wire circuit between two points and only those two points. A point-to-point connection can be either a dial-up type connection or a dedicated connection which belongs to the user on a monthly basis. A point-to-point connection is shown in Fig. 4-2.

B.

Multipoint/Multidrop

A multipoint/multidrop circuit is one which connects three or more points on a common line. There is usually a single master site and a series of slave sites connected on such a circuit. An example of such circuits is shown in Fig. 4-2. In the past this type of circuit was sometimes called a multistation circuit, but this is no longer the

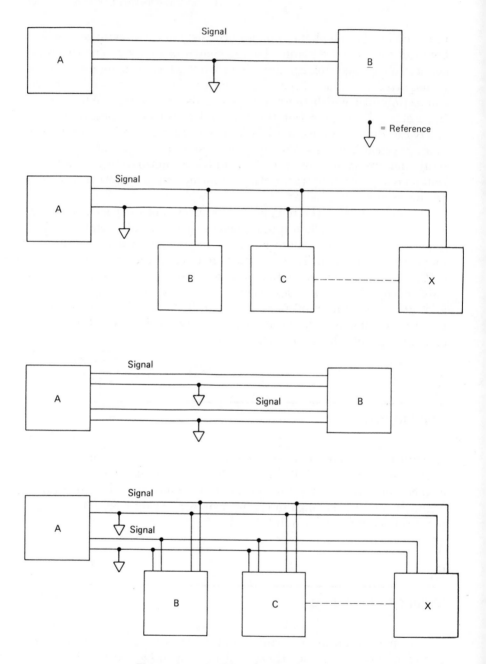

Figure 4-1. Half/Full Duplex Circuits

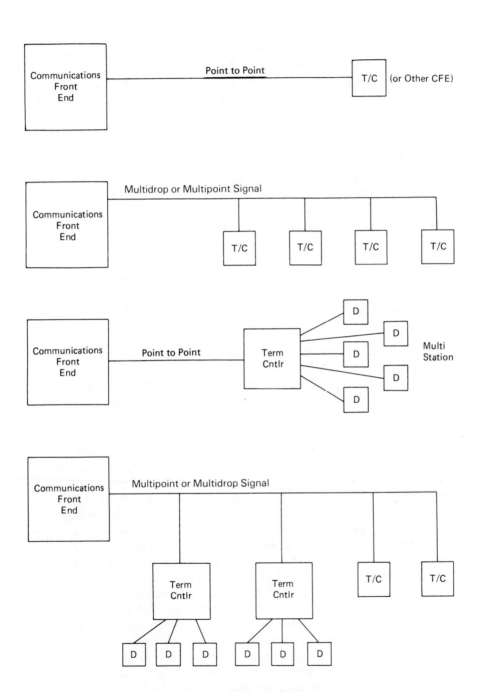

Figure 4-2. Circuit Definitions

case, as multistation referred primarily to teletype configurations where any teletype on a line could talk to other teletypes on that same line directly. This is different in a multipoint/multidrop configuration where there is a definite master/slave relationship in that the master is the only site that can talk to the individual slave sites. If a slave site wants to transmit a message to another slave site, it must first go through the master site where it will be rerouted out onto the same circuit to go back to the second slave site. Multipoint circuits must be leased because only under very limited conditions with special equipments, can a multipoint circuit be dialed (these cases usually involve dialing of multiple locations and patching the individual dialed lines together for a temporary connection).

C.

Dial Network

The dial network (DDD) is where the standard telephone type of dial connection is made. Either a rotary dial or the newer touch tone dialing can be implemented, and there is a direct connection between the end user locations, both at the remote and central site ends, where a circuit known as a *local loop* connects the user site to the closest telephone company serving office. All of the dial arrangements are made from that local serving office regardless of the length of the call. There are many levels of telephone company service office, especially with long haul capabilities, and the telephone company equipment will automatically route the call via the most efficient means for telephone company equipment utilization. This means that it is quite possible for a call which may only be required to go from San Francisco to Los Angeles to actually be routed through some midwestern or eastern cities if equipments used by the phone company determine that is the best route to take at that particular time. The user still only pays for the air line mile difference between the two cities but actually has no control over the route which the switching centers may take to get the call from one location to the other. If any problems are encountered on a particular line on the dial network, the call should be hung up and then redialed as the probability of getting the same physical connection is almost zero. All dial-up calls are point to point and are half-duplex circuits. Again, under very limited conditions with special equipments, a full-duplex circuit can be dialed. It is done by the dialing of two separate half-duplex circuits which are then configured in a point-to-point arrangement as if they were a full-duplex circuit. What must be considered here is that if the terminal is going to operate in a half-duplex mode (described in Chap. 7) then connecting them together with a full-duplex circuit may be unnecessary.

D.

Dedicated

Dedicated lines are also called private lines and leased lines, but all mean the same thing. A dedicated line is obtained from the telephone company on a monthly basis for unlimited utilization based on a distance between the individual points to be connected. A dedicated line can either be point to point or multipoint. A dedicated line cannot be dialed except under special conditions, as they are two different types of service. A dedicated line is also the only kind of line which can have conditioning applied to it. Conditioning is described in Chap. 13. As a general rule, if the traffic volume is such that a dedicated line is warranted, it pays to get a full-duplex line instead of a half-duplex line. The difference in rates is only about 10 percent, and the capability for utilization of a full-duplex protocol and/or the elimination of modem turn-around time is then available (modem turn-around time is described in Chap. 7).

QUESTIONS

1. Draw a half-duplex circuit point to point and multipoint.
2. Draw a full-duplex circuit point to point and multipoint.
3. What is the circuit name which connects the user's location to the telephone company serving office?
4. What kind of circuits make up the connection in a dial-up environment?
5. What are three names for circuits which can be obtained from a carrier on a monthly basis?

chapter

5

MODEMS
AND MODULATION

A.

Background

In the computer environment today, the means of moving signals from one part of a device to another is usually accomplished by sending digital pulses which are in the form of either square waves or actual pulses. This mechanism works extremely well for short distances and over wires which are of a relatively small gauge (diameter). Once the signals have to be transmitted over longer distances, a whole series of options opens up to the user. These options result from the fact that the square waves and/or pulses cannot travel down a metallic wire without in some way degrading. This degradation takes the form of rounding off of the rise and fall time of the signal, as well as loss of total energy level of the signal itself. The losses are caused by the fact that the metallic wire has a resistance associated with it that in effect consumes some of the energy initially injected into the line and therefore cannot be available at the end of the line. The reason why the round-off of the square wave signal occurs is that mathematically an electrical square wave signal is made up of many, many different frequencies, of which the very high frequencies give the squareness to the signal. The characteristics of the metallic wire are such that the very high frequencies are the ones which are degraded the most as the wire gets longer. With the loss of the higher frequencies, the square wave or pulse loses its sharp rise and/or fall times and therefore gets rounded.

B.

Purpose/Basic Theory /Baseband/ Sampling Time vs. Frequency

It is the rounding off of the signal, in conjunction with the loss of energy, which is interpreted at the receive end with much less reliability than what would have been recognized with the original signal, because the degraded electrical signals cannot trigger the detection circuitry at the same points as the original signal would have if it had been received in its originally generated form. This results in all kinds of distortions and loss of information which means that some other technique must be used for transmitting the digital signals over longer distances.

The distance over which a signal must travel is probably the key criterion in determining the method which must be used for that transmission. Close behind this criterion, however, is the transmission rate of the information which must be accommodated. The four most common methods of transmitting data, each more expensive than the previous one, are listed here.

1. Direct connection by wire
2. Line drivers which reshape distorted pulses
3. Limited-distance modems (short-haul modems), which are in effect simplified versions of conventional modems. (Some versions may utilize digital signaling techniques.)
4. Standard telephone line modems

The RS-232C specification, which is an industry standard interface specification, limits direct wire connections to fifty feet for transmission rates of 56,000 bits per second. Therefore, at this rate, for distances greater than fifty feet the first consideration should be given to the line drivers. It should be noted that longer distances can be tried first without the line driver and only if the output is not what is desired, then put in the line drivers. The consideration for use of line drivers at lower speeds will permit an increase in distance over which transmission throughput will still be effective. Individual line drivers generally provide adequate performance for between 500 and 5000 feet for data rates of up to 9600 bits per second. Above this distance for most applications, consideration must be given to either short-haul modems or regular telephone modems. Another factor to consider is that various line drivers can be installed in series on a particular telephone line for transmission in one direction. This means that with a full-duplex connection there can be transmission in both directions with line drivers in sequence along the route. Obviously, as you add more line drivers the probability for malfunction increases as well as the cost.

Once the distance and the data rate exceed the capacity of line drivers, the next device which can be used is the short-haul modem. The short-haul modem is good for distances between 5000 and 100,000 feet where the trade-off is cost versus distance. These short-haul modems are used mostly for private line, hardwired links, but some can operate over local loop voice grade telephone lines provided that there are no loading coils between the two points, and the total distance the signal must travel can be guaranteed to be within the range of the modem (usually limited to about twenty miles or connection of both ends to the same telephone company serving office). The bandwidth of the short-haul modem must also be within the range of the telephone line capability, and the power level must meet the Bell standard. A more detailed explanation will be given later in this section.

The last form of transmitting data is the conventional telephone line modems. These come in many different forms at different speeds, but all are primarily designed to operate on what is known as a 3002 voice grade line. There are different modes of modulation which are used at the various transmission rates, and these will be described in detail later in the paragraphs covering that particular kind of modem.

Modulation is the technique which modifies the form of an electrical signal so that the signal can carry information on some form of communications media. The signal which does the carrying is called a *carrier,* and modulation will change some of this carrier's form in a predetermined manner at the transmit end so that the change of form which represents the information can be detected at the receive end. The specific device that performs the conversion at the transmit end is called a *modulator,* and the device that detects the information at the receive end from the modulated carrier is called a *demodulator.* Combining the two, which are needed for both transmit and receive at the same end, we have the name MODEM (MOdulator DEModulator).

Under most conditions the carrier is a single frequency signal that would be continuous if not for the fact that the information is modifying that signal. The three methods which are used to modify the signal are to change its height (amplitude), change its frequency, or to change its phase. The higher transmission speed modulation schemes may use more than one form of modulation to convey multiple bits of information at the same time. ──── CARRIER

The information which is to be modulated onto the carrier is called the *baseband signal.* Since this text deals with the transmission of digital information, we will consider the schemes which modulate digital signals onto the carriers for transmission over a telephone line. The digital information is binary in nature in that it has only two possible states, a zero and one (space and mark). Figure 5-1 shows a series of different types of digital signals with their most common name, any one of which can be used to modulate a carrier. Most commonly encountered plus and minus voltage levels are in a range of 3 to 25 volts, with the minimum level that can be modulated without the possibility of an error being called the *modulator slicing level.*

Once the digital bits are modulated onto the carrier, they must be demodulated at the receive end and converted back to digital form reliably. In order to be detected with this high degree of reliability, the sampling of the data must be done during the time that the digital bit is "most stable." The most stable time is at the midpoint of the digital bit. It is most stable here because the rise and fall time degradations as well as the impairment called *jitter* (forward and backward movement of the start of each digital cycle) have the least amount of impact here. This will be described further in the section on signal detection under each of the types of modems.

In the theory of modulation one must understand the relationships of the three functions of time, frequency, and amplitude. This is shown in Fig. 5-2 where we have a three-dimensional view of the signal relationships. The amplitude of the signal is drawn along the "Y axis," its frequency is positioned along the "X axis," and if at the same time a time relationship is needed, time can be identified along the "Z axis." Time and/or frequency are frequently drawn in relation to amplitude alone as is shown in the top two figures of the diagram.

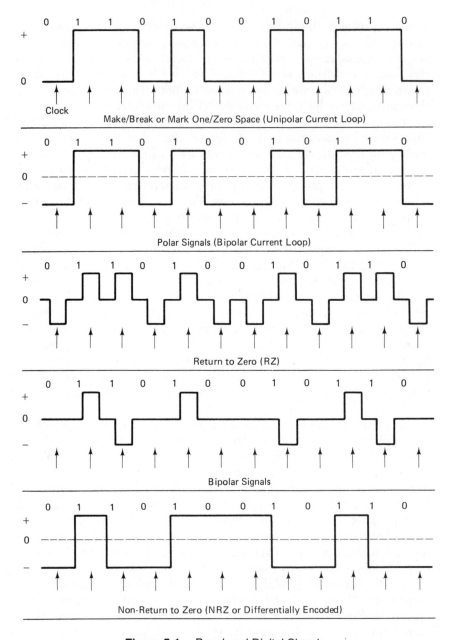

Figure 5-1. Baseband Digital Signals

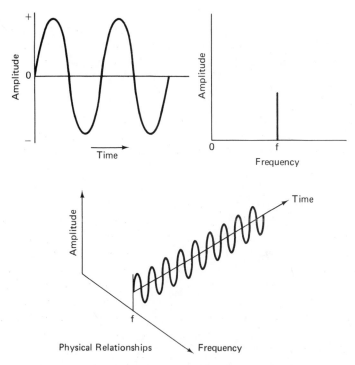

Figure 5-2. Time/Frequency/Amplitude Relationships

The different types of modulation will show changes in amplitude and frequency over a period of time which results in the specific modulation scheme being used. These are described in the next section.

C.

Modes of Modulation—AM, FM, PM, Pulse, Other Analog

Figure 5-3 shows a simplified version of amplitude, frequency, and phase modulation schemes. Each scheme is identified so that one particular state indicates the presence of a zero bit on the digital side while the other state indicates the presence of a one bit on the digital side.

In the case of *amplitude modulation,* it can be seen that a specific frequency represents a one bit when it is of a higher amplitude and that the same frequency at a different point in time and at a lower

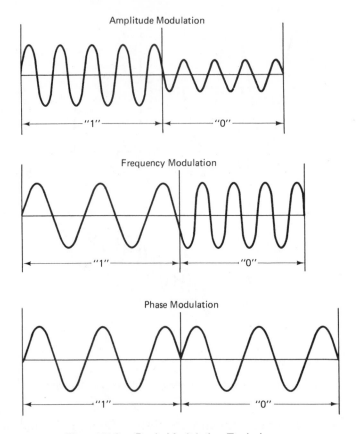

Figure 5-3.   Basic Modulation Techniques

amplitude represents the zero bit. The change in signal amplitude from lower to higher and then higher back to lower is indicative of the one bits or zero bits which are inserted into the modulator at the transmit end and then detected and output by the demodulator at the receive end. This is a continuously running sequence where the demodulator puts out zeros and ones in direct relation to the amplitude of the signals which it receives over the telephone line. In general, this technique is used for modulation over a telephone line in the range of 300 bits per second up to 1200 bits per second where each of the two amplitudes represents a single bit.

The second form of modulation shown is *frequency modulation*. In this particular case the frequency is one particular value for a zero bit and, at a different point in time, a different frequency for the one bit. The change in frequency occurs exactly in the same kind of relationship as the change in amplitude for amplitude modulation. Each time the specific frequency representing either a zero or one bit is detected, that particular digital bit is output out of the demodulator. Frequency modulation is commonly used in the range of 50 bits per second up to 2000 bits per second.

The third basic type of modulation is called *phase modulation*. This particular form of modulation is probably the hardest form to understand from a conceptual point of view if the reader is unfamiliar with the methods for representing a particular sine wave or frequency with respect to time. A simple but accurate description of a sine wave of a particular frequency is that it starts from what is known as the baseline and conforms to a curve which is known as a sine wave. When it reaches its peak (all frequencies are described the same way), it is at its 90-degree point. When it comes back down to the baseline, it is at its 180-degree point. When it goes to its full amplitude in the negative direction, it is at its 270-degree point, and when it comes back to the baseline it is now at its 360-degree point, or the zero-degree point for starting the next cycle. This occurs over a period of time with the amount of full cycles per second being called the frequency. A full cycle consists of going from a zero-degree point to the full positive amplitude, back through the baseline to the full negative amplitude, and then back to the baseline, at which point it starts a new cycle. For a particular frequency this continues without interruption. As can be seen in the phase modulation description of Fig. 5-3, at the 180-degree point of the third cycle, instead of continuing on in the negative direction, the frequency instantaneously starts at the zero point again. This means that the signal, changed by 180 degrees in phase at a particular instant of time, has started a whole new series of cycles at the same frequency and amplitude. The "phase shift" can be related directly to digital input at a modulator so that one particular phase can be the zero bit while a phase change of 180 degrees can now be the one bit. In actuality, phase modulation techniques are such that four different phases can be recognized very reliably, and with four different and recognizable phase differences, each individual phase can be defined to represent two separate bits. For example, first phase can represent bits zero-zero, the second phase zero-one (90 degree displaced), the third phase can indicate a one-zero bit combination, while the fourth phase displacement can indicate a one-one bit configuration. This is known as multibit modulation or, specifically, dibit modulation. Phase modulation is more expensive to implement than either amplitude or frequency modulation and is used only in those applications where higher transmission speeds are necessary. Therefore, the same frequency, displaced only by phase, can indicate two bits at a time. This enables the transmission of 2400 bits of data per second over a voice grade line, where the signal only changes 1200 times per second. Thus, phase modulation is the predominant technique used for transmitting data at 2400 bps.

In order to obtain the higher speed transmission rates (2400 bits per second and above) it is necessary to use a multibit modulation scheme, because the voice grade line can only support a frequency range of 300 to 3300 cycles, giving a theoretical limitation in the best case of somewhere around 6000 bits per second (Shannon's Law). The practical limitations, however, indicate that a range of approximately 1200 to 2000 bits per second is realistic with a single change of amplitude, frequency, or phase. These practical limitations have to do with the circuitry presently available to generate and then detect the differences in amplitude, frequency, and phase. For amplitude and phase a minimum of one cycle is needed while two or more are needed for detecting a new frequency accurately. The multibit modulation schemes utilize both amplitude and phase modulation, as well as a combination of the two.

If you are able to generate and then detect the same frequency with four different levels of amplitude then each amplitude level could identify two different bits in the same manner as the four different phase displacements did. If there were eight levels of amplitude that could be generated and detected, you would have the capability of three digital bits of information represented by each particular amplitude. By the same token, if there were sixteen levels of amplitude which could be generated and detected, you would have four digital bits of information represented by each individual amplitude. With the present capability of equipment and with the types of line degradations which are present in the existing transmission environment, eight different amplitude levels are usually the maximum being used (representing three digital bits), but in some of the short-haul modems the full sixteen levels are utilized, giving four unique bits per amplitude level. It should be noted that amplitude modulation is by far the most sensitive to line degradation effects and therefore would be the most error prone. Phase modulation would be the least error prone, but the present level of technology allows only for eight phase displacements to be detected reliably, allowing a maximum of three bits per individual phase displacement.

Using phase and amplitude modulation techniques where we have a combination of multiple phases and multiple amplitudes, we can get up to 19.2 kilobits per second transmission. The simplified versions of multibit modulation are shown in Fig. 5-4, but it should be noted that the multibit frequency modulation scheme shown is not used for the high-speed transmissions.

When analyzing a line for error-characteristic purposes, special emphasis must be placed on the fact that the higher the transmission rate, the more bits are carried for each individual amplitude at a

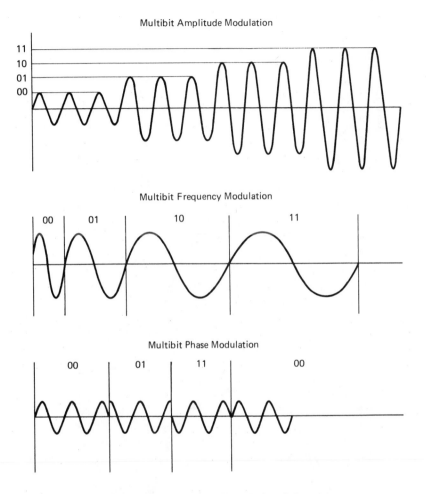

Figure 5-4.   Multibit Modulation Schemes

particular phase. This means that for a 1200 change per second carrier there are two bits per signal change at 2400 bps, four bits per signal change at 4800 bps, and eight bits per carrier frequency at a particular amplitude and phase at 9600 bps. The reason this emphasis is so critical is that the noise which normally exists on a transmission line, which used to affect only one bit at a time at the lower speeds, now can affect up to 8 bits at one time with the same type and magnitude of degradation. This particular phenomenon will be discussed further in the section on transmission integrity.

Recently there have been some technological advances that have changed the mode whereby the techniques for modulation have been implemented in unique situations. For example, in Fig. 5-5 we have a diagram of modulation technique which is called *split channel*. The

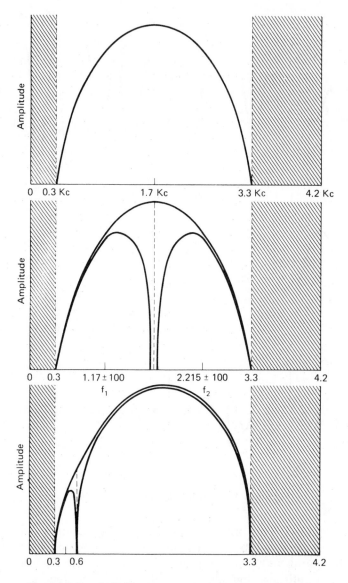

Figure 5-5. Split Channel and Reverse Channel Modems

voice grade line is divided up into two separate segments (as shown in the middle diagram) where each segment can support a data transmission rate of 1200 bits per second (using FM in each segment), while in the bottom diagram an uneven two-segment split is shown, where 2400 bits per second can be transmitted in the larger segment and up to 150 bits per second can be transmitted in the smaller segment. This is the capability which exists on a two-wire circuit and allows for either two-way transmission on a single wire at the same time or, in the case of a full-duplex circuit (four wire) we have the capability of transmitting two completely independent full-duplex data transmissions. These are also called *split channel, backward channel,* or *out-of-the-band modems.* Any one of the names is applicable, although out-of-band to some people indicates outside the voice grade line frequency spectrum and is therefore not as applicable as one of the other three names.

A whole different form of modulation called *pulse modulation* exists and is used for transmitting digital information directly. It is used by the telephone company as well as other users who must transmit digital type information. Pulse modulation requires a differ-

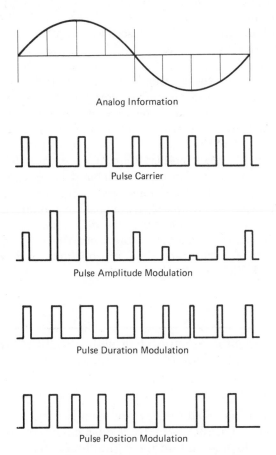

Analog Information

Pulse Carrier

Pulse Amplitude Modulation

Pulse Duration Modulation

Pulse Position Modulation

Figure 5-6. Pulse Modulation Techniques

ent set of modulation/demodulation equipment as well as different transmission facilities (not on voice grade lines). A description of three forms of pulse modulation is shown in Fig. 5-6 where, for purposes of simplicity, we have an analog signal (a sine wave) which is sampled at different points in time with a particular pulse carrier. The first type of pulse modulation shown is called *pulse amplitude modulation* (PAM), which gives a different height digital pulse for each different height of the analog signal it measures. The second type of pulse modulation is called *pulse duration modulation* (PDM), which gives a thicker pulse relative to the magnitude of the analog signal at sampling time, and the third one is called *pulse position modulation* (PPM), which has more pulses per unit time depending on the amplitude of the signal. These types of modulations are normally used to convert analog signals to a digital form for transmission by the newer digital equipments used by the telephone company.

The final mode of modulation to be described also has to do with analog modulation and in effect describes the modes of modulating a particular carrier by an analog signal. Some of these methods are shown in the Fig. 5-7. The top diagram shows both information sidebands as well as the carrier being transmitted. The second diagram shows both of the sidebands being transmitted but not the carrier. This is called *double sidebands suppressed carrier* (DSBSC). The third diagram represents what is known as single sideband, which only has one of the sidebands (lower) transmitted which carries all of the information. In the last diagram *vestigial sideband* (VSB) is shown where only a portion of the sideband is transmitted and the entire information portion is regenerated at the receive end. VSB is a very efficient form of an analog transmission modulation technique but also an expensive one. For purposes of this particular text a more detailed explanation is not applicable since the techniques used for transmission over voice grade lines are adequately described under the regular AM, FM and PM sections.

D.

Modes of Operation—Serial, Parallel, Synchronous, Asynchronous, Half Duplex, Full Duplex, Line Interface

When modems are described they are usually identified as serial or parallel modems. Parallel is really a misnomer because all modems are truly serial devices, in that the digital bits enter the modulator in

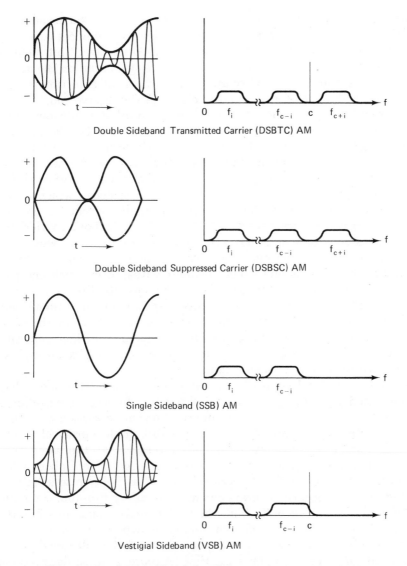

Figure 5-7. Analog Modulation Schemes (not used for data)

serial form and come out of the demodulator in serial form. The reason why some modems are called parallel is that they may have more than one input which in effect shares the voice grade line, and you have more than one signal being transmitted at the same time on the same line in the same direction. This is both a split channel technique as described in the previous section and a multiplex type of operation, which will be described under multiplexers. So for purposes of this section, all modems will be considered serial devices where the information, even though it may be combined in a multibit modulation scheme for higher transmission rates, is still serial on the digital side, where the digital information comes in a bit at a time on the transmit end and comes out a bit at a time at the receive end.

Probably the two most confusing terms in all of data communications are *Half Duplex* (HDX) and *Full Duplex* (FDX). The primary reason for this confusion is the fact that there are two completely separate and independent functions which can be defined by the terms half and full duplex. The first definition is the type of transmission line being used, while the second is the protocol, which moves data over that transmission line. A half-duplex circuit is nothing more than a two-wire circuit provided by the telephone carrier (the two wires consist of a signal wire and a reference wire, where the signal wire is the only one which carries the signals on it), while a full-duplex circuit is one which has four wires, over which one pair may be used to transmit information in the opposite direction. As was seen in the previous section, however, split channel modems will allow for transmission of information in both directions at the same time so circuit and data movement definitions must be kept separate. Simply stated, from a circuit point of view half duplex means two wires, while full duplex means four wires.

From a protocol point of view, we have another definition of half duplex and full duplex which is described as follows: A half-duplex protocol is one which transmits information one direction at a time between the same two points, while a full duplex protocol is one which transmits information in both directions at the same time between the same two points. Note that nothing is said about what kind of circuit the protocol operates over. That is because a half- or full-duplex protocol can operate on either a half- or full-duplex circuit. Over and above these definitions the modem definition enters into the situation, in that a half-duplex modem is one which can transmit and receive only in one direction at a time, while a full-duplex modem can transmit and receive at the same time. A more detailed definition of half- and full-duplex operations is contained in the sections on protocols (Chap. 7).

The second most confusing terms used in the data communications industry are the terms *synchronous* and *asynchronous*. The basic difference between the two is that asynchronous data has extra bits at the beginning and the end of each character which define the start and stop positions of each individual character being transmitted, while synchronous transmission does not have any of these

overhead bits on a character basis but carries start and end characters on a message basis. Asynchronous and synchronous can be
defined as follows:

Asynchronous "Character framed data" This is a transmission
where each character has one start and one or more stop bits
which allows the information to be transmitted a character at a
time or contiguously.

Synchronous "Message framed data" This is a transmission where
the sequence has a predefined start and stop sequence (bits or
characters) while the information contained in it is transmitted
contiguously.

A diagram as well as the utilizations of both synchronous and
asynchronous transmissions are shown in Fig. 5-8.

Asynchronous Transmission — Character-framed data

Each character has a very specific start and end bit sequence. Baudot Teletypes
have one start bit and $1\frac{1}{2}$ stop bits while the Model 33 Teletype has 1 start bit
and 2 stop bits.

ST	1	2	3	4	5	6	7	8	SP	ST	1	2	3	4	5	6	7	8	SP	ST	1	2	3	4	5	6	7	8	SP

Characters may be transmitted one at a time or contiguously.
Transmission is usually up to 2000 bps but may be up to 2400 bps.
Almost always used with half-duplex protocols.
Start bit is always a "0" or "space".
Stop bit or bits is always a "1" or "mark."

Synchronous Transmission — Message-framed data

Each message has a predefined start and end sequence. For transmissions using
ASCII code this sequence consists of an SOH character to start and an EOT
character to end. In addition to the SOH start character there must also be one
or more SYNC characters preceding the SOH so that the modems will have
sufficient time to go through their bit synchronization process.

SYNC	SYNC	SOH	BYTE 1	BYTE 2		BYTE x	EOT

Transmission is based on characters of a specific length in a predefined code set.
If transmission is in straight binary stream, external hardware and software is
    required to determine information content of message – message must still
    have SOH and EOT definitions and must also have appropriate shift to and
    from binary stream characters.
Used for transmission speeds of 2400 bps and above
If SOH is not recognized the rest of the message will not be recognized either
On multidrop lines messages from remote locations must be preceded by SYNC
    characters but messages from master may not have to be if master transmits
    continuously (SYNC characters between messages).
Multidrop lines are not commonly used at 9600 bps or above
Synchronization is time dependent so modems will require more time to
    synchronize as the transmission rate is increased
Messages may be sent contiguously but must be preceded by an SOH and
    succeeded by an EOT.
May be used with both half-duplex and full-duplex protocols

Figure 5-8. Synchronous/Asynchronous Transmission

The last major feature to be considered when modems are involved is the line interface. This interface consists of the RS232C digital interface and the analog line interface which are both described later in this chapter. For purposes of description, the RS232C interface is a digital interface containing twenty-five separate wires, of which twenty-two have specifically defined signals on them. The analog interface is the interface between the output of the modulator and the transmission line at the transmit end and the transmission line and the input to the demodulator at the receive end. These interfaces are defined in decibels (dB) of signal levels. From the transmit side they are injected on the line with a specified allowable signal power level within the range of zero plus or minus 4 dB, while at the receive level the specification level is minus 16 plus or minus 4 dB. It should be noted however that typical levels are never set greater than 0 dB.

E.

Short-Haul Modems

As was briefly described in Section B of this chapter, short-haul modems (SHM) are used when direct connections can be made in the range of about 5000 to 50,000 feet (one to ten miles). Some units can go up to twenty or twenty-five miles but the transmission rate on those lines usually has to be somewhat less. The time to consider a short-haul modem is when the application is somewhere between a line driver and a telephone type modem. The cost advantage of an SHM increases with the data rate because two major functions required by standard telephone line type of modems can be eliminated or alleviated. At low data rates the cost differences are not great, while at the high speeds the differential may be many thousands of dollars.

One of the primary telephone line modem functions that can be eliminated by the use of an SHM is the correction circuitry required for long distance transmissions using standard analog demodulation processes. This is normally required in a standard modem because the carrier for the demodulator may not be exactly at the same frequency as the carrier for the modulator, thus causing some kind of delay distortion which will degrade the quality of the received transmission. The second function which can be alleviated by the use of an SHM is the amount of noise rejection required, which is one of the important criteria in selecting the type of modulation scheme to be used. Because of the relatively limited distance of an SHM the noise rejection requirement is much less compared to a regular telephone grade line.

Some of the limitations of an SHM were described in Part A (private line/hardwired link only), but the real problem is that some SHMs may have modulation techniques with inherent design deficiencies (put in for cost-saving reasons) so that certain specific bit patterns may cause temporary loss of synchronization. The user should always verify with other users of the same equipment as to whether this type of problem was encountered in their implementation and if so, at what transmission speeds.

For short distance transmissions using an SHM (distance means the actual length of the wire between the two points), the error rates for most units are as low as one bit error in every 10^8 bits transmitted; but the error rates increase very rapidly with respect to distance, and therefore the user must also study very carefully the total cable length between the two facilities he wants to transmit between, especially if they go through a telephone company serving office which may add significantly to the total distance between the points. An excellent way to verify the effective transmission rate is to borrow or rent the unit to be considered, and then test it before actual implementation.

Since the speed and distance are the two most critical factors in the use of an SHM, very close attention should be paid to those characteristics. For gross calculation purposes, Fig. 5-9 shows a typical length in miles versus data transmission rates for different size wire. Also in the same figure is a block diagram of an SHM. Note that it is possible for an SHM to be either an analog or a digital device (modulate means analog and encode means digital).

F.

Digital Modems

It is an interesting anomaly that while digital information has been transmitted over the voice grade line using analog signals, the telephone company has turned toward the use of digital techniques to transmit the analog signals which make up the voices in a telephone conversation.

To understand the reason for this we have to take a look at the equipment which has been used in telephone transmission for many years. They were originally all amplifiers that worked similarly to

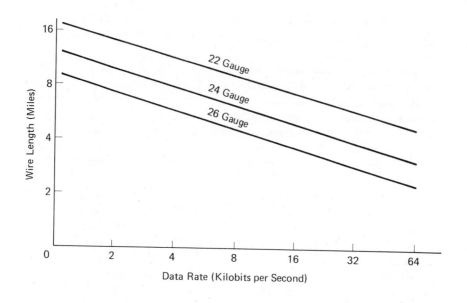

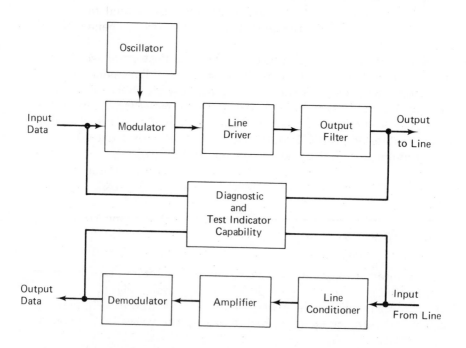

Figure 5-9. Distance vs Data Rate—SHM Block Diagram

the amplifiers on a home high fidelity audio system. As is obvious to the owner of such a system, when there are defective records the amplifiers make the noise louder at the same time they make the signal louder. The telephone transmission system does exactly the same thing for analog signals, in that the signal received at the end of a telephone line has, in addition to a voice signal, such noise items as crosstalk, background noise, and other distortions. Once the noise has been introduced it cannot be eliminated; therefore the information content of the voice is somewhat degraded, because the noise is amplified at each of the same relay sites where the signal is. Finally, the system performance is limited by those external additions of noise which may become so great that the signal cannot be detected uniquely from the noise. In a digital transmission, however, a receiver only has to determine whether the signal is present on the line at a given moment to determine whether a one or a zero exists, and this task is made much easier by the fact that the digital signal can be regenerated along the line before the degradation becomes so bad that the receiver cannot detect the unique signals. Therefore, while the analog amplifier cannot improve the quality of the signal going through it, a digital regenerator can restore the signal to an exact replica of the transmitted signal, and with digital regenerative repeaters there is no limit to the transmission distance. Also, because of the regeneration, the signal-to-noise ratio of the facility used may be relatively much poorer than would be required on an analog circuit.

In order to utilize a digital transmission capability, a site must have what is called a *digital modem*. This digital modem is not truly a modem in that it takes the digital signal from the computer and converts it to a digital signal which can be transmitted over the communication line, regenerated as often as required, and then delivered to the end location. Today there are both AT&T and non-Bell carriers offering digital data transmission services. AT&T calls their version of a digital modem a digital service unit (DSU).

The digital data system offered by the telephone company is either a private line, point-to-point or multipoint, full-duplex transmission or a dial-up switched service offering. It has synchronous data transmission rates of 2400, 4800, 9600, and 56,000 bits per second. The digital service unit provides the customer with an interface mechanism which is designed for plug-to-plug interchangeability with existing modems using the RS232C interface at the speeds of 2400, 4800, and 9600 bits per second. It also provides plug-to-plug compatability for existing modems using the CCITT recommendation V.35 interface at a speed of 56,000 bits per second. The digital system takes advantage of the existing and planned hierarchy of the telephone company network equipment for digital transmissions.

Along with the private line transmission there is a switched 56,000 bits per second service offered by the telephone company. The DSU used in this configuration also uses the V.35 interface and offers connections for automatic calling units, multiline hunting group arrangements, and other related features for switched-line services. It should be noted that digital transmission can only occur where the local facilities, as well as the local telephone company service office, have the capability to handle the digital transmissions. In most cases this means internal wiring may have to be coaxial wire as opposed to twisted copper pairs.

G.

Modem Selection

When a user selects a specific modem for his application, there are two criteria which pretty much determine the kind of modem which he must select. Those two criteria are the speed of transmission and the distance over which the data must be transmitted. The distance will determine whether a direct connection, line driver, short-haul modem, or a regular modem must be used. The speed will be determined by the quantity of data which must be transmitted per unit time. Another key criterion will be whether the modem will be used on a point-to-point circuit or in a multidrop environment. The reason for this is that the multidrop environment today cannot support data rates any greater than 4800 bits per second with a reasonable data throughput. In a point-to-point environment the speeds may range anywhere from 50 bits per second up into the multimegabit range for short distances, but for practical communications over the telephone company network, it can be assumed that common transmission rates in the range of 300 bits per second up to 50 kilobits per second will be used for analog, while for digital transmission the rates are most commonly 2400 bits per second up through 56 kilobits per second.

Once the required speed of a particular transmission line has been determined, the modems to match that line can be selected. Modems are available from both the telephone company and third party vendors. In general, the telephone companies will rent their modems, while other vendors will either rent, lease, or sell theirs. The advantages and disadvantages of going from one to the other are predominantly price and service. The telephone companies provide the most extensive service to the user, while third party vendors vary quite a bit in the capability for support once a set of modems has been installed on a user's site. As a matter of fact, probably the most important feature to consider once the speed has been determined is maintenance capability. If a modem is down and must be serviced, the user becomes totally dependent on the service time and capability of the vendor. For that reason it is extremely important to consider the service capabilities of the vendor who will be servicing the modems at all sites at which they will be installed.

An overriding consideration which must be taken into account at this time is the error rate, because if the available facilities cannot support the transmission throughput required, the entire network or quantity of lines must be reevaluated. Therefore, the user must try to set up some form of test which can validate that the necessary amount of data can be reliably moved between the required locations within the required time frame. Vendor claims cannot be taken at face value, because available carrier facilities may be physically incapable of supporting the required transmissions due to age, in-house wiring limitations, serving office equipments, etc. Testing, using the anticipated equipment and facilities, is the only true way to verify quality of effective data throughput.

When selecting a modem for leased lines it is also necessary to insure that all ends of the communication line have the same modem from the same vendor. You cannot mix and match in a practical sense except in dial-up situations.

Once the basic criteria for speed and compatability have been determined (assuming the digital side interface is one of the standards such as RS232C), there are a whole series of subtopics which must be evaluated. It should be noted that most vendors also have varied capabilities in this area, so the direct trade-off values are not always obvious. Unless there is a mandatory requirement for one of the subtopics, they should not have an overriding influence on the user's selection of a modem, but some of the topics to consider are as follows:

- Diagnostic capabilities
- Multiple speed capabilities
- Operational signal output monitoring
- Levels of conditioning required
- Ease of changing options

Last but not least the price must be considered. Only with all other items being equal should price be the overriding factor, because in most cases the technical requirements must be met first. When two or more units can perform the same functions (including maintenance), then pricing is important. Pricing is also dependent on the options desired by the user, so it is very important to determine which of the options you must have as mandatory requirements and those which are simply *nice to haves*. If, after going through a particular selection sequence, it is determined that the total cost of the modems will be too high for the allowable budget, then the user must make the arbitrary cutbacks in option capability, error rate, diagnostic capabilities, or he must start considering techniques which will reduce the total amount of modems while at the same time maintain response time integrities (such as multiplexing, dial-ups, etc.).

For purposes of comparison with AT&T modems, the 100 series of Bell modems go up to 300 bits per second, while the 200 series go between 600 bits per second and 9600 bits per second, and the 300 series goes from 19.2 kilobits per second up to 230.4 kilobits per second. Many commercial publications have, on an annual basis, a listing and matrix which will describe the capabilities of the various offerings which can then be compared with the offerings from AT&T. When making the selection of AT&T versus third party, a general criterion to consider is the quality of personnel which will be maintaining the system at the user's facility. If the user has technically qualified personnel, he will be in a much better position to utilize third party modems than if his personnel were not as qualified and would therefore have to rely on the telephone company to determine whether there were line problems, modem problems, or a combination. During this time the facility or line may be down, and business may be lost.

H.

Electrical Interfaces—Loop Current, RS232C, DAA, Acoustic Coupler, ACU

In the evolutionary development of communications capabilities, one of the first methods for electronic transmissions was the presence or absence of a current in a transmission line. When a current was flowing it represented a signal which could be used to light a light, close a relay, activate a magnet, or perform any one of the other functions required for what was known as telegraph operation. Also, when used with mechanical teleprinters the current flowing in the line would indicate a specific "bit" of information, which would be considered part of a code and therefore be used to generate specific characters or provide controls within the printing device. The most common form of current flow, current loop, is 20 milliamperes. The most common use for 20 mA current has been for the transmission of binary serial asynchronous data. In the mechanical teleprinters, the current is switched on and off for transmission or recognition of information by a series of carbon brushes rotating over a copper commutator. The commutator has individual segments which relate to the specific bits, and as the brushes make contact with each of the segments of the commutator (the brushes rotate around the com-mutator), a current will flow during the time the brushes are in contact with that segment if a voltage is present at that particular segment controlled through a switch. At the receive end, an equiva-lent commutator/brush arrangement exists which is started by the "start" bit of the transmitter and rotates at the same rate as the transmitting brushes. Because the receiving brushes will be in the same segment area as the transmitting brushes, if a current is flowing through the line from a particular segment at the transmit end, then the current will also flow through the segment at the receive end. This is the mode whereby individual bits within a character (a character is one complete revolution of the commutator) can be transmitted over the wire.

The carbon brushes rotating over a commutator have two signifi-cant disadvantages. The first is that there is significant noise intro-duced on the line from the contact imperfections between the brushes and the commutator, and second, a specific minimum cur-rent, usually 18 mA, must be maintained in order to keep the surfaces of the commutator relatively clean. The interface with such a device must include circuitry to suppress the noise generated by the brushes/commutator and also some kind of filter which will reduce the signals generated from "contact bounce," which occurs when the machines are switched from a local mode of operation to line trans-mission modes.

As was stated previously, a minimum current of 18 ma has to be maintained through the commutator contacts, but due to internal dissipation parameters the upper limit of current is usually 25 ma. Taking this into account, we can look at the available interface with a data processing device. This type of interface may have voltages of +5 and −15 volts available (it should be noted that others are available and can be used). Because there is approximately 1 volt loss at various points in the internal loop, we can assume that of the total 20-volt difference (between the +5 and −15 volts), that only 19 volts are available to generate the necessary line current. If the total interface resistance is approximately 750 ohms we will have slightly over 25 ma of current available for line transmission. If we also assume that 26 AWG gauge copper wire is used for transmission, we can have up to 7300 feet of this wire before its resistance totals 300 ohms. Note that this particular transmission requires a "full loop," which means the teleprinter could be located half that distance away or 3650 feet away. This also assumes that external interference has not affected the operation.

By taking higher initial voltages additional wire resistance can be made available which would increase the length of the wire which would be used and, in turn, increase the distance at which the printing device can be located. It is just this approach which is used by the common carriers and other users who have to cover long distances with loop current transmission, and this type of transmission scheme is usually limited to rates below 150 bits per second.

There are some other considerations, especially when interfacing with foreign countries, where a specific mode of generation of current loop is important. Some countries require that the common carrier provide the loop current, while the hardware merely switches or detects it. In other countries the communications site provides the current and must therefore have the capability for adjusting it. In either case there are two variations, *polar working* and *neutral working*. In polar working, a "mark" is current flow in one direction while a "space" is current flow in the other direction. In neutral working a "mark" is the presence of current, and the "space" is the absence of current. The currents used in most telegraph systems are typically 20 ma, but another common value is 60 ma.

For most computer to teleprinter interfaces that will use loop current, the distance between them will not be more than 1500 feet. Therefore, the low voltage current approach is desirable because it is cheaper and easier to maintain and only for the longer distances using a common carrier will the higher voltage interfaces be used. The high and low voltage interfaces are not compatible with each other even though there is the same amount of current in the overall loop.

As the evolution of interfaces progressed and AT&T with its associated operating companies was, for all practical purposes, the only provider of communications services, the modems which were developed at AT&T became industry standards. Even though they are still pretty much the industry standard, both users of the modems as well as independent modem manufacturers who offered equipments for private line use had to know what the electrical characteristics of the computer and/or terminal had to be in order to interface with the modem. The result was that the Electronic Industries Association (EIA) in conjunction with the Bell System, the independent modem manufacturers, and the computer manufacturers, developed a standard for the interface between the data communications equipment (provided by the carrier) and the data terminal equipment (provided by the data processing hardware manufacturers). This standard, which uses serial binary interchange, is called RS232, and the C revision reflects the latest version. There are some newer standards such as RS422 and RS423 which have been developed for both high speed and/or digital interfaces, but RS232C is still the standard to which modem/computer equipment interfaces are designed. For purposes of this text and by EIA definition, the modem may also be referred to as the DCE, while the data processing hardware will be referred to as DTE.

For interface with circuits in foreign countries, the CCITT has also established a standard which is very closely aligned with RS232C and it is called V.24.

When defining the RS232 standard there are really three specific items which are defined. They are:

1. The electrical signal characteristics.
2. A functional description of the interchange circuits.
3. A list of standard subsets of specific interchange circuits for specific groups of communication system applications.

NOTE: A specific connector is not defined. Typically what this means is that the interface is defined for every specific signal and, in addition, has adequate definition for the combinations and permutations of different types of modems (private line, leased line, dial up, etc.) which are known at this time. Table 5-1 defines the RS232C interface for different types of communication paths.

The definitions of each of the interface signals, their relationship between the CCITT and the EIA circuit equivalents are shown, and listed below will be the functional descriptions of each one of the signals.

Circuit AA   Protective Ground   This is a conductor which shall be electrically bonded to the equipment frame and may be further connected to external grounds as required by local codes.

Circuit AB   Signal Ground   This is a conductor which establishes the common ground reference potential for all interchange circuits except circuit AA. It may be connected or removed as required at local installations to meet local codes or minimize addition of noise.

TABLE 5-1

RS-232C INTERFACE

Electronic Industries Association
RS-232C Interface

PIN NO.	CCITT EQUIV.	CIRCUIT	DIRECTION	DESCRIPTION	A	B	C	D	E	F	G	H	I	J	K	L	M	Z
1	101	AA	Both	Protective Ground	-	-	-	-	-	-	-	-	-	-	-	-	-	-
7	102	AB	Both	Signal Ground	x	x	x	x	x	x	x	x	x	x	x	x	x	x
2	103	BA	To-m	Transmitted Data	x	x		x	x	x		x		x	x	x	x	p
3	104	BB	To-T	Received Data			x	x	x		x		x		x	x	x	p
4	105	CA	To-m	Request to Send		x		x	x	x		x		x		x	x	p
5	106	CB	To-T	Clear to Send	x	x		x	x	x		x		x		x	x	p
6	107	CC	To-T	Data Set Ready	x	x	x	x	x	x	x	x	x	x	x	x	x	p
20	108.2	CD	To-m	Data Terminal Ready	d	d	d	d	d	d	d	d	d	d	d	d	d	p
22	125	CE	To-T	Ring Indicator	d	d	d	d	d	d	d	d	d	d	d	d	d	p
8	109	CF	To-T	Received Line Signal Detector		x	x	x	x	x	x	x	x	x	x	x	x	p
21	110	CG	To-T	Signal Quality Detector														p
23	111	CH/CI	Either	Data Signaling Rate Selector/Indicator														p
24	113	DA	To-m	Transmitter Signal (DTE) Element Timing	s	s	s	s	s	s	s	s	s	s	s	s	s	p
15	114	DB	To-T	(DCE) Element Timing														
17	115	DD	To-T	Receiver Signal Element Timing (DCE)			s	s	s	s	s	s	s	s	s	s	s	p
14	118	SBA	To-m	Secondary Transmitted Data							x	x	x	x	x	x	x	p

16	119	SBB	To-T	Secondary Received Data	x					x	x	x	x	p
19	120	SCA	To-m	Secondary Request to Send		x				x	x	x	x	p
13	121	SCB	To-T	Secondary Clear to Send			x		x	x	x	x	x	p
12	122	SCF	To-T	Secondary Received Line Signal Detector			x	x	x	x	x	x	x	p

Circuit BA   Transmit Data   These are the signals generated by the DTE and transferred to the local DCE. The DTE shall hold circuit BA in a mark condition between characters or words and at all times when no data is being transmitted. In all systems the DTE shall not transmit data unless a mark condition is present *on all of the following four circuits* when implemented:

1. Circuit CA (request to send)
2. Circuit CB (clear to send)
3. Circuit CC (data set ready)
4. Circuit CD (data terminal ready)

All data signals that are transmitted across the interface on circuit BA during the time a mark condition is maintained on all of the four above circuits, when implemented, will be transmitted to the communications channel.

Circuit BB   Receive Data   These are signals which are generated by the local DCE and transferred to the local DTE. Circuit BB shall be held in the mark conditions at all times when circuit CF is in the OFF condition. On a half-duplex circuit, circuit BB shall be maintained in the mark condition when circuit CA is in the mark condition and for a brief interval following the mark to OFF transition of CA to allow for the completion of transmission and decay of line reflections.

CA   Request to Send   This signal is used to prepare the local DCE for data transmission, and on a half-duplex channel, to control the direction of data transmission of the local DCE. On one-way only channels or full-duplex channels, the mark condition maintains the DCE in the transmit mode. The OFF condition maintains the DCE in a nontransmit mode. On a half-duplex circuit the mark condition maintains the DCE in a transmit mode and inhibits the receive mode. The OFF condition maintains the DCE in the receive mode. The DCE initiates the necessary actions and indicates completion of them returning circuit CG to the mark condition. The mark condition indicates to the DTE that data may be transferred across the interface on circuit BA. A transition from mark to OFF directs the DCE to complete the transmission of all data which was previously transferred on circuit BA and then assume a nontransmit mode or a receive mode as appropriate. DCE then turns circuit CB to the OFF condition when it is ready to again respond to a subsequent mark condition of circuit CA. (Notes: A nontransmit mode does not imply that all line signals have been removed from the communications channel. When circuit CA is turned OFF it shall not be turned to the mark condition again until circuit CB has been turned OFF by the DCE. A mark condition is required on CA as well as CB, CC, and where implemented, CD, whenever the DTE transfers data across the interface on circuit BA. It allowed to turn CA to the mark condition any time that circuit CB is in the OFF condition regardless of the condition of any other circuit.

Circuit CB   Clear to Send   The signals on this circuit are generated by the DCE to indicate whether the DCE is ready to transmit data. The mark condition of CG combined with the mark condition on circuits CA, CC and where implemented CD, is an indication of the DTE that signals transmitted on circuit BA will be transmitted to the communications channel. The OFF condition indicates to the DTE that data should not be transferred on circuit BA. The mark condition of circuit CB is a response to the occurrence of a simultaneously mark condition on circuits CC and circuit CA, delayed as may be appropriate to the DCE for establishing a communications channel (including the removal of the MARK HOLD clamp from the Receive Data Interchange Circuit of the remote data set) to a remote DTE. Where circuit CA is not implemented in the DCE with transmitting capability, circuit CA shall be assumed to be in the mark condition at all times, and circuit CB shall respond accordingly.

Circuit CC   Data Set Ready   The signals on this circuit are used to indicate the status of the local DCE. A mark condition on this circuit indicates the following:

1. The local DCE is connected to a communications channel ("OFF HOOK" in switched service) and,
2. The local DCE is not in test, talk, or dial mode, and,
3. The local DCE has completed, where applicable, any timing functions required by the switching system to complete call establishment and the transmission of any discrete answer tone.

Where local DCE is not transmitting an answer tone, or where the duration of the answer tone is controlled by some action of the remote data set, the mark condition is presented as soon as all of the above conditions or conditions one, two and the first part of three are satisfied. The circuit shall be used only to indicate the status of the local DCE. The mark condition shall not be interpreted as either an indication that the communication channel has been established to a remote location or the status of any remote equipment.

The OFF condition shall appear at all other times and shall be an indication that the DTE is to disregard any signals appearing on any other circuit with the exception of circuit CE. The OFF condition shall not impair the operation of circuit CE or CD. When the OFF condition occurs during the progress of a call before circuit CD is turned OFF, the DTE shall interpret this as a lost or aborted connection and take the necessary action to terminate the call. Any subsequent mark condition on circuit CC is to be considered a new call.

Circuit CD   Data Terminal Ready   Signals on this circuit are used to control switching of the CDE to the communications channel. The mark condition prepares the DCE to be connected to the communications channel and maintains the connection established by external means (e.g., manual call origination, manual answering, automatic call origination). When the station is equipped for automatic answering of received calls and is in the automatic answering mode, connection to the line occurs only in response to a combination of a ringing signal and the mark condition of circuit CD. However, the DTE is normally allowed to present the mark condition of circuit CD whenever it is ready to transmit or receive data except as indicated below.

The OFF condition causes the DCE to be removed from the communications channel following the completion of any "in process" transmission from circuit BA. The OFF condition shall not disable the operation of circuit CE. In switched network applications, when circuit CD is turned OFF, it shall not be turned to a mark condition again until circuit CC is turned OFF by the DCE.

Circuit CE   Ring Indicator   A mark condition of this circuit indicates that a ringing signal is being received on the communications channel. The mark condition shall appear approximately coincident with the mark segment of the ringing cycle (during rings) on the communications channel. The OFF condition shall be maintained during the OFF segment of the ringing cycle (between rings) and at all other times when ringing is not being received. The operation of this circuit shall not be disabled by the OFF condition on circuit CD.

Circuit CF   Receive Line Signal Detector   The mark condition on this circuit is presented when the DCE is receiving a signal which meets its "suitability" criteria. These criteria are established by the DCE manufacturer. The OFF condition indicates that no signal is being received or that the received signal is unsuitable for demodulation. The OFF condition shall cause circuit BB to be clamped in the mark condition. On half-duplex circuits, this circuit is held in the OFF condition whenever circuit CA is in the mark condition and for a brief interval of time following the mark to OFF transition of circuit CA.

Circuit CG Signal Quality Detector   Signals on this circuit are used to indicate whether or not there is a high probability of an error on the received data. A mark condition is maintained whenever there is no reason to believe that an error has occurred. An OFF condition indicates that there is a high probability of an error.

Circuit CH Data Signal Rate Selector (Using DTE Source) Signals on this circuit are used to select between the two data signalling rates in the case of a dual rate synchronous modem or the two ranges of data signalling rates in the case of a dual range nonsynchronous modem. A mark condition shall select the higher data signalling rate or range of rates.

Circuit CI   Data Signal Rate Selector (DCE Source)   Signals on this circuit are used to select between the two data signalling rates in the case of dual rate synchronous modems or the two ranges of data signalling rates in the case of dual range non-synchronous modems. A mark condition shall select the higher data signalling rate or range of rates.

Circuit DA Transmitter Signal Element Timing (DTE Source) Signals on this circuit are used to provide the timing information relative to the transmitted signals. The mark to OFF transition shall nominally indicate the center of each signal element on circuit BA. When circuit DA is implemented in the DTE, the DTE shall normally provide timing information on circuit DA whenever the DTE is in the "power on" condition. It is allowable for the DTE to inhibit timing information on circuit DA for short periods provided circuit CA is in the OFF condition. (This may be done for maintenance purposes.)

Circuit DB Transmitter Signal Element Timing (DCE Source) Signals on this circuit are used to provide the DTE with timing information. The DTE shall provide a data signal on circuit BA in which the transitions between signal elements normally occur at the time of the transitions from OFF to mark conditions of the signal on circuit DB. When circuit DB is implemented in the DCE, the DCE shall normally provide the timing information on this circuit whenever the DCE is in a "power on" condition. It is allowable for the DCE to inhibit timing information on this circuit for short periods provided circuit CC is in the OFF condition. (This may be done for maintenance purposes.)

Circuit DD   Receiver Signal Element Timing (DCE Source)   Signals on this circuit are used to provide the DTE with receive signal timing information. The transition from mark to OFF condition shall nominally indicate the center of each signal element on circuit BB. Timing information on circuit DD shall be provided at times when circuit CF is in the mark condition. It may, but not necessarily, be present following the mark to OFF transition of circuit CF.

Circuit SBA   Secondary Transmitted Data   This circuit is equivalent to circuit BA except that it is used to transmit data via the secondary channel in reverse channel modems. The DTE shall hold circuit SBA in the mark condition during intervals when characters or words and at all times when no data is being transmitted. In all systems the DTE shall not transmit on the secondary channel unless a mark condition is present on all of the following circuits where implemented: SCA, SCB, CC, CD. All data signals that are transmitted across the interface on circuit SBA during the time the above conditions are satisfied shall be transmitted to the communications channel. When the secondary channel is used only for circuit assurance or to interrupt the flow of data in the primary channel (less than 10 baud capability), circuit SBA is normally not provided, and the channel carrier is turned to a mark condition or OFF by means of circuit SCA. Carrier OFF is interpreted as an "interrupt condition."

Circuit SBB   Secondary Received Data   This circuit is equivalent to circuit BB except that it is used to receive data on the secondary channel. When the secondary channel is used only for circuit assurance or to interrupt the flow of data on the primary channel, interchange circuit SCF is usually provided instead of circuit SBB. In that case, the mark condition shall indicate circuit assurance or noninterrupt condition. The OFF condition shall indicate failure or interrupt.

Circuit SCA   Secondary Request to Send   This circuit performs the same function as circuit CA, except that it performs that function for the secondary channel.

Circuit SCB   Secondary Clear to Send   This circuit performs the same function as circuit CB except that it performs those functions for the secondary channel.

It should be noted that the definitions provided here are standards which are used worldwide, but that does not mean that these are the only signals which can be provided on the individual pin assignments. For those modem equipments which do not use all of the defined parameters for their operation, the vendors sometimes use the same pins for other functions (not defined within the RS232C interface). These modems are then not compatible with modems which are using the standard interface and which are also using the functions which had been predefined on those leads. The user should always verify with the vendor, both AT&T and third party vendors, as to whether their modems are first RS232C compatible, and second, do they use any of the leads for defining some other signal which is unique to their own operation.

One last item relative to RS232C. It is also sometimes compared to MIL-STD-188C in the U.S. military environment. MIL-STD-188C specifies a lower level current at the interface than RS232C so that less electromagnetic radiation is generated.

The next major interface which is involved in many networks is the Automatic Call Unit (ACU), which is represented by the 801 series of AT&T devices. The interface specification for this unit is EIA RS-366. The definition of the interface is shown in Table 5-2 and the sequential operation of an ACU with a modem and DTE is shown in Fig. 5-10. The DTE and its interface with the ACU are responsible for four separate functions:

1. Ensuring that the DCE is available for operation
2. Provide the telephone number to be dialed
3. Decide to abandon the call if unsuccessful
4. Supervise the call to determine when to abandon the connection. This is usually done by the modem after the call has been established.

In order to perform the first task, the PWI signal is referenced to determine whether the ACU has the power on. The DLO signal is then referenced to determine whether the communications line is presently in use. To initiate control of the communication line, the CRQ (Call Request) lead must be activated. To do this and to obtain dial tone, the DTE interface checks to determine that the ACU has power on and that there is no one else using the line. If these conditions are met the DTE turns on the CRQ. At the same time the data terminal ready signal may also be presented at the interface to the modem. The communications line is now placed in the "Off Hook"

TABLE 5-2

AUTOMATIC CALL UNIT INTERFACE BELL SERIES 801

PIN. NO.	CIRCUIT	DIRECTION	DESCRIPTION
1	FGD	Both	Frame Ground
2	DPR	To ACU	Digit Present
3	ACR	To Term.	Abandon Call & Retry
4	CRQ	To ACU	Call Request
5	PND	To Term.	Present Next Digit
6	PWI	To Term.	Power Indication
7	SGD	Both	Signal Ground
8			Unassigned
9			Unassigned
10			Unassigned
11			Unassigned
12			Unassigned
13	DSS	To Term.	Data Set Status
14	NB1	To ACU	Digit Lead
15	NB2	To ACU	Digit Lead
16	NB4	To ACU	Digit Lead
17	NB8	To ACU	Digit Lead
18			Unassigned
19			Unassigned
20			Unassigned
21			Unassigned
22	DLO	To Term.	Data Line Occupied
23			Unassigned
24			Unassigned
25			Unassigned

condition by the ACU, and the telephone switching equipment returns a dial tone to the ACU.

Once the dial tone has been recognized it is time to undertake the second task, which is providing the telephone number to be dialed. The lead called PND is activated from the ACU to the DTE which, when ON, indicates that the ACU is ready to be told which digits are to be dialed. The digits-to-be-dialed information is presented from the DTE to the ACU over the four leads referred to as NB1, NB2, NB4, and NB8. The transfer of information on the digit leads is provided in parallel. At the same time the strobe signal is provided by the DPR lead. With most ACUs it is permissible for the interface to present the digit information and the DPR simultaneously, but in all cases the

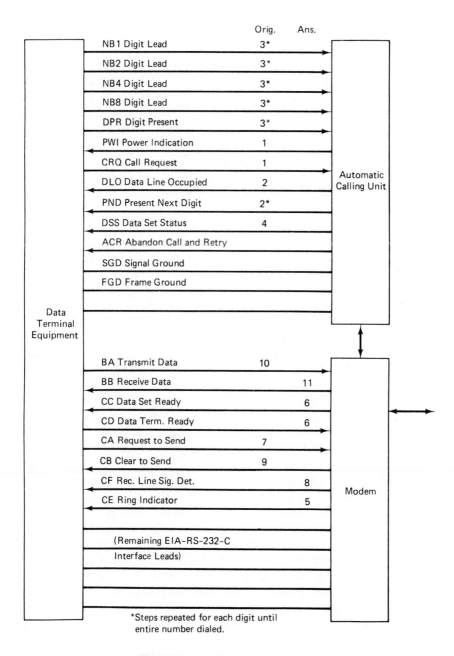

Figure 5-10. Operation of ACU

DPR must not be provided unless the appropriate information is presented on the digit leads. The ACU next indicates that it has accepted the digit for dialing by negating the PND lead. The digit lead information and the DPR signal must not be changed until this negation occurs.

The ACU then reasserts PND when it has completed dialing the digit. The DTE may then present new information on the digit leads and then reassert DPR to indicate that the new digit should be dialed. The process of presenting digit information proceeds until the last digit has been dialed, at which time the DTE places the EON code on the digit leads. Having dialed the number, the ACU and modem are now ready for the third function, which is abandoning the call if unsuccessful.

When the EON code is presented on the digit leads an "abandon call timer" is initiated. If the call is answered by a data terminal, a tone is received by the ACU, and the abandoned call timer is turned off. If the call is not answered or is answered by something or someone other than a data terminal, the timer continues running, and after 10-40 seconds (selectable) the ACU initiates signal ACR (Abandon Call) which directs the DTE to disconnect. The call is disconnected by turning off signal CRQ. If the call is successfully answered by a data terminal, the ACU transfers control of the line to the modem, which continues to hold the connection under the control of the data terminal ready lead which must be provided by the DTE at the time. The call request lead may then be dropped without disconnecting the call while the modem interface, in conjunction with the DTE, then controls the assertion of data terminal ready and disconnects the call when appropriate.

There are two interfaces which, although they are not standards, must be reviewed in relation to the transmission of information. The first of these is the acoustic coupler, which is almost always an inductive device that converts the bits of specific characters to multiple tones which can be transmitted on a communication line. In conjunction with either rotary or touch tone calling systems, the acoustic coupler can be utilized as an interface between a data terminal to transmit information from that terminal to a central site. The most prevalent use of this type of interface is with portable terminals which can then be used at any location where such a calling system exists.

The last of the interfaces is known as the *Data Access Arrangement,* DAA, which is required on all devices that are not certified for use with direct connection into the DDD network. The DAA was required to prevent any harm which might result from nonstandard interfaces connecting to the communications network. There are three types of DAAs; a manual type, voltage type, and contact type. They are shown in Fig. 5-11 along with the definition of the individual signals. The CDT is a manual coupler which must have a telephone set provided. All telephone calls are manually made and answered, and then the data key is actuated for data transmission. In the meantime, the CBS and CBT are both automatic couplers which make the telephone set optional. The interface leads are voltage type in the CBS unit and contact closure type in the CBT unit, and the power supply may be supplied by the user or the telephone company

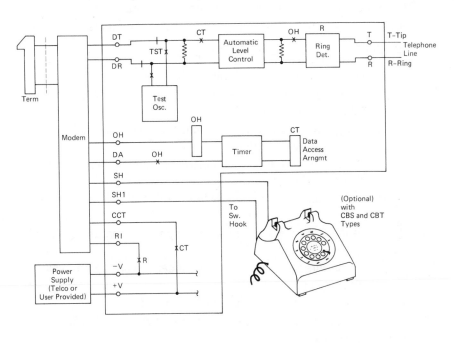

Manual CDT	Type Voltage CBS	Contact CBT	Direction	Function
DT	DT	DT	Both	600-Ohm Transmission Leads.
DR	DR	DR	Both	600-Ohm Transmission Leads.
*	OH	OH	To DAA	Control of "Off Hook" Relay.
*	DA	DA	To DAA	To Request Data Cut Through.
*	RI	RI	To Modem	Ringing Signal Present.
*	SG	*	Both	Signal Ground (CBS only).
*	CCT	CCT	To Modem	DAA Data Path Cut Through.
*	SH	SH	To Modem	Status of Hook Switch.
*	*	SH1	To Modem	SH Return (CBT only).
*	*	+V	To DAA	Positive DC Power (CBT only).
*	*	−V	Both	Return for DC Power and common for all contacts except SH, SH1 in CBT.

* Not Used in This Unit

Figure 5-11.   Data Access Arrangement Configurations

in the case of the CBT. Since these devices are no longer necessary with certified units and will probably be eliminated within the near future, a further detailed analysis of their operation is not provided.

QUESTIONS

1. What are the two primary degradation criteria which affect the quality of information transmission°

2. What are the four most common methods for transmitting information over wire communications facilities°

3. What primary functions are performed by modems on electrical signals°

4. Draw a single cycle modulation diagram for each of amplitude, frequency, and phase for the digital bit sequence of 01011100.

5. Draw a dibit modulation sequence using single cycle modulation for the digital bit sequence of 01011100.

6. Draw a frequency bandwidth diagram for a typical F1/F2 modem and a reverse channel modem.

7. Name three different types of pulse modulation techniques and draw a diagram of each.

8. Define half duplex and full duplex from both a circuit and a protocol point of view.

9. What are the definitions of the terms *asynchronous* and *synchronous?*

10. What are the three secondary potential capabilities to be evaluated when selecting a modem?

11. What is the concept of loop current operation?

12. What four specific areas of definition are provided in RS232?

13. What is a DAA?

chapter

6

DATA CODES

A.

Background

There are many different code sets which are available today that are used for both data processing functions and data communications functions. For this particular section of text we will concentrate on those codes which are used for data communications purposes. In effect, this means that we will be discussing the various code sets which enable one automated machine to talk to another automated machine. Even though a message may be destined to go from one human to another human who has to read the ultimate text, the physical function of moving the information from one machine to another will most likely be accomplished by using one of the code sets defined in this chapter.

One of the definitions of information is *any signal or set of signal elements which performs a particular message or communication, especially one assembled and processed by automatic machines.* A totally predictable event will contain no information since the receiver already knows what is to be transmitted. Therefore, information is a quantitative term which is measured by the degree to which it clarifies an unknown quantity.

In data communications the smallest element of information is the *bit,* a term derived from the contraction of "binary digit." The machines which we are discussing are used to store and carry this information in a binary manner. A binary manner means on or off, mark or space, yes or no, etc. Each of the individual items of information, whether a one or a zero, contains a specific piece of information and is called a bit.

Some very confusing terms which have evolved in the data communications environment are *bits per second* and *baud.* Although there is a very specific difference between these two terms, the newer modes of communication have further blurred the meanings. Originally, baud was defined as the quantity of the smallest increment of signal changes on a communication line which appear on that line at the maximum transmission rate per unit time (seconds). This is the maximum quantity of signal changes which can appear on the line in one second. It can be specified by dividing the time span on the smallest signal into one second. It should be noted that these signal changes do not necessarily pertain to information regarding specific characters. They may contain signals which establish the start and stop positions of the characters and therefore do not convey any user information with those changes, but the signals are required because they do contain very important machine control information. This means the amount of user information bits transmitted is less than the quantity of signal changes which occur on the line per unit time. At the other end of the spectrum, today's modems carry multiple user information bits with each signal change giving the exact opposite effect.

As described above, the baud rate is calculated by taking the reciprocal of the length of time in seconds of the shortest signal used in creating a particular piece of information for transmission. This can also describe each of the bits for information purposes when each signal change identifies one information bit, but for those codes or transmission sequences which require additional overhead bits to define the beginning and the end of characters, the total amount of signals transmitted may not accurately describe the actual amount of information bits transmitted.

To give an example of this we can use the Baudot Code, which is used on all teletypes up to and including the Model 28. Baudot Code

(Baudot will be specifically described later in this chapter) has five information bits, one start bit, and a stop bit which is one and one-half bit times as long as either the start or information bits. It is also a code which is transmitted by teletypewriters at a rate of 10 characters per second. If 10 characters total are transmitted every second there will be a total of 75 bit times transmitted on the communication line. Of these, there will be 50 information bits (5 bits of information for each of the 10 characters), 10 start bits and an equivalent total of 15 stop bits (1½ for each character). Therefore, the baud rate (total amount of signal time on the line) is 75 (75 baud). On the other hand, the bit per second rate, which describes the actual user information, is only 50 bits per second. Therefore, a 75 baud line using Baudot Code is the same as a 50 bit per second line.

This particular type of definition was important during the time that low-speed teletype equipments were being used, and the transmission rate of information (bps) was always less than the baud rate, because there always had to be start and stop bits for the information bits. This is an asynchronous type transmission. As soon as synchronous transmission came about, where we no longer had to have a start and stop sequence for each of the individual characters, the baud and bit per second rate came to mean the same thing. Today, however, with the multibit modulation schemes as described in Chap. 5, we have the individual changes of amplitude or frequency or phase (signal changes) identifying more than one information bit. For example, in a multibit (dibit) modulation scheme, there are two bits of information contained in four different phases, each phase change (signal change) which contains two bits of information is in reality the equivalent of the baud rate, but the information transfer is actually twice the signal change rate and therefore twice the baud rate. The end result of all of this is that in today's higher speed modems (2400 bps and above), the true bit per second information transfer rate is greater than the baud rate (exactly the opposite of what it was on the low-speed teletype lines).

For these reasons the bit per second and baud rate are being confused even more extensively today and in turn, the terms are used almost entirely interchangeably today. A communication line which is described as a 2400 baud line is actually a facility which can accommodate 2400 bits per second, and it is up to the user to decide whether he will be sending synchronous information, where each bit is truly user information, or asynchronous information, where each character may have start and stop bits. For the ASCII Code, where we have 8 information bits, and for asynchronous transmission, with usually one start and one stop bit, a 2400 baud/bit per second communication line will support 300 characters per second synchronously or 240 characters per second (10 bits per character) asynchronously.

The final result of all of these definitions is that even though there is a semantic and technical difference between the terms *baud* and *bits per second,* they are used interchangeably today. It is therefore up to the user to determine what his mode of transmission (synchronous or asynchronous) will be, and from that, to determine what the useful amount of information to be transmitted down the line will be. Interchangeability of terms should definitely not be promoted, but in this case, where such interchange already exists, the use may be tolerated as long as the users of the terms are aware of the difference and know exactly what the other user is saying.

B.

Code Sets and Purpose—BAUDOT, BCD, EBCDIC, ASCII, etc.

Getting back to the code definitions, the first real code that was used in electronic data communications was *Morse Code.* Samuel Morse also developed the code which bears his name when he developed the telegraph system. This code is based on what are known as "dots" and "dashes." A dot was a single short bit, while a dash was a single long bit. For those instances where short and long could not be identified, a dot was still a single entity while the dash was two quick dots. So a dot followed by some time frame was still a dot, while two quick dots would indicate a dash.

Even during the time when Morse was developing his code, he was interested in the efficiency of information transmission. He reasoned that the most often used characters in the English alphabet, if represented by the least amount of dots and dashes, would decrease the total amount of time it took to transmit a particular message. He therefore went to a friend who owned a printing shop (at that time all printing was set a character at a time) and borrowed the type box where all of the individual characters were stored. He counted the characters in each of the type box slots, and those where the most characters of a particular letter were stored were chosen to be the least amount of dots and dashes. As we all know, E is the most commonly used letter in the English alphabet and it is therefore represented by a dot, T a dash, etc. The entire code is represented in Fig. 6-1.

Morse Code

A	• —	N	— •	1	• — — — —
B	— • • •	O	— — —	2	• • — — —
C	— • — •	P	• — — •	3	• • • — —
D	— • •	Q	— — • —	4	• • • • —
E	•	R	• — •	5	• • • • •
F	• • — •	S	• • •	6	— • • • •
G	— — •	T	—	7	— — • • •
H	• • • •	U	• • —	8	— — — • •
I	• •	V	• • • —	9	— — — — •
J	• — — —	W	• — —	0	— — — — —
K	— • —	X	— • • —	.	• — • — • —
L	• — • •	Y	— • — —	,	— — • • — —
M	— —	Z	— — • •	?	• • — — • •

Baudot Code

Character Case		Bit Pattern	Character Case		Bit Pattern
Lower	Upper	5 4 3 2 1	Lower	Upper	5 4 3 2 1
A	—	0 0 0 1 1	Q	1	1 0 1 1 1
B	?	1 1 0 0 1	R	4	0 1 0 1 0
C	:	0 1 1 1 0	S	'	0 0 1 0 1
D	$	0 1 0 0 1	T	5	1 0 0 0 0
E	3	0 0 0 0 1	U	7	0 0 1 1 1
F	!	0 1 1 0 1	V	;	1 1 1 1 0
G	&	1 1 0 1 0	W	2	1 0 0 1 1
H	#	1 0 1 0 0	X	/	1 1 1 0 1
I	8	0 0 1 1 0	Y	6	1 0 1 0 1
J	Bell	0 1 0 1 1	Z	"	1 0 0 0 1
K	(	0 1 1 1 1	Letters (Shift)↓		1 1 1 1 1
L	)	1 0 0 1 0	Figures (Shift)↑		1 1 0 1 1
M	.	1 1 1 0 0	Space (SP) =		0 0 1 0 0
N	,	0 1 1 0 0	Carriage Return <		0 1 0 0 0
O	9	1 1 0 0 0	Line Feed ≡		0 0 0 1 0
P	0	1 0 1 1 0	Blank		0 0 0 0 0

1 = Mark = Punch Hole
0 = Space = No Punch Hole

Figure 6-1.   Code Sets–Baudot

Morse Code lasted as the primary communication code for many years, until Emile Baudot developed the Baudot Distributor. This unit provided for the transmission of five consecutive units of information (bits) representing a character of information to be transmitted on a line between two electro-mechanical devices. A receiving station could identify the five bits of information which were generated electrically at the transmitting station, because the receiving device would have an identical distributor with a commutator rotating at the same speed. Because both ends started at the same time and were rotating at the same speed, the commutators would be in the same relative position at both ends. If the distributors were segmented and the segments electrically isolated from each other, signals could be sent from segments on the transmit end to correlating segments on the receive end. If a signal existed on the line the bit was a 1, while if there was no signal on the line, the bit was a 0. This particular distributor was capable of transmitting these asynchronous characters ten times a second. This is really where the basic teletype transmission rates evolved from. What is called Baudot Code, which is really International Telegraph Alphabet (ITA) # 2, is also shown on Fig. 6-1 and is still in heavy use throughout the world today. As an inherent part of its design, Baudot Code used five information bits/characters (32 combinations). Because of the "transmission medium," start and stop bits were required to move the characters reliably. If there was an error in the transmission, the human at the receive end could always request the human at the transmit end to retransmit the message. For these reasons Baudot Code has two very major drawbacks to its use in a totally automated environment where machines must use the information without human intervention.

These two drawbacks are first, there is no parity or inherent method of validating transmission integrity, which means a machine has no way to tell if an error has occurred, and second, the code is a sequential one. Sequential means that a particular control character defines the subsequent series of characters for a period of time until a new one of the special control characters is recognized. The two control characters which identify the bit configurations in Baudot Code are *letters* (LTRS), which is represented by an arrow pointing down, and *figures* (FIGS), which is represented by an arrow pointing up. These two characters do the same thing that the shift lock on a typewriter would do. The lower case or LTRS shift meant that all characters after it were alpha characters, as shown by the lower case under the Baudot description, and when a FIGS character was recognized it meant that all succeeding characters would be looked at in the upper case mode, which are all of the numerics and the special characters as shown in the code description. For teletypes, where the means of storage is paper tape with holes punched in it, if a particular FIGS or LTRS character was missing, an entire portion of a paper tape message would have to be physically cut out, repunched correctly, and then reinserted, or repunched entirely. This obviously required great time and effort so in actuality all of the characters in error were usually repunched so that they were eliminated (all LTRS characters). The result of all this was that the entire sequence of transmitting Baudot Code via punched paper tape was a slow and tedious process.

If an error was not recognized by the human at the transmit end but was recognized by the human at the receiver, it would have to be re-requested by the receiver, at which time either just the error section or the entire message would have to be retransmitted. Note again, that this is primarily a human to human type communication. So even though Baudot was used for many years, it was used in an environment where human to human communication was the object. As technology evolved and machines had to start communicating with other machines without humans involved, better and more efficient codes had to be evolved for transmitting information, so that the machines themselves could recognize the information and automatically request a retransmission when necessary in the event of an error being received. This led to the development of many other codes which were designed usually with specific hardware devices in mind and which are described in the remainder of this chapter.

In parallel with the development of data communication codes, when data processing first evolved, the data processing machines used their own codes. One of the first codes used was the *Binary Coded Decimal,* which is shown in Fig. 6-2. Binary Coded Decimal (BCD) was used to perform calculations internally within a data processing device. As can be seen there are no alpha characters, so this code is not usable as a communications code and cannot be used for anything but storing of numeric information.

As soon as the data processing requirement came about to communicate with humans and therefore print characters on some type of printing device, the *Binary Coded Decimal Interchange Code* (BCDIC) was developed, which is shown also on Fig. 6-2. This code could be used for complete communication between a human and a machine, but it was not good for machine to machine communications purposes because there was no parity bit in it. Therefore it suffered from one of the same drawbacks that Baudot did, in that a machine could not recognize an error that had occurred during transmission.

The parity problem was corrected by using the *Extended Binary Coded Decimal* (Extended BCD) code, which was also called the *Paper Tape Transmission Code* (PTTC). This is the code that was first developed for the IBM Selectric type typewriters, where a typewriter could be used to create information in a hard copy while, at the same time, generate a code for transmission over a communication line. This code had six bits for information and a parity bit which would enable a transmission device to determine whether an error had occurred within a particular character. As can be seen, however, PTTC was a sequential code in that it had the upper and lower case characters. Therefore, even though the communications error detection part of the code was now acceptable, the fact that upper and

Binary Coded Decimal

Numeric (Decimal)	Binary Equivalent	BCD Code
0	0	1010
1	1	0001
2	10	0010
3	11	0011
4	100	0100
5	101	0101
6	110	0110
7	111	0111
8	1000	1000
9	1001	1001
10	1010	0001 1010
11	1011	0001 0001
12	1100	0001 0010
13	1101	0001 0011
14	1110	0001 0100
15	1111	0001 0101
16	10000	0001 0110
20	10100	0010 1010
63	111111	0110 0011
64	1000000	0110 0100
225	11111111	0010 0101 0101
256	100000000	0010 0101 0110

Binary Coded Decimal Interchange Code

Bits			3	0	0	0	0	1	1	1	1
			2	0	0	1	1	0	0	1	1
			1	0	1	0	1	0	1	0	1
6	5	4									
0	0	0		SP	1	2	3	4	5	6	7
0	0	1		8	9	0	# / =	@ / ,	:	>	√
0	1	0		SP	/	S	T	U	V	W	X
0	1	1		Y	Z	=	,	% / (	γ	\	+++
1	0	0		–	J	K	L	M	N	O	P
1	0	1		Q	R	!	$	*	]	;	
1	1	0		& +	A	B	C	D	E	F	G
1	1	1		H	I	?		¤ /)	[	<	‡

Commercial Usage ⟋ Scientific Usage

Example:
Bits: 6 5 4 3 2 1
1 1 0 0 0 1 = letter "A"
0 0 0 0 1 0 = number "2"

Figure 6-2. Code Sets—BCD and BCDIC

lower case were required made efficient utilization of this code less than optimum. Extended BCD is shown in Fig. 6-3.

The next code which was used extensively was *Extended Binary Coded Decimal Interchange Code* (EBCDIC). EBCDIC had the capability of accommodating 256 combinations because it was an 8-bit code. The standard definition for EBCDIC is shown in Fig. 6-4. A seemingly step backwards was taken from a communications viewpoint because even though more bits were available to be used for character representation, there were no bits set aside for parity detection. In order to overcome this absence of parity, and because not all of the defined characters were required, many users took EBCDIC and established their own code using EBCDIC as a base and identified the particular characters with an odd or even parity. This meant that if two or more users who were using EBCDIC had defined their parity differently, they could end up with a different interface and be incompatible even though they were using the same code set. This also became a problem when the characters that had to be eliminated in order to accommodate the establishment of parity were redefined themselves to a different bit configuration than the other users. Therefore, in an environment where users have been using EBCDIC at different locations, a very detailed analysis should be made, when the time comes to integrate these different sites, to determine each particular character configuration and its definition, to make sure that all definitions are the same. Otherwise, even though both sites are using the same code, they may not be able to talk to each other.

The next level of code to be developed was the *American National Standard Code for Information Interchange* which is also called ANSCII or ASCII. This code was first developed in 1963 and was specifically oriented towards communications processing. In 1967 the code was changed to accommodate different functions which existed in newer equipments. The 1967 version is called ASCII II and is the code that is referred to as ASCII today. ASCII code, which is a 7-bit code plus 1 bit for parity giving 8 bits, is shown in Fig. 6-5 where the 7 bits for information are described completely. The eighth bit, which is a parity bit, could be either odd or even depending on what the user desires. ASCII is now the most extensively used communications code in the United States and has even become a government standard. Even the military establishment, which for years generated codes of its own which were more efficient for their particular applications, has now adopted ASCII as their standard.

Something of the same problem exists for ASCII utilization, however, as does for EBCDIC, where codes were redefined for parity

	Bits 6	0	0	0	0	1	1	1	1
	5	0	0	1	1	0	0	1	1
	4	0	1	0	1	0	1	0	1
3 2 1									
0 0 0		SP / SP	: / 4	/ 2	' / 6	= / 1	% / 5	; / 3	/ 7
0 0 1		− / −	M / m	K / k	O / o	J / j	N / n	L / l	P / p
0 1 0		¢ / @	U / u	S / s	W / w	? / /	V / v	T / t	X / x
0 1 1		+ / &	D / d	B / b	F / f	A / a	E / e	C / c	G / g
1 0 0		* / 8	PN / PN	) / Ø	UC / UC	(/ 9	RS / RS	" / #	EOT / EOT
1 0 1		Q / q	RES / RES		BS / BS	R / r	NL / NL	! / $	IL / IL
1 1 0		Y / y	BY / BY	EOB / EOB		Z / z	LF / LF		/ ,	PRE / PRE
1 1 1		H / h	PF / PF		LC / LC	I / i	HT / HT	¬ / .	DLE / DLE

Upper Case ⟶ (top)
Lower Case ⟶ (bottom)

Example:

Bits: P 6 5 4 3 2 1

0 1 0 0 0 1 1 = letter "A"
1 1 0 0 1 0 0 = number "9"

Non-Printing Characters

SP – Space
PN – Punch On
RES – Restore
BY – Bypass
PF – Punch Off
BS – Backspace
P   – Parity Bit
RS – Reader Stop
NL – New Line

LF – Line Feed
HT – Horizontal Tab
EOT – End of Transmission
EOB – End of Block
UC – Upper Case
LC – Lower Case
IL – Idle
PRE – Prefix
DLE – Delete

Figure 6-3. Code Sets–Extended BCD

Bits 8765 ↓ \ 4321 →																
4	0	0	0	0	0	0	0	0	1	1	1	1	1	1	1	1
3	0	0	0	0	1	1	1	1	0	0	0	0	1	1	1	1
2	0	0	1	1	0	0	1	1	0	0	1	1	0	0	1	1
1	0	1	0	1	0	1	0	1	0	1	0	1	0	1	0	1
0 0 0 0	NUL	SOH	STX	ETX	PF	HT	LC	DEL			SMM	VT	FF	CR	SO	SI
0 0 0 1	DLE	DC_1	DC_2	DC_3	RES	NL	BS	IL	CAN	EM	CC		IFS	IGS	IRS	IUS
0 0 1 0	DS	SOS	FS		BYP	LF	EOB	PRE			SM			ENQ	ACK	BEL
0 0 1 1			SYN		PN	RS	UC	EOT					DC_4	NAK		SUB
0 1 0 0	SP										¢	.	<	(	+	|
0 1 0 1	&										!	$	*	)	;	¬
0 1 1 0	−	/										,	%	_	>	?
0 1 1 1											:	#	@	'	=	"
1 0 0 0		a	b	c	d	e	f	g	h	i						
1 0 0 1		j	k	l	m	n	o	p	q	r						
1 0 1 0			s	t	u	v	w	x	y	z						
1 0 1 1																
1 1 0 0		A	B	C	D	E	F	G	H	I						
1 1 0 1		J	K	L	M	N	O	P	Q	R						
1 1 1 0			S	T	U	V	W	X	Y	Z						
1 1 1 1	0	1	2	3	4	5	6	7	8	9						□

PF – Punch Off
HT – Horizontal Tab
LC – Lower Case
DEL – Delete
SP – Space
UC – Upper Case

RES – Restore
NL – New Line
BS – Backspace
IL – Idle
PN – Punch On
EOT – End of Transmission

BYP   – Bypass
LF   – Line Feed
EOB   – End of Block
PRE   – Prefix (ESC)
RS   – Reader Stop
SM   – Start Message
Others – Same as ASCII

Figure 6-4. Code Sets–EBCDIC

purposes. Not all of the control codes or special characters defined in ASCII were used by all users who, for their own applications, needed other functions to be redefined. In those cases they took the standard ASCII definitions and redefined them for their own purposes. This in turn means that two or more users who developed a modified ASCII code independently and are now trying to talk to each other, may have characters which are undefined or defined differently in the other users' environment. Of all the problems encountered with the utilization of ASCII code, this is by far the most prevalent. When implementing a particular communication system (unless there are special requirements), the use of ASCII code is recommended in the format that exists in Fig. 6-5. If changes are necessary they must be uniform throughout the environment where the code will be utilized. One final point to mention on ASCII code is that many of the terminal vendors today are using ASCII code for the creation of individual characters from the keyboard; but instead of using the eighth bit for a parity character, they are using the other 128 combinations for defining the special functions to be used in the local environment, such as generating special format controls, peripheral accesses, local data processing, etc. If one of these terminals is used, the user should be aware of the potential ramifications if the same terminal is to be used in a communications environment also.

C.

Control Codes

In order to use a code set efficiently in a data communications environment, the user must be able to transmit not only the alpha/numeric type information, but also transmit the necessary controls to identify to the receiver what is to be printed, how it is to be printed, and also what to do in the event special actions are to be taken. In order to control the transmission of information, a series of characters must identify the different portions of the message and what to do with the text from a recognition point of view. The characters that perform this function are called control characters or control codes and are shown in Fig. 6-6 for ASCII. As can be seen there are twenty-seven different controls, each with a specific function defined. Within these controls there are different functions to which the controls relate. There are first the controls used in transmission of individual characters and these are identified by the letter A. These are characters which are usually sent on an individual basis and have to do with bits being transmitted on the line which do not affect the information content.

The second type of control character (labeled B) is a character that defines the various parts of a message being transmitted. The individual segments of a message, as well as the controls for going to different codes in the middle of a message transmission and blocking of information within the message, are all defined within this particular segment of control characters. The third set of control characters (labeled C) involves the controls on the line that identify whether a particular terminal is to transmit or not and whether a message was received correctly or not. Many of the terminal vendors today use these particular single character codes for controls in a different mode than described here as a standard, and when these codes are used they should be analyzed in detail to determine their specific function

American
National Standard Code
for
Information Interchange

Bits				7	0	0	0	0	1	1	1	1
				6	0	0	1	1	0	0	1	1
4	3	2	1	5	0	1	0	1	0	1	0	1
0	0	0	0		NUL	DLE	SP	0	@	P	`	p
0	0	0	1		SOH	DC1	!	1	A	Q	a	q
0	0	1	0		STX	DC2	''	2	B	R	b	r
0	0	1	1		ETX	DC3	#	3	C	S	c	s
0	1	0	0		EOT	DC4	$	4	D	T	d	t
0	1	0	1		ENQ	NAK	%	5	E	U	e	u
0	1	1	0		ACK	SYN	&	6	F	V	f	v
0	1	1	1		BEL	ETB	'	7	G	W	g	w
1	0	0	0		BS	CAN	(	8	H	X	h	x
1	0	0	1		HT	EM	)	9	I	Y	i	y
1	0	1	0		LF	SUB	*	:	J	Z	j	z
1	0	1	1		VT	ESC	+	;	K	[	k	{
1	1	0	0		FF	FS	'	<	L	\	l	:
1	1	0	1		CR	GS	—	=	M	]	m	}
1	1	1	0		SO	RS	.	>	N	∧	n	~
1	1	1	1		SI	US	/	?	O	—	o	DEL

Example:
Bits: P*7 6 5 4 3 2 1

1 1 0 0 0 0 0 1 = letter "A" (Odd Parity)
0 0 1 1 1 0 0 0 = number "8" (Odd Parity)

P* = Parity Bit

Figure 6-5. Code Sets—ASCII

and how it relates to the user's operation of the machine. It should also be recognized that many of the control characters such as those listed as "separaters" are redefined by users when not required and, in turn, may mean something totally different. This is one of the primary areas where users of ASCII code may be incompatible with each other, because codes defined for special purposes may be defined differently at the different locations.

ANSCII Code Set Abbreviations

A — NUL (Null)	The all zeros character, used for time or media fill.
A — SYN (Synchronous Idle)	Used for character synchronization in synchronous transmissions.
A — DEL (Delete)	Used to erase in paper tape punching.
B — SOH (Start of Header)	Used at the beginning of routing information.
B — STX (Start of Text)	Used at the end of header or start of text.
B — ETX (End of Text)	Used at end of text or start of trailer.
B — EOT (End of Transmission)	Used at end of transmission; i.e., end of call.
B — SO (Shift Out)	Code characters which follow are not in the code set of the standard code in use. (Predefined as to which code you shift to.)
B — SI (Shift In)	Code characters which follow are in the code set of the standard code in use.
B — DLE (Data Link Escape)	Used to change the meaning of a limited number of contiguously following characters.
B — ETB (End of Transmission Block)	Used to indicate end of a block of data.
B — CAN (Cancel)	Disregard the data sent with.
B — EM (End of Medium)	End of wanted information recorded on a medium.
B — SS (Start of Special Sequence)	As named.
B — ESC (Escape)	Used to extend code.
B — FS, GS, RS, US	(File, Group, Record, Unit Separators)
C — ENQ (Enquire)	Used as a request for response; "who are you."
C — ACK (Acknowledge)	Used as an affirmative response to a sender.
C — BEL (Bell)	Used to call for human attention.
C — DC1, DC2, DC3, DC4	(Device Controls) Characters for the control of auxiliary devices; i.e., start, pause, stop.
C — NAK (Negative Acknowledge)	Used as a negative response to a sender.

Figure 6-6.   Control Codes

D.

Format Effectors

Along with the control codes shown in Fig. 6-6 there is another set of codes which are called format effectors. These format effectors are contained within a particular message and pertain to the control of the printing device which will be printing out the message. The format effectors consist of those characters defined in Fig. 6-7 and, as can be seen, these particular control codes permit the capability of controlling a printing device for the printout of forms using tabs or form feeds, so that the total transmission does not require extra characters transmitted as blanks or no characters, when particular formats such as columnar printing are required.

It should be noted here, however, that for the Baudot teletype mode of operation, there are times where particular sequences of control characters have different functions. For example, a message may be started by using the sequence (carriage return/line feed) (carriage return/line feed) CR/LF CR/LF where two or more of these particular sequences mean the start of a message, and in other environments the characters ZCZC used in sequence may mean start of message. Some users who still have Baudot teletypes will use these character sequences for start of message, while end of message may also be a unique set of characters such as NNNN. The receiving hardware will recognize the special sequence as being the end of the message and will then start looking for a new start of message sequence.

Even though many of these particular control code sequences involve the use of Baudot teletypes, users in the ASCII environment may also have to consider the use of sequential characters as meaningful controls for interface purposes. This may mean, however, extensive use of additional hardware because if those additional controls are necessary, they may not be contained uniquely within the individual ASCII characters such as SOH, STX, ETX, and EOT. If another unused control character cannot be redefined to specify the new required function, a sequence may have to be used, but because of the cost, this should be avoided if at all possible. Baudot sequences can never be used with ASCII machines, so they cannot be used on the same communication line.

BS	(Backspace)	Moves a printing device back one space on the same line.
HT	(Horiz. Tab)	Moves a printing device to the next predetermined position along a line.
LF	(Line Feed)	Moves a printing device to the next printing line.
VT	(Vertical Tab)	Moves a printing device to the next predetermined printing line.
FF	(Form Feed)	Moves the paper to the next page.
CR	(Carriage Return)	Moves the printing device to the left margin.
SP	(Space)	A format effector, used to separate words.

Figure 6-7. Format Effectors

E.

Relative Efficiencies

In order to get an idea of the relative utilization of the different codes, Fig. 6-8 was generated and provides a summary of the different code sets as well as the communications efficiency ratings for them. The year the code was developed is shown on the first line and then the number of bits which define a character. The mode of primary transmission is shown next as to whether it is asynchronous with stop/start bits or used both ways. Next shown is the amount of characters which are defined within that code set, then whether parity is implemented, and the type which is used most often. The next two identification lines show first the efficiency of the bit utilization, where the total amount of bit configurations possible is looked at compared to how many of those configurations are defined

Code \ Function	Baudot	BCD	BCDIC	PTTC	EBCDIC	ASCII
Year Developed	1930 (Update)	1950	1951	1960	1962	1967 (Update)
Bits/Char	5 Info No Parity	6 Info No Parity	6 Info No Parity	7 Info 1 Parity	8 Info No Parity	7 Info 1 Parity
Async S/S Bits or Sync	1 Start $1\frac{1}{2}$ Stop	Sync	Sync	1 Start 1 Stop	Sync	1 Start 1 or 2 Stop or Sync
Number of Standard Characters	58	64	64	128	256	128
Parity	None	CRC	None	LRC	Bisync-CRC Batch-LRC	Async-LRC Sync-CRC
Relative Efficiency of Bits	3	2	1	3	2	1
Efficiency for Data Communications	3	4	4	2	4	1

Figure 6-8.   Code Set Efficiencies

for either characters or controls. As can be seen, both BCDIC and ASCII are rated number one because every single one of their bit configurations are defined, while BCD and EBCDIC are rated second because they do not have all of their bit configurations for each code which must be preceded by a control character defining which of either the upper or lower case the particular code being transmitted belongs in.

The second efficiency rating is the efficiency for data communications purposes. First is ASCII, which is number one both because it has parity capability and is not a sequential code. PTTC is rated second because it has parity even though it has both upper and lower case (sequential). Baudot is rated third, because even though for sequential purposes it is the same as PTTC, it does not have as many of the potential characters defined and therefore is rated below the PTTC code. BCD, BCDIC, and EBCDIC are rated last because they do not have a parity capability. It should be noted that if the user puts parity in EBCDIC so that the machine can recognize transmission errors, then EBCDIC would be rated number two between ASCII and PTTC. Overall, then, it is obvious that ASCII with parity is the best self-contained code in widespread use today to use for data communications.

QUESTIONS

1. Why is a data code required?
2. Describe the differences between "bauds" and "bits per second."
3. What are the two major drawbacks to the use of Baudot as a communications code?
4. What was the first code used in computers? Why was it not applicable for use as a communications code?
5. What code problem does a user face when establishing a connection between two locations for the first time even when those locations use the same basic code?
6. What is the reason for establishing control codes in a code set?
7. What are format effectors, and what do they do?

PROTOCOLS

When talking to different users and different vendors, as well as reading the different textbooks which are available on the subject, one comes up with many different definitions of a protocol. Not only are there different definitions of the term protocol itself, but there are many different ways in which the classifications of the different portions of the protocol can be defined. Because this particular text is a user-oriented text and will probably be used in conjunction with the understanding of and design and operation of an entire network, the approach taken here is to define the functions of a protocol, describe the different methods in which a protocol can be implemented, and then provide an example which will give the reader a practical idea as to how the protocol functions in the real world.

For purposes of definition in this text, a protocol will be defined to have two major functions:

1. HANDSHAKING This is the sequence which occurs on the communications facilities between the communication equipments (modems) and establishes the fact that a circuit for transmission of

information is available and operational. The signals which describe the electrical interface between the modem and the user equipment (RS232) were described in Chap. 5. This chapter will describe those functions of a protocol which move the information and the techniques for doing so, as opposed to the interface-only digital signaling control which was described in Chapter 5.

2. LINE DISCIPLINE   The line discipline is the sequence of operations which actually transmits and receives the data, handles the error control procedures, handles the sequencing of message blocks, and provides validation for information received correctly. This is the portion of the protocol which most vendors call a protocol.

The line discipline portion of the protocol can be further segmented to describe the sequence for movement of the data and may be called half duplex (HDX), which means transmission in one direction at a time regardless of the facilities which are available, full duplex (FDX) which means transmission in both directions at the same time between the same two points, and a brand new term full/full duplex (F/FDX) (which the author has newly defined to describe a unique capability), meaning the transmission of information in both directions at the same time on a *multidrop line*—specifically where a master site can be transmitting to one point on the multipoint line, while the master site can, at the same time, be receiving from a different point on the multidrop line.

The F/FDX protocols are defined as full-duplex protocols by the vendors, typically SDLC from IBM. They are capable of transmitting in both directions at the same time between the same two points. (IBM has started calling SDLC a Multi/Multipoint Protocol) but a separate definition is given for the full/full duplex type capability because it is this mode of operation on a multidrop line which gives these particular protocols a significant advantage in a distributed network where some terminals on multidrop lines can have high volumes of traffic destined for the central site, while others on the same line can have high volumes of traffic destined to them from the central site. Without the capability of transmitting and receiving from different terminals on the same line, the effective line utilization decreases significantly. This decrease is due to the fact that if only one terminal location can communicate with the central site on a multidrop line and there is a long message in one direction from that terminal, all other terminal locations on that line must wait their turn before they will be able to communicate with the central site. So, for the special limited case of multidrop lines with the newer data link control type protocols, the new definition of full/full duplex protocol will be used.

The handshaking for both dial and dedicated circuits will be described, as well as bisync, which is a half-duplex protocol, and SDLC, which is both a full-duplex protocol for point-to-point circuits, and also a full/full duplex protocol for multipoint circuits.

A.

Half Duplex

The line discipline portion of a half-duplex protocol, as was described above, is one which allows data transmission to occur in one direction at a time between the same two points. For all practical purposes, the relationship will always be a master/slave type arrangement where one end will determine who transmits and when. Half-duplex protocols are almost always used at the lower speeds (up to 2400 bps), are sometimes used up to 9600 bps, and almost always on dial-up circuits. For those applications which are "interactive" a half-duplex protocol is more applicable, because each transmission, regardless of which way it goes, is dependent on the previous transmission. As such, the functions which occur can only occur in sequence giving a one-way-at-a-time operation, which fits perfectly within the definition of a half-duplex protocol.

A very important advantage of a half-duplex protocol is that a single block of information will be transmitted and then a positive acknowledgment must be received prior to the transmission of the next block. What this means is that only one buffer has to be allocated at the remote site and one buffer at the central site for transmission of information. In full-duplex protocols the additional buffers required and the management of them adds a significant level of complexity. The relative advantages and disadvantages of this mode as opposed to the full-duplex mode where multiple buffers are required is described further in Chap. 12.

In order to understand the half-duplex mode of operation better, bisync will be described here in a little more detail because it is the most commonly used form of a half-duplex protocol. It is very important to remember that all during the time this chapter discusses the types of protocols, at no time will there be a mention of the type of circuit over which these protocols will be transmitted. A single section at the end of the chapter will tie the protocols together with the circuits to show how the definitions of the protocols and circuits are used, and it will in turn help to eliminate the confusion in this area, which is probably the most misunderstood area of definition in all of data communications.

Bisync, an IBM developed protocol, has been in use since 1966 for communication primarily between computers and terminals, but is also used from computer to computer, especially in a dial-up mode. It is a half-duplex protocol which uses special characters to delineate the different fields of a message and to control the required protocol functions.

Figure 7-1 shows the format of a typical bisync message. The header portion is optional, but if it is used it begins with a start of header character and ends with a start of text character. The sync (SYN) characters are required in order to establish a mechanism whereby the individual message control and information characters can be identified. This will be described in detail later on in this section. The SOH and STX characters are special format control characters, and the specific bits required to form them uniquely are found in ASCII and EBCDIC, which are the two most common codes used with bisync. The contents of the header are specified by the user, except for status and test request messages. The text portion is variable in length and may contain bits which are not character oriented. In order to do this, the character recognition logic of the receiver has to be turned off so that a data pattern resembling either ETX or one of the other special characters will not confuse it. To turn off the character recognition at the receiver, the bit-oriented data is delimited by a DLE (data link escape character) STX, and DLE ETX or DLE ETB; these special characters indicate the end of the text field and the beginning of the trailer section, which contains only the block check character or characters. The line discipline portion of bisync employs a rigorous set of rules for moving the data between transmitter and receiver. A typical sequence between a terminal station and a computer on a point-to-point line is shown in Fig. 7-1. Note that the individual functions which occur on the transmission line occur one way at a time. This is a true half-duplex protocol.

To detect and correct for errors occurring during transmission, bisync uses either a combination vertical/longitudinal redundancy check sequence (VRC/LRC) or a cyclic redundancy check (CRC), depending on the information code being used (parity checking will be described in Chap. 12). For ASCII, a VRC check is performed on each character, and an LRC check is performed on the entire message. In the case of ASCII, the LRC in the trailer field of the message is a single 8-bit character. If the code is EBCDIC, no VRC check is made;

Bisync Message Format

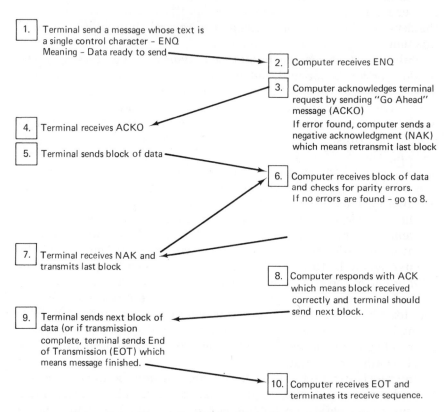

Figure 7-1. Bisync Contention Mode Format and Sequence

instead a 16-bit CRC is calculated for the entire message. When errors are detected, a negative acknowledgment sequence (NAK) is transmitted back to the originator (shown in Fig. 7-1). To correct the error, bisync requires that the block be retransmitted in its entirety (1 block storage at a time). It is up to the user to determine how many retransmissions will be tried before it is assumed that the line is nonoperational or that the originally transmitted message contained an inherent error.

When a transmitted block check matches the block check calculated at the receiver, the receiver sends a positive acknowledgment, ACK 0 for an even numbered block or ACK 1 for an odd numbered block. This alternating between ACK 0 and ACK 1 checks for sequence errors and can detect duplicated or missing blocks. The acknowledgment messages are sent as separate control messages rather than being incorporated within a specific data message. If the reader requires a more detailed description of the specific bisync sequences for all cases of operation, IBM provides a complete operational sequence document and there are many other texts, including those from vendors, which also do the same.

B.

Full Duplex

A full-duplex protocol is one which will move data in both directions at the same time between the same two locations. This method of data movement is functionally the same whether the circuit is point to point or multidrop. In a point-to-point circuit either end can be the master site, although in most instances the user has predetermined that one of the ends will be the master and the other the slave. For a multidrop circuit, there can be only one master site and all the rest of the locations on the line must be slave sites. The term *terminal* is being used to identify remote sites which, for the most part, use some form of lower level capability data processing; but a multidrop network configuration could also have a series of different computers connected to a single line for which a single predefined location can serve as the master site.

Since there are a multitude of full-duplex protocols which permit transmission in both directions at the same time between the same two points, with no single type being a *de facto* standard such as bisync is for half-duplex protocols, a specific sequence of data movement descriptions will not be provided. For a better understanding of full-duplex operation, however, the SDLC example given in the next section can be a full-duplex description when transmitting between two points at the same time in both directions. This can be done because the full/full duplex definition for SDLC described in this chapter is a more complex sequence, and point-to-point operation can be considered a subset of it.

C.

Full/Full Duplex—SDLC

As has been stated previously in this chapter, a full/full-duplex protocol is a special case for a standard full-duplex protocol. Only the newer DLC (data link control) protocols have the capability of transmitting to one remote location while receiving from a different remote location over a multidrop line (protocols doing this have been written by individual users, but none are available as a product offering). The method most widely used to implement this technique is IBM's SDLC—which stands for Synchronous Data Link Control.

There are other protocols which do very much the same things as SDLC and are produced by the other major mainframe vendors. Burroughs has BDLC, Honeywell has HDLC, and CDC has CDC DLC, but these, if available, are part of a complete system offering. Digital Equipment Corporation (DEC) has a protocol named Digital Data Communication Message Protocol (DDCMP), which functionally performs the same operations as SDLC but in a different mode. Whereas SDLC is defined as a bit-oriented protocol, DDCMP is defined as a character count protocol. Although there is a difference of opinion, especially between the vendors, the fact that one protocol is bit oriented while the other is character oriented really makes very little difference to the user; because the protocols almost always come with hardware, firmware, software, and ancillary support. The user therefore, when selecting a vendor, has no real choice. He gets what the vendor has, and the capabilities are comparable anyway. Since SDLC and DDCMP are different in operation and incompatible with each other and SDLC is being implemented by many different vendors while DDCMP is unique to DEC, SDLC will be described in detail here along with an example.

Figure 7-2 depicts the format of SDLC as well as the functional characteristics which make up the pieces of the format. SDLC is described by IBM as being a bit oriented, full duplex, serial by bit transmission, centralized control, synchronous, data communications message protocol. In reality, SDLC is not only a full-duplex protocol, but as described previously it can function as a full/full duplex protocol when in a multidrop environment. In addition, the centralized control concept can be carried further to a "buss" arrangement, whereby any CPU on an interconnected common buss at the same physical location can be a master, while any other is a slave, as long as they first go through a synchronization sequence where the

SDLC is a bit oriented, full/full duplex, serial by bit transmission, centralized control, synchronous, data communications message protocol.

Flag	Address	Control	Info	CRC Frame Check Sequence	Flag

Flag is always 01111110 (If a sequence of 5 "1" bits occurs in the middle of a transmission, the transmitter "stuffs" a "0" bit and the receiver removes it.)

Address is the Station Address on a particular line.

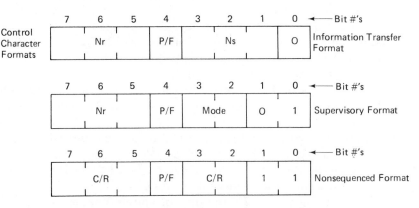

Ns is Sending Sequence Number = 000 through 111 and then repeats

P/F is Primary Station Poll when = 1 from Primary Station

      Secondary Station Final when = 1 from Station on the line

Nr is Receiving Sequence Number = 000 through 111 and then repeats

Mode is Receive Ready (RR) when 00

      Receive Not Ready (RNR) when 10

      Reject (REJ) when 01

C/R is Command from Primary Station or Response from Secondary Station

      Nonsequenced Information (NSI) = 000–00 ⎫

      Set Normal Response Mode (SNRM) = 001–00 ⎪

      Disconnect (DISC) = 010–00   ⎬ Commands

      Optional Response Poll (ORP) = 100–00 ⎪

      Set Initialization Mode (SIM) = 000–10 ⎭

      Nonsequenced Information (UI) = 000–00 ⎫

      Nonsequence Acknowledgment (UA) = 110–00 ⎪

      Request for Initialization (RIM) = 000–10 ⎬ Responses

      Command Reject (FRMR) = 001–10 ⎪

      Request Online (DM) = 000–11 ⎭

Info is Information = Variable Length for Information Transfer

      Prohibited for Supervisory Format

      Variable Length for Nonsequenced Format with NSI

      Fixed Format with CMDR

CRC = Cyclic Redundancy Check Remainder

Figure 7-2. SDLC-Format

machine which wants to transmit initiates the synchronization sequence with the CPU with which it wants to communicate with as a slave. With respect to this buss operation, IBM does not support any configuration other than a predefined master/slave relationship.

There are two major features to consider with respect to the limitations of SDLC as a protocol. First of all, the definition of SDLC does not provide for any of the handshaking procedures which are required to establish the communications link. IBM leaves that up to the user. In any synchronous transmission, in which mode SDLC was designed to operate, there must be sufficient time allowed preceding the message so that the receiving modem will be synchronized to the transmit modem, providing reliable bits to the receive hardware. Without the synchronization time, and possibly even some sync characters, it is quite possible that the address and the control bytes of SDLC will not be recognized (because the flag character is not recognized), and therefore the entire message will be lost. In reality therefore, the SDLC definition from IBM only describes the line discipline portion of the protocol and leaves the handshaking sequence up to the user to implement. (RS232C is defined as the electrical interface specification to be used.)

By referring to Fig. 7-2 the line discipline functions of SDLC will be described. The first set of bits to be generated in the format is called a *flag*. The configuration of this flag byte is always 01111110, and this sequence will never be repeated again throughout the entire message transmission until the end flag with the same configuration is transmitted. In order to ensure this operation every time, when a sequence of five 1 bits in a row is recognized by the transmit hardware after a start flag is generated (except when the end flag has to be generated), an extra 0 bit will be added to the bit stream between the fifth 1 bit and the next bit, regardless of whether that next bit is 0 or 1. This technique is called *zero stuffing*. The hardware at the receive end will always remove a 0 which is detected after five consecutive 1 bits before being passed on to the recognition logic and therefore will end up being transparent to the user.

SDLC itself is totally transparent to the user, in that all of the bits which are added to the front and the back of the message at the transmit end will be removed at the receive end, so the user will get back his original bit stream starting with the first user character to be generated and ending with the last user character to be generated. In this manner SDLC can be looked on as a functional black box into which a user at the transmit end inserts his information in a serial bit form and receives out at the receive end the same serial bit stream exactly the way he put it in. This is even more evident from a hardware viewpoint, because SDLC is almost always implemented via a separate interface at both ends of the line which, in reality, is a printed circuit board (or two of them) which performs all of the SDLC functions transparently to the user. Each of the functions which will be described below is accomplished by the software and firmware which is supplied as part of the SDLC interface.

Since the flag sequence will only occur at the beginning and the end of the message, it is relatively easy to view them as both a "start of message" and an "end of message" delimiter. The only other time 01111110 can occur in sequence is due to a transmission error somewhere between the two flags. If this is the case, the receive hardware assumes that the second flag was preceded by a 16-bit CRC check sequence. When the calculated CRC at the receive end is compared with the assumed CRC which resulted from the transmission error, they will be found to be different, and therefore the message is determined to be in error and will have to be retransmitted. A further description of this will be given later.

The next byte after the start flag is the *address byte,* which consists of 8 bits giving 256 combinations. It should be recognized that this particular address refers to the address on a particular communication line. It has nothing to do with the address which the user may define for his system. The address byte allows 128 unique addresses to be accommodated on every single individual communication line in the network, but because the probability of using that many on one line is extremely remote (16 being a practical limit), many of the other vendors who have SDLC type protocols have taken bits from the address byte to use for other functions. These other functions could be used for more control or for transmission of more blocks of information before an acknowledgement must be received. (This will be described under control byte definition.) Since the address byte on a link is unique to that link, there must be a table somewhere which will convert the user's defined mnemonic and/or logical addresses to the specific link address on that particular line. This information must be provided to the SDLC interface so that the link address can be inserted correctly. (Note that a sequence of five 1 bits occurring in a row even in the address byte will result in the addition of a 0 bit after that fifth 1 bit but will be removed prior to being given back to the decode logic at the receive end).

The third byte of the format is really the heart of the protocol. It is called the *control byte.* The control byte can have any one of three different formats depending on what is to be transmitted. As can be seen from Fig. 7-2, if bit "0" is a 0, this is called an *information transfer format.* If bits "0" and "1" are a 1 and a 0, it is a *supervisory format,* and if bits "0" and "1" are a 1 and a 1, it is called a *nonsequenced format.* When bit "0" is a 0, the next three bits identify the sequence number of the block being transmitted (by either the master or the slave). Since there are 8 combinations available with 3 bits, this means that no more than 8 blocks of information can be sent before this segment will start repeating itself. Therefore, it would appear that the maximum limitation of blocks which can be sent prior to the repeating of message identification would be 8. In reality however, only 7 blocks can be transmitted before an acknowledgment for at least one of the blocks must be received. The eighth block identification is reserved for positive acknowledgment of the preceding seven, because, as will be seen in the example later, the mechanism whereby SDLC informs a transmitter that a block has been received in error is to use that sequence number to request a retransmission. Therefore, if 8 blocks are transmitted there would be no unique way to tell whether all 8 blocks were received correctly or only the first block was actually received in error. (The example provided later will show this clearly.)

The next bit location in the control character is the same for all three formats; it is called *P/F bit.* What this means is that when being transmitted from the master location it is called a P bit and if set to one, identified as a *poll message.* If set to 0 this is not a poll message, and the slave which is being addressed should not answer. If coming from a slave location it is called an *F bit* (final message of a sequence), and if it is a 0, then at least one more block of information will be following the block in which this control character is contained. If the F bit is a 1, this block will be the last block in the present sequence to be transmitted by that slave site. Since the F bit occurs at the very beginning of a block being transmitted by a slave site, the firmware at the master site can use this information to interrupt its transmission of a multiblock sequence of information to another location on the same multidrop line at the end of the block in progress, wait for the end of the incoming transmission from the slave site that is in the process of receiving, and at that time, poll a different location on that line for information to be brought in from that new location. As soon as the newly polled site begins to transmit to the master, the master can go back and finish the interrupted multiblock transmission to the original slave site to which it was transmitting. This is the mechanism whereby the full/full duplex capability is implemented in a multidrop environment. In a point-to-point environment this mode of operation is transparent, except that the master, after receiving the F bit as a 1, can poll the slave site again at the end of that block.

The last three bits of the control byte contained in the information transfer format is the next block number which the transmitting end (master or slave) expects to get from the other end the next time a transmission takes place. As we will see, this is the mechanism whereby acknowledgments are accomplished.

For the supervisory format, where bits "0" and "1" are a 1 and a 0, the next two bits are defined as the "mode," shown in Fig. 7-2 as being either receive-ready, receive-not-ready, or reject. These are controls which are used to identify whether a particular terminal can receive or not. The P/F and Nr bit segments are the same as for the information transfer format.

Nonsequenced Format (Now Called Unnumbered) The nonsequenced format is defined by bits "0" and "1" of the control byte being 1 and 1. When the nonsequenced format is identified, then bit numbers 2, 3, 5, 6, 7 must be looked at together as being a command or a response. These commands/responses are shown in the bottom half of Fig. 7-2 in the brackets assigned for each. Nonsequenced formats are used primarily for establishing the initial synchronization and for ultimate disconnecting of a terminal site.

The next segment in the SDLC format is what is known as the *information portion*. This is the segment of the transmission which is the total user transmission and starts with the user's first character and ends with the user's last character. If the user has, in addition to the SDLC capability, his own capability for error detection, it will also be included in this segment before the user EOT and the SDLC CRC. This CRC (cyclic redundancy check) is described in Chap. 12, in which all of the transmission integrity functions are included. It is also called the frame check sequence and guarantees, to an extremely high reliability, the fact that the transmission is correct.

After the SDLC CRC is the final flag byte. This final flag identifies the end of the present block and a new flag sequence must be transmitted to initiate the next message or block.

A couple of further comments on the information portion of the format:

1. It is of a variable length (multiples of 8 bits).
2. It is prohibited for the supervisory format.
3. It is of variable length for the nonsequenced format when used with VI (nonsequenced information).
4. It is of a fixed format with the use of the command reject (FRMR) response by a slave to the master.

Probably the best way to understand the concepts of SDLC is to go through a specific example describing the functions being performed. There are two examples provided and are shown in Figs. 7-3 and 7-4. The example which will be described in detail is Fig. 7-3. This is the easier one to understand for the first-time user because the functions will happen sequentially in what is really a half-duplex mode of operation. The desirability of SDLC operating in a half-duplex mode is very low from a transmission efficiency point of view and it is therefore shown here only for explanatory purposes. It should be noted, however, that those applications upgraded from HDX protocols may retain the same hardware and therefore operate SDLC in a HDX mode. After going through the sequence of operations in Fig. 7-3 the reader should be able to go through on his own the example shown in Fig. 7-4 where the true full/full duplex operation is depicted.

There are four major functions described in Fig. 7-3. They are an initial synchronization sequence, a two-way transmission without an error, a two-way transmission with an error and a retransmission, and finally, a disconnect command. The functions are described by identifying the individual format segments, expanding out the control byte, and then describing the operation which has occurred. The left-hand column shows the transmission from the master site to the slave site, and the arrow shows the direction in which the transmission occurs. To the right of the arrow is a column which shows what the slave is transmitting back to the master, and to the right of the vertical line is the description of what has occurred. It must be noted that, where applicable, the initial synchronization sequence required for handshaking must take place prior to transmission of the initial flag character. This may not be required on point-to-point transmissions between the master and slave sites as long as there is a high percentage of traffic (to keep synchronized), but it is mandatory to be transmitted each time a slave site initiates a transmission on a multidrop line.

We start off with a transmission from the master to the slave with the flag byte, the address (B), and then the control byte which starts off with a 10 (a supervisory format). With the P/F bit coming from the master set as a 1, this is a poll. The CRC and end flag follow, and as can be seen under "remarks," the master has polled site B. Coming back from B now we have the flag, and notice here the slave identifies himself. If the slave were to put in the master's address it would be redundant information, because the slave can only talk to the master. Therefore, in each case when a slave transmits to the master in the address byte, the slave site puts its own address. The control byte starts off with an 11, which identifies the transmission as a

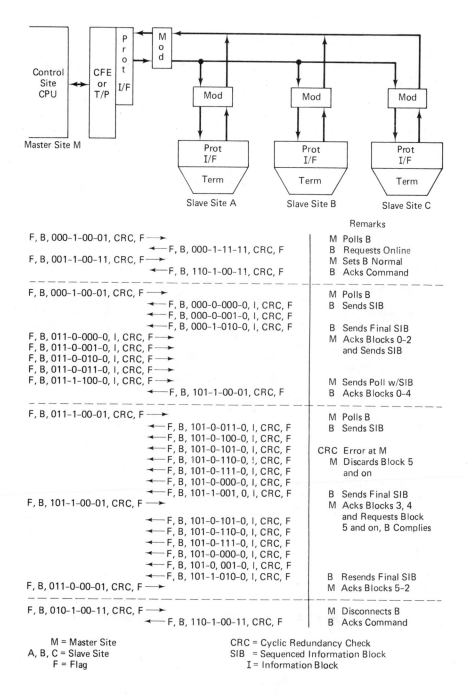

	Remarks
F, B, 000-1-00-01, CRC, F ⟶	M Polls B
⟵ F, B, 000-1-11-11, CRC, F	B Requests Online
F, B, 001-1-00-11, CRC, F ⟶	M Sets B Normal
⟵ F, B, 110-1-00-11, CRC, F	B Acks Command

F, B, 000-1-00-01, CRC, F ⟶	M Polls B
⟵ F, B, 000-0-000-0, I, CRC, F	B Sends SIB
⟵ F, B, 000-0-001-0, I, CRC, F	
⟵ F, B, 000-1-010-0, I, CRC, F	B Sends Final SIB
F, B, 011-0-000-0, I, CRC, F ⟶	M Acks Blocks 0-2
F, B, 011-0-001-0, I, CRC, F ⟶	and Sends SIB
F, B, 011-0-010-0, I, CRC, F ⟶	
F, B, 011-0-011-0, I, CRC, F ⟶	
F, B, 011-1-100-0, I, CRC, F ⟶	M Sends Poll w/SIB
⟵ F, B, 101-1-00-01, CRC, F	B Acks Blocks 0-4

F, B, 011-1-00-01, CRC, F ⟶	M Polls B
⟵ F, B, 101-0-011-0, I, CRC, F	B Sends SIB
⟵ F, B, 101-0-100-0, I, CRC, F	
⟵ F, B, 101-0-101-0, I, CRC, F	CRC Error at M
⟵ F, B, 101-0-110-0, !, CRC, F	M Discards Block 5
⟵ F, B, 101-0-111-0, I, CRC, F	and on
⟵ F, B, 101-0-000-0, I, CRC, F	
⟵ F, B, 101-1-001, 0, I, CRC, F	B Sends Final SIB
F, B, 101-1-00-01, CRC, F ⟶	M Acks Blocks 3, 4
	and Requests Block
⟵ F, B, 101-0-101-0, I, CRC, F	5 and on, B Complies
⟵ F, B, 101-0-110-0, I, CRC, F	
⟵ F, B, 101-0-111-0, I, CRC, F	
⟵ F, B, 101-0-000-0, I, CRC, F	
⟵ F, B, 101-0, 001-0, I, CRC, F	
⟵ F, B, 101-1-010-0, I, CRC, F	B Resends Final SIB
F, B, 011-0-00-01, CRC, F ⟶	M Acks Blocks 5-2

F, B, 010-1-00-11, CRC, F ⟶	M Disconnects B
⟵ F, B, 110-1-00-11, CRC, F	B Acks Command

M = Master Site	CRC = Cyclic Redundancy Check
A, B, C = Slave Site	SIB = Sequenced Information Block
F = Flag	I = Information Block

Figure 7-3. SDLC-HDX Operation Sequence

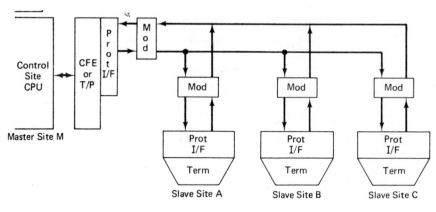

Master Site M

	Remarks
F, B, 000-1-00-01, CRC, F ⟶	M Polls B
⟵ F, B, 000-1-00-01, CRC, F	B Has No Send Data
F, C, 000-1-00-01, CRC, F ⟶	M Polls C
⟵ F, C, 000-0-000-0, I, CRC, F	C Sends SIB to M
F, B, 000-0-000-0, I, CRC, F ⟶	M Sends SIB to B
⟵ F, C, 000-0-001-0, I, CRC, F	
F, B, 000-0-001-0, I, CRC, F ⟶	
⟵ F, C, 000-1-010-0, I, CRC, F	C Sends Final SIB to M
F, C, 011-0-00-01, CRC, F ⟶	M Acks Blocks 0-2 to C
F, B, 000-1-010-0, I, CRC, F ⟶	M Sends Final SIB to B
⟵ F, B, 011-1-00-01, CRC, F	B Acks Blocks 0-2 to M
F, A, 000-1-00-01, CRC, F ⟶	M Polls A
⟵ F, A, 000-1-00-01, CRC, F	A Has No Data to Send
F, B, 000-1-00-01, CRC, F ⟶	M Polls B
⟵ F, B, 011-0-000-0, I, CRC, F	B Sends SIB to M
⟵ F, B, 011-0-001-0, I, CRC, F	
F, B, 000-0-011-0, I, CRC, F ⟶	M Sends SIB to B
⟵ F, B, 011-1-010-0, I, CRC, F	B Sends Final SIB to M
F, B, 011-1-100-0, I, CRC, F ⟶	M Sends Final SIB to B
	and Acks Blocks 0-2
⟵ F, B, 101-1-10-01, CRC, F	B Acks Blocks 3, 4
	and Advises is Busy
F, C, 011-1-00-01, CRC, F ⟶	M Polls C
⟵ F, C, 000-1-00-01, CRC, F	C Has no Data to Send
F, A, 000-1-00-01, CRC, F ⟶	M Polls A
⟵ F, A, 000-1-00-01, CRC, F	A Has No Data to Send
F, B, 011-1-00-01, CRC, F ⟶	M Polls B (Still Busy?)
⟵ F, B, 101-1-00-01, CRC, F	B Has No Data to Send
	and is Normal

M = Master Site	I = Information Block
A, B, C = Slave Sites	CRC = Cyclic Redundancy Check
F = Flag	SIB = Sequenced Information Block

Figure 7-4. SDLC-F/FDX Operation Sequence

nonsequenced format, which by looking at Fig. 7-2 will be seen as a "request for on line." With the P/F bit set as a 1 from the slave, the master knows that this is the final block being transmitted from the slave, and there will be no blocks after it. This is followed by the CR and the end flag. B has requested on line.

The master now transmits flag, the address of B, the control byte starting with 11 (which means a nonsequenced format), and a set normal command. With the P/F bit being a 1, this is also a poll. This is followed by the CRC and flag. B then comes back and sends a flag, his own address, a nonsequenced control byte format acknowledging the command, and the P/F bit a 1, which says this is the final block of this sequence, followed by the CRC and end flag. These four steps now complete the sequence which establishes initial synchronization between the master and the slave, and this sequence must now occur between the master and every other slave site on the line to establish a basic synchronization of buffers. With this logic synchronization complete, the master and the slaves now know which messages are being transmitted and which ones are to be acknowledged. If desired at this point in time, the reader should draw a line across the page under the fourth line, and these four steps can be referred to as a typical synchronization sequence.

Next let us take a look at a transmission sequence where information must be passed in both directions. Remember we are showing this in a half-duplex arrangement for simplicity. In actuality the transmissions would be occurring in both directions at the same time. Figure 7-4 has this mode in the example, and it should be recognized that the arrows in opposite directions could be taking place at the same time in Fig. 7-4 but cannot take place at the same time in Fig. 7-3.

The master starts off by sending a flag byte, B address, and then a supervisory format with a poll included. In other words, the master polls B. The assumption is made that B has three blocks of information to send, so he returns flag, his own address, and then an information format which has as the sending sequence number (Ns) 000. Note here that the P/F bit is a 0, which means that there is at least one more block coming after this block is completed. The Nr is 000 which means the slave will expect to receive block 000 from the master when the master transmits information. "I" stands for an information block regardless of the length. This is followed by CRC and a flag. B then sends block 001 and block 010. Along with block 010 the P/F is set to a 1, which tells the master that this is the last block to be transmitted. The master waits for the end of the transmission, and in the meantime has put together a five-block message which must be sent to B.

We now have a flag byte and an address for B. In the control byte we have a 0 which specifies an information format and then 000 for the first block to be transmitted. The P/F bit is next and is a 0 which means this is not a poll, and then Nr which is set to 011. The fact that the master expects to get block number 011 from the slave the next time the slave transmits tells the slave that all blocks up the 010 have been received correctly. In this mode SDLC has acknowledged three blocks of information being received from the slave site with a single transmission, and in actuality up to 7 blocks can be acknowledged this way. Either individual or multiple block sequences can be acknowledged in this manner. The master then sends his information block followed by a CRC and a flag.

Following this transmission block are blocks 001, 010, 011, and 100. Along with block 100 is a poll in the P/F bit position so that B is being polled. B does not have a message to send back to the master at this time, so it acknowledges by transmitting a flag, his own address, and a supervisory format acknowledging blocks 000 through 100 by putting into the control byte in position 6, 7 and 8 (Nr), a 101. This is followed by the CRC and a flag. Between the line drawn above and this description line is a two-way transmission without an error. If desired, the reader should draw a line here under "B ACKS blocks 0 to 4" across the page, which will indicate a successful two-way transmission. Again, remember that in a true SDLC operation these transmissions would be occurring at the same time in a full-duplex mode.

Next let us take a look at a transmission where an error is recognized. The master sends out to site B a flag, B address, a supervisory format with a poll, a CRC, and a flag. B now has an 8-block message to send. B starts transmitting by sending a flag, his own address, and an information format starting with block 011 (note the block identification continues on). Block 100 is then sent, 101, 110, 111, 000 (wrap around now), and 001. Along with 001, the P/F bit is sent as a 1, because up to this point in time no acknowledgment has been received, and because this means 7 blocks have been transmitted, the slave must stop transmitting until it gets an acknowledgment. An assumption is made that an error has been detected in block 101 at the master site.

To initiate the retransmission sequence the master therefore sends back a flag, B address, and a supervisory format which indicates in the Nr segment that the next block expected is block 101. Included within this message is a poll. Since B has transmitted not only 101, but all succeeding blocks through 001, by definition of the SDLC protocol operations, B recognizes that 101 was received in error. Also by definition of the protocol, not only must block 101 be transmitted, but all blocks after 101 which had been transmitted must also be retransmitted. This is known as the *Go back N Technique* and is therefore significant in that only a maximum of 7 buffers must be available to store the 7 blocks of information at both ends of an SDLC communication link. For those other vendor protocols like SDLC, where many more blocks can be in transit before an acknowledgment is received, they will need that many more buffers at either end to store information for the case where acknowledgments have yet to be received.

B, recognizing that block 101 was received in error, now transmits blocks 101, 110, 111, 000, 001, *and* block 010. B can send block 010 now because the first two blocks of the original sequence were acknowledged as part of the previous transmission, and there were only 6 blocks in this sequence to be transmitted. The master answers back now with an acknowledgment indicating that the next block to be received is 011. This tells B that all blocks through 010 have been received correctly now, and therefore no additional retransmissions are required. The reader can now draw a line under "master ACKS blocks 5-2," and this sequence can be considered a two-way transmission where one of the sequences contains an error.

The last two lines show a disconnect command which is used when a terminal site is to be taken out of service in an orderly manner. The master sends a flag, B address, a nonsequenced format which is interpreted as a disconnect command, followed by the CRC and a flag. Included within this transmission is a poll. B then answers back with a flag, his own address, and a nonsequenced format which acknowledges the command, and at the same time he indicates this is a final transmission. At this point in time B disconnects, and now a brand new synchronization sequence must be initiated before the master can talk to B again.

A true full/full duplex operation is depicted in Fig. 7-4, although no error transmissions are shown. When the reader goes through the sequence, he should keep in mind that when arrows are in two different directions, those transmissions may be occurring at the same time. This is the way true SDLC will operate on a multidrop line.

D.

Dial/Dedicated Handshaking

Up to this point we have been discussing the line discipline portion of a protocol. What is even more critical, before the data transmission can start, is to have a valid circuit established which can support the information transmission. The technique for validating the availability and operability of a circuit is called *handshaking*. There are different modes of handshake which are applicable to the different kind of circuits involved. The circuits were described in Chap. 4, where the differences between dial-up and dedicated lines were discussed. This section will cover the details of the handshaking procedure as they apply to both types of circuits.

Four of the most common handshaking procedures are shown in

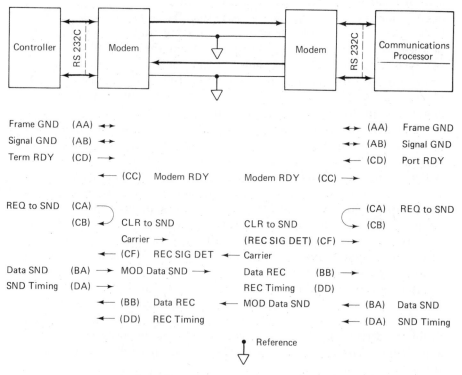

Figure 7-5.   FDX Private Line Handshaking

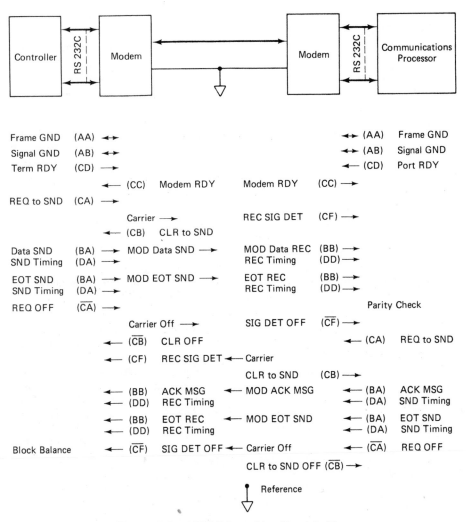

Figure 7-6. HDX Private Line Handshaking

Figs. 7-5 through 7-8. Figure 7-5 shows the procedure which takes place at RS232C interface for a private-line full-duplex circuit operation. Figure 7-6 shows the RS232C interface for a half-duplex private-line interface. (Note that in most cases a user, when leasing a line, will get a full-duplex line and not a half-duplex line because of the minimal difference in cost.) Figure 7-7 describes the RS232C interface for a dial-up half-duplex mode of operation, and Fig. 7-8

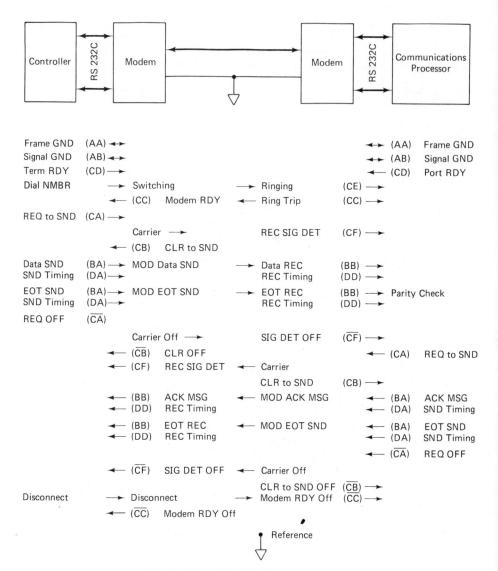

Figure 7-7. HDX Dial-Up Handshaking

describes the handshaking sequence which occurs on a full-duplex leased line with reverse channel. These are some of the handshake sequences on typical point-to-point type connections, but in reality very much the same sequence takes place on a multidrop private line between the master and each of the remote sites. Once the handshaking is complete and the circuit is confirmed, information can be

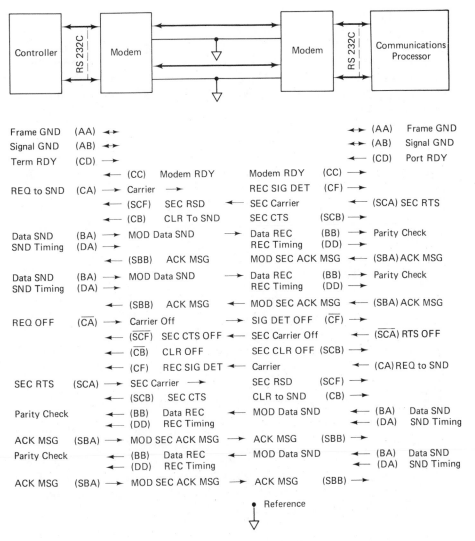

Figure 7-8. FDX Reverse Channel Handshaking

passed back and forth until one of the ends decides to terminate the sequence.

Because the descriptions are presented in the same format and at the same level of detail, all of the sequences will not be described. The only one that will be described is Fig. 7-5, which is the full-duplex private line.

The handshaking sequences are described with respect to their relationship at the RS232C interface which was described in detail as to its operation in Chap. 5. Referring then to Fig. 7-5 we find on the left-hand side of the page the definition of the signal and its designation, the direction of the signal transmission between the controller and the modem (designated by the arrows), the functions which occur on the modem (or line), the arrows depicting the direction of signal at the central site end, and finally the definition of the signals at the central site.

Starting off at the top line, we have the frame ground which ties both the modem and the controller together at each end. Then we have the signal grounds that do the same thing. At the remote end the "terminal ready" signal is sent to the modem, while at the same time, the "modem ready" signal is sent back to the terminal. This indicates that both units are capable of operation. At the other end of the line, at the same time, we have "modem ready" being transmitted to the central site controller port and the control port indicating to the modem that it is ready.

From a digital viewpoint, therefore, both ends are ready to transmit in both directions. If we assume that both ends would like to transmit at the same time, the digital side of the interface will initiate the "request to send" signal. At the modem, only because this is full duplex, the signal is "strapped" back to the "clear to send" signal interface so that the digital side is now ready to transmit. The carrier now comes up in one direction on one pair of wires and in the other direction on the other pair of wires, indicating that the transmission line will now be transmitting data.

From the remote end you have data being sent via Pin BA over the line and being output on Pin BB at the central site, while at the same time Pin BA at the central site will be sending data out on the line, which will be output from Pin BB at the remote site. At exactly the same time that the data is being sent, both ends are also sending timing information through Pin DB. The timing information is combined with the data in the modulator so that the modulated carrier will contain sufficient information for the demodulator to determine both. This will come out as phase-corrected receive timing at the receive end so it can be used by the DTE equipment to recognize the data reliably.

When each one of the ends comes to the end of this transmission (could be at different times), the "request to send" will be removed, which in turn takes the carrier off the line, and the link now waits for the next "request to send" to come up. If during or between transmissions, the modem-ready signal is no longer being detected, it is assumed by the DTE that the line is no longer available and the transmission is terminated. Also, when the carrier comes up there is a signal called *receive line signal detect* that indicates a carrier is on the line. The same functions, unique for their particular handshaking sequence, are shown in Figs. 7-6 through 7-8.

E.

Protocols vs Circuit Types

Sections A through D of this chapter described the sequence of events that is required to transmit information on a communication line. The two steps which are involved are first the handshaking and then the line discipline of the protocol. All during the description no mention was made as to the type of circuit over which these protocols would operate. This was done intentionally, because the protocol really is independent of the type of circuit in almost all cases except the full/full duplex mode of operation, because they are on a multidrop line. When operating in a point-to-point mode, however, even the DLC type protocols can operate on the two available circuit types.

As was described in Chap. 4, the two basic types of circuits are the half-duplex circuit, which is a two-wire circuit, and a full-duplex circuit, which is really a four-wire circuit. Any one of the protocols can operate on each of the described circuit types, because now the capability exists, as was described in Chap. 5 under modems, to transmit in both directions on the same physical signal line. In order to describe these combinations better, the matrix shown below in Fig. 7-9 identifies the combinations of protocol and circuit which can be implemented by the user.

As can be seen from the matrix, there are five entries which describe the possible combinations of circuits over which the different types of protocols can function. Naturally the handshaking portion will be different because of the difference in timing relationships

	Circuit	Protocol
1	HDX	HDX
2	FDX	HDX
3	FDX	FDX
4	HDX	FDX
5	FDX	F/FDX (Multidrop Line)

Figure 7-9.   Protocol vs Circuit Matrix

between two-wire circuits and four-wire circuits (no turn around required).

At first we have a half-duplex circuit and a half-duplex protocol. This is a typical mode of operation on any dial-up circuit where a half-duplex protocol is used. There will be transmission in one direction at a time over the single signal wire. The transmission will go first in one direction, then the modem will turn around, and the transmission will go back in the other direction. The sequence will continue until the total transmission required is completed. Functionally, the exact same thing would happen on a half-duplex leased circuit.

The second line shows a full-duplex circuit with a half-duplex protocol. The protocol is exactly the same half-duplex protocol as would be used on the first line, but in this case the transmissions which occur in each direction, one way at a time, occur on different pairs of wires. What we have in this case is two unidirectional pairs of wires which carry the transmission in one direction only. These circuits are functionally the same as the half-duplex circuits above except that there are two of them between the transmitting and receiving locations. The full-duplex circuit can only be available in leased configurations (except in special circumstances as described in Chap. 4), and for multidrop lines the FDX protocol operates independently between the master site and each of the remote sites on the same line but not at the same time.

The third line shows a full-duplex circuit and a full-duplex protocol. This situation occurs again on leased lines because the circuit is full duplex. For the full-duplex protocol, however, the data transmissions take place in both directions at the same time, between the same two points. Regardless of whether the circuit is a point-to-point circuit or a multidrop circuit, the protocol will operate only between the master site and a single slave site. As such, a point-to-point circuit can be considered the limiting case of a multipoint circuit where there is only a single point connected to the master site. For the case where two computers will be connected to each other on a point-to-point arrangement, the full-duplex protocol which is used can be either a defined master/slave relationship or a master/master relationship, where the individual transmission session is set up on an "as required" basis when one of the master locations has a message to send to the other master location. Note that this definition also applies to the DLC type protocols when they operate in a point-to-point configuration (except for IBM where one end is always defined as the master).

The fourth line of the matrix shows a full-duplex protocol operating on a half-duplex circuit. This means that data is transmitted in both directions at the same time, between the same two points and on the same physical signal line. This operation was also described in Chap. 5 when describing reverse-channel modems. The most common use of this type of arrangement is on a dial-up line, using buffered terminals, where it is a time-saving operation to transmit in both directions at the same time (saving modem turn-around time). The modems which operate in this environment are called F1/F2 or reverse-channel modems. The voice grade line is divided into two equal segments for F1/F2 operation and unequal segments in the reverse channel mode of operation. Each of the segments uses different modulation carrier frequencies, and for F1/F2 operation each segment is capable of supporting a 1200-bit per second transmission rate, and can therefore operate on a single two-way circuit where information is passing in both directions at the same time.

A somewhat analogous description of this kind of operation is if a person stands near a body of water and drops in a rock at one end, then walks a few feet and drops another rock in at the other end, the ripples which are caused by each of the rocks pass each other going in opposite directions and can be seen in their entirety at the other end. Functionally this type of operation occurs on a reverse-channel modem. The ends of the transmission line are comparable to the two locations where the rocks were dropped into the water. The different frequencies crossed each other in each direction although neither one is destroyed. The same situation functionally exists on the communication line where both transmissions can be seen at the same time as a composite signal. When the signal gets to the other end there is a filter arrangement on the line which permits only the signals which are transmitted from the far end to be passed through, while the signals on the same line transmitted from the transmit end are filtered out.

The fifth line of the matrix shows a full/full duplex protocol operating on a full-duplex circuit. As was previously stated the full/full duplex operation can only occur on a multidrop line which has to be a leased line. Also the full-duplex circuit must consist of the two independent half-duplex circuits in order that the master can use one of the circuits to talk to the single slave site while another slave site can talk back to the master on the other circuit (pair of wires).

Because of all of the different combinations of circuits and protocols it is mandatory that the people using the terms use them correctly. There is no question that these two terms (half duplex/full duplex) are the most confusing terms in the data communications business. This is caused by the fact that both the circuit and the protocol must be defined, and there can be all the possible combinations for them.

Another point to mention here is that a full-duplex protocol can operate in a mode where only one end transmits at a time. Even though the capability exists to transmit in both directions at the same time, if the transmission only goes in one direction at a time the full-duplex protocol is really operating in a half-duplex mode. This is another point of confusion for the users, so the terms must be accurately and adequately defined when discussing them with other people.

Finally, if reverse channel modems are used on an FDX circuit, there are two fully independent paths available on each circuit. This means that in reality two separate FDX transmissions can take place on a single FDX circuit. Either two separate FDX protocols can be operated, or more often two separate functions, such as data on 1 FDX protocol and diagnostics on the other FDX protocol, can be implemented independently.

QUESTIONS

1. Describe the two primary functions of a protocol.
2. Define the information flow using a half-duplex protocol.
3. Define the information flow using a full-duplex protocol.
4. Define the information flow using a full/full duplex protocol.
5. Draw a functional format of SDLC and briefly describe the functions of each segment.
6. Draw a matrix of the available combinations of circuits and protocols which may be used together. Describe the flow of information of the specified circuits.

FORMATS

By far, one of the most critical functions which has to be implemented in a data communications system is the format of the message to be transmitted. It is the format that tells the logical processing equipment at either end of the communication line what to do with the message and how to do it. Part of the format may also involve the sequence of operations (handshaking) which must be completed to permit modem synchronization and network routing. Data formats can only be recognized after the communications equipment has completed its handshaking (described in Chap. 7) and is therefore more applicable to the system-level design, but because the code type, length, and transmission validation technique are also involved, the format must be considered as an integral part of any data communication system.

There are three fundamental segments of a data transmission format. They are the *header,* the *text portion,* and the *trace* or *tail segment.* Since all applications may be implemented differently, a generalized format is shown in Fig. 8-1. It should be recognized that not all of the functions which will be described are necessary for all

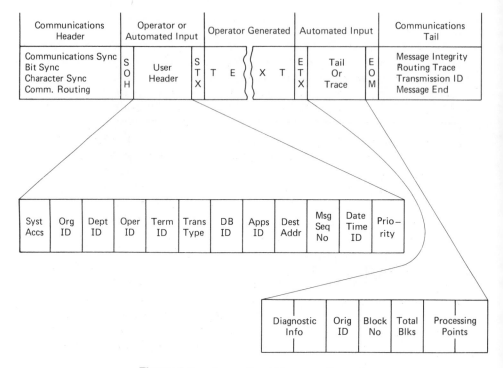

Figure 8-1. Generalized Message Format

applications, while other applications may require additional functions. What is included here is a basic format which contains the majority of the key functions which must be considered when designing the format, then the user can select those which are applicable to his situation and add those which are required over and above what is described here.

Another factor to consider relative to formats is that in a network, especially a hierarchial network (as described in Chap. 15), the lower level communication links can have complete formats defined for them, while at the same time the links at the upper levels and/or between central processing sites may add on additional information fields to create a *super format*. These super formats will allow the movement of entire blocks of information from low-order processing locations, so that when the information reaches its intermediate or ultimate destination, all of the original information is available for processing, and the super format information is used for the multiple link routing (interprocessor) and error detection capabilities which they may provide.

A.

Header

In referring to Fig. 8-1, we see at the left two portions of a sample message header. The first portion is the communications header which is used to establish the fact that communication link exists both electrically and logically and provides the capability for synchronization in synchronous transmission (handshaking). It also provides the capability for the communications hardware at the receive end to establish bit and character synchronization when necessary. In a high level communication link, where messages have been routed from a lower order processing location, there may also be a communications routing segment in the communications header which will provide for the information to determine the necessary routing between the higher order links.

Once the communications header has been identified we have a user header which is initiated by a character which is identified as a "start message." In the case of ASCII this is known as the SOH (Start of Header) character. The user header is terminated by an STX (Start of Text) character, and it is up to the user to determine the information which is to be contained within the header. This portion of the individual items of information within the user header can be bits, bytes, words, combinations of them, or any other sequence which the user finds convenient and feasible to be implemented. The information can be either operator generated or automatically generated by software and/or firmware. Each of the potential segments of the header will be described below as to its application and probability of use.

System Access This particular segment can be considered a "password" type of segment, where the potential accessor of the system must identify himself as an authorized user of the system. Depending on the type of equipment involved, this system-level access can be detected and validated at the remote terminal, the nodes, the central site processors, or even at the data base manager. This access type identification will permit at least a first-level identification as to whether a particular user is authorized to utilize the facilities of the system. For those applications where dial-up connections are made this type of password is just about mandatory. Also if the situation exists where dedicated lines are used primarily, but dial-up is used for backup capability, even if not used at all sites, this system access level identification will still be required because the user must not allow his data to be compromised by an unauthorized user.

Organization ID/Department ID   These two levels of identification specify the specific organization within the user environment which is trying to access the system facility. Neither of these may be required, one of them may be required, both of them may be required, or even further level definitions within the organization might be required at this level. This type of ID provides the capability for the control of who, within the spectrum of authorized users, will be allowed to access the different types of data bases which may be available within the system. For example, in those situations where all users are not allowed to access all data bases (manufacturing operations not allowed to access financial information or personnel files, etc.), this level of identification will allow the data base management system to determine which users are authorized to access not only specific data bases, but even records within a single data base. In the future, however, it may also be desirable to have a sublevel organization ID which will permit certain users to access specific applications while other users will be excluded.

Operator ID   In all systems today which are network oriented, and where many terminals out in the field can be used by different personnel, it is becoming increasingly more critical to identify the specific operator who is using a terminal. This identification is necessary not only for security and accessing purposes, especially where the data base access must be limited to specific operators within specific organizations, but it is also necessary to identify those users who may be utilizing the system in an unauthorized manner or are making an inordinate amount of accesses which may indicate a possible training problem. Since all tracking and auditing relies ultimately on identifying the individual who is trying to access the system, this is one of the most important functions to be included in the header of a message. The information may be entered in each message by the operator or after a log-on procedure can be inserted automatically by terminal software or firmware.

Terminal ID   The first four segments of the header described thus far may or may not be entered by an operator. Obviously it is quite possible for an unauthorized user to obtain a valid operator's number and try to access the system illegitimately. By installing a terminal ID at each individual terminal location in hardware or firmware, an additional level of security can be implemented by forcing specific operators to use only previously authorized terminals for their accesses. The result of this specific implementation means that if an unauthorized user has a valid operator's number, that unauthorized user must also get a terminal which is authorized to accept inputs with that operator ID. This capability allows the system manager to limit the accessibility into the system at all remote levels, and by changing both the operator IDs and the terminal IDs in a predetermined manner, any compromise of the system will only last until the next change occurs, when the authorized users obtain a new ID number to be used with an authorized terminal ID again. Terminal ID can also be used to prevent users who are otherwise authorized to use the system from accessing specific data bases. For example, if payroll information should not be available to terminals used on the production floor, specific limitations can be imposed within the data base manager, so that access to the payroll files can only be from the specifically identified payroll access terminals. This is a powerful level of system security capability because it is nonoperator dependent.

In the newer distributed processing networks, for the processing CPUs to determine what is supposed to be done with a message, the type of transaction it contains must be defined (the transaction types will be defined in Chap. 13). Since specific types of transaction must be processed differently by the various CPUs, it is necessary to identify as soon as possible the specific type of transaction so that it can be routed to the appropriate CPU for processing. If all applications are performed by the same set of CPUs at a particular location, it may not be required. The transaction may not have to be specified, but management and applications functions are processed in different CPUs, so this transaction-type definition is extremely important for handling of messages at those sites efficiently.

Data Base ID/Applications ID   Since the newer systems today are going more and more towards the use of minicomputers, not only are the data bases being segmented but the applications are also being performed in separate CPUs. For those situations where different data bases reside with different CPUs and different applications are performed by different computers, it is necessary to identify both the data base and the application to which a particular message is applicable, so that the proper inter and intra site routing functions can be performed. These definitions can be used in conjunction with the transaction type to identify final destination address in those networks where it is desired to have the terminal operator transparent to where his data is physically resident. This capability is known as *implied addressing,* and even though it takes more software to implement, it relieves the operator from having to determine where the appropriate application or data base resides.

Destination Address If the system design is such that implied addressing is not incorporated or the requirement for terminal-to-terminal communications exists, then it is necessary to have a destination address segment in the header included. Even for those cases where implied addressing is involved, there may be situations when an operator must communicate with some administrative and/or control location, and it may therefore be necessary to have both the implied addressing and destination address capability included in the same format.

Message Sequence Number Some form of message sequence number identification must be incorporated into a communication system so that the users of the system, both manual and automated, will have a means of identifying whether duplicate transmissions are being received and/or whether messages are missing. In all networks where multiple paths for messages exist, it is quite possible for a message to take one particular path to get to its ultimate destination and for the acknowledgment to take a different path. It is also possible for a message being transmitted to be received in error while the negative acknowledgement for that message is lost or held up on the way back to the transmitter. For example, if there is no way for the data base manager to determine whether a particular "update" has been received, it is quite possible to apply the same update to a record twice or to lose an update completely. This can happen in a typical banking situation in the following manner. A customer goes into one of the bank branches and wants to cash a check. The teller inquires against the data base to determine whether there is enough money in the account to cash the check. Once the amount is validated, the teller will cash the check for the customer, and the customer will leave the bank. During this time the teller will go back into the system with an update which debits the account for the amount of the check. The update can be made to the data base, but the acknowledgment coming back to the terminal can be held up in a queue, lost, garbled, etc., so that the terminal operator never gets an acknowledgment. If, after the appropriate time out, the operator retransmits the message, the file will be updated again, having, in effect, two checks being debited to the same file instead of just one. Now, the acknowledgment for the first update comes back, and it appears to the operator that the second transmission has now been acknowledged.

In the meantime, another transaction, such as a deposit, takes place for a different customer. A file update transaction is transmitted into the system which, for the typical reasons in a communications network, does not get to the file for update immediately, but the acknowledgment from the second transmission of the previous transaction now comes back and appears to the operator to be an acknowledgment for the deposit update. As far as the operator is concerned, everything is all right within the file, but we have, in actuality, two records which are erroneous.

One of the means of overcoming this particular situation is to identify each particular transaction with the terminal ID and message sequence number, so that the data base manager will be in a position to compare the new update on a particular record with the previous update. If they are the same then the second one is acknowledged without changing the file. There is, of course, a probability of error here too, in that in between the first and second update being received by the data base manager, an update from another source can come into that record (a deposit or check at a different branch or a previously written check cleared through the system). The data base manager now looking at the sequence numbers which appear to be different will process both if only the single previous transaction is stored.

A brute force solution to this situation would be to have the previous two transactions stored, but the same type of sequence can be described (where a third input is processed between the two which are stored), so some limit has to be placed by the user on how many of the previous transactions will be stored. It must be recognized that all of this storage of previous transactions adds a significant amount of overhead to the system in processing time, and especially in information storage on the peripherals. An alternative approach might be to require an operator to reinquire into the data base anytime an acknowledgment is not received for a transmission, to validate whether an update has already reached the file. This too is not foolproof in that the original update can be held up in a queue somewhere, while the new inquiry, taking a different path, can go into the data base, and look at the data in its original unchanged state. The operator will then initiate a new update, while in the meantime the first update, having overcome its delay in the queue, will update the file. Shortly thereafter, the second update comes in and updates the file again. The risk factors involved in implementing these different methods must be evaluated by the user to determine which single method, or combination of methods, must be incorporated to provide the least amount of exposure in the customer environment. Without some form of message sequence number identification, however, this becomes an almost impossible task. For that reason, it is quite possible that additional levels of message ID must be incorporated within the header of a message so that the data base manager can determine whether or not to apply an update to a file.

Date/Time ID   As one of the additional levels of message ID which can be used to validate the applicability of a particular update, a date/time ID can be put in the header portion of a message. The data base manager can then be designed so that date/time comparisons must be made, and they must always be in sequence before an update to the file can be made. This requires a new date/time stamp be put on each message when it is transmitted and therefore requires some kind of real-time clock to be installed at all of the terminal locations. This too is not a totally clean method, in that multiple terminals at different locations can be trying to access the same record for the updating purposes and because of propagation delays or queues, may arrive out of sequence. For this particular case, the terminal ID can be used with the sequence number and the date/time stamp to determine whether a particular update should be made. Here again, the user must determine how much identification is required within the message to provide the least tolerable amount of exposure to erroneous file handling.

Priority   For the communications network where there are multiple paths and multiple transmission lines, terminals or lines being down is a day to day possibility. When these conditions occur, queues of messages destined for those terminals or lines will build up. Over a period of time these queues can become very long. When the failed unit becomes operational again, the messages must be sent out one at a time, on a first in/first out basis, unless some form of priority scheme has been established for permitting urgent messages to be transmitted first. Without some form of priority scheme, it is quite possible for urgently required information to wait its turn after lower priority information (which may also take a long time to transmit) and therefore not arrive at the destination in time to be of any use. For example, the response to an inquiry where an operator is waiting should take precedence over a batch type transmission which will go to a printing device at the remote site. For some applications this may not be a problem because of the fact that the system is "transaction driven," which means that only terminal operators are accessing the system and are waiting for responses. If the responses do not come, the operators have procedures either to reinquire or to use alternate methods of obtaining the information. In the future, however, for those applications where there will be information transmitted from the terminal locations for batch type processing and in turn require long printouts, it may very well be possible for priority to be required.

A typical example of this type of problem can be looked at in the airline environment where the passenger manifest is transmitted to the boarding station where the flights are being boarded so the airline service agents can identify the passengers with valid reservations. If for some reason, a manifest is being held up due to a long transmission, and there was no priority scheme implemented, it would be of no use to the service agent if the manifest came after the flight had left. Therefore, with a priority scheme which would allow passenger manifests to precede other predefined low priority transmission, the problem can be overcome. A single bit will allow two levels of priority, while two bits will allow four levels of priority. It should be noted that priority handling software is one of the items which makes the communications software more complex. If not necessary in the beginning, the user should evaluate in detail his long-term requirements to determine whether the priority capability should be implemented at the beginning of the design, when it is easiest to do so.

As was said previously, the above items do not necessarily all have to be implemented, and there may be others which should be implemented over and above these. They are being presented so that the user can at least evaluate the criteria which must be incorporated, and this list can be used as a check list for incorporation of the required functions. Another point to remember is that the sequence of these individual segments is not necessarily critical and can be changed according to the user requirements. Also, one or more of the segments, if applicable, can be put in the trace portion of the message which will be described in Part C of this chapter. By the same token, one or more of the segments in the trace can be put in the header if it is so desired. The reason for putting information in specific sequences in the header or the trace portion of the message is that the decoding of each of the segments can be done in firmware instead of software, and if the segments always occur in the same location relative to the control characters (SOH, STX, ETC, EOM), the firmware can be used to detect the same locations every single time for the same quantity of characters, which reduces the amount of software that must be used to perform those functions. This in turn allows the applicable software required to be accommodated in less main memory of the CPU.

B.

Text

The text portion of the message format is the information which the operator has generated for transmission to the location where it is to be processed (or from the CPU back to the operator as a response), and it may contain a fixed or variable amount of characters. Almost all systems today use variable length text portions with a maximum limitation, which is usually based on buffer size. Also, the text portion itself may contain multiple blocks of information which can be processed separately by the applications CPUs. Within the ASCII code set there is an ETB (end of text block) character which can be used to segregate the different message blocks. As long as all of the blocks pertain to the same function described by the header and the trace, they can be accommodated within the same text portion. If, however, there are different applications, updates, inquiries, etc., they must be transmitted using different message sequence numbers, because they may very well be applicable to different data bases, locations, and so on. The text portion of a message is terminated by the insertion of an ETX (end of text) character which, at the same time, defines the start of the tail or trace portion of the message format.

C.

Trace

The tail or trace portion of a message, just like the header, consists of two parts. The first part is applicable to the information being transmitted. It is used to identify various functions which will be useful primarily in the analysis mode of message handling. The analysis mode means the tracking of the message through the system, as well as any diagnostic information which pertains to the generation of transmission of that message. The diagnostic information is shown as being two separate segments. In all likelihood this will be many segments or one very long segment, where information is contained such as the amount of times this block had to be retransmitted, the amount of operator-generated errors this message had in its generation, the amount of time this message was stored at the original terminal, and so on. Because of the possible length of the data collected, many users take the diagnostic information created at the remote sites, store them locally on some random access type storage media (such as floppy discs), and subsequently transmit the information to a central site for processing later in a batch mode. This is very important for analyzing the efficiency of the network operation and can also provide a very extensive capability to determine the quality of the operators which are using the system. Too many errors in generation or retransmissions because of format problems may or may not be transmitted with each message. If the quantity of information is too long it should not be sent as overhead, because its extra potential contribution to transmission errors can then be eliminated.

Originating ID For those instances where the diagnostic information will be stored for subsequent transmission, some form of identification must be included with that diagnostic information to define the key parameters of how the message was handled, such as terminal ID or operator ID. Originating ID therefore must be used with the diagnostic information, when it is processed later, and can be related back to the specific location and operator being analyzed.

Block Number/Total Blocks For those cases where messages must be broken up into smaller blocks for buffer or transmission length purposes, some block number identification must be provided, so the ultimate receiver can put all the blocks back together to reassemble the original message and know for certain that all of the blocks have been received. By identifying the block number, as well as the total blocks in a particular message, the receive equipment can perform that function. It is also possible that block number and total blocks could be contained in the header portion instead of the tail portion.

Processing Points Because many of the routing functions in a network depend on the quality and/or loading of the network at the time of transmission, it is quite possible for a message to take a different path each time it goes between two network end points. In addition, the message can go through many different processing points where the routing software at that point must determine the next location where the message must be sent. It is also quite possible for the message to be transmitted from one location, and due to some hardware and/or software problem, the message keeps going between two or more CPUs in a "round robin" effect, so that it never gets to its desired destination. There has to be some limited number of locations to which a message can be transmitted before it must be considered lost. Once this number has been reached, the message has to be sent to an administrative type of location where an operator can determine what is to be done with it. In order to store all of the different locations where a message can be processed, a segment of the trace portion of the message must be added at each processing location to store the location ID to show where the message has been. This will also be of great use when it comes to the tracking of lost messages to determine what kind of software problems may have been encountered (could also be hardware type).

In a typical network situation, for a message which is generated to go through many different CPUs before it finally reaches its ultimate destination a limit is established and then exceeded during routing, then the message is considered to be lost and routed to the administrative location for human analysis. Naturally, this kind of situation is an error condition, and what complicates the matter is that the routing sequence may not repeat itself, because in transmitting the second time a totally different set of conditions may exist for network loading. Still, for analysis and diagnostic purposes, it is necessary in all multiple CPU processing location situations for the CPU processing a particular message to leave its stamp on that message so that malfunctions and/or errors can be corrected by analysis. The user portion of the trace information is then terminated by an EOM (end of message) character which is sometimes called EOT (end of transmission).

Once the user portion of the tail or trace has been completed, there may also be a communications tail or trace which is oriented towards the communication link control. This may consist of a message parity type function such as CRC, a communications routing trace for network use only, a transmission ID for link-to-link transmission of the message, and then a message end which tells the communications equipment that this transmission is truly over (may be part of the handshake procedure). This communications trace is transparent to the user except for the situation where transmission errors are detected which require retransmissions. This in turn causes the propagation time to increase. The user is unaware of the reason for this propagation delay, and therefore the communications tail can be considered transparent from a processing point of view.

To summarize the pieces which make up a particular format, we have the user-oriented functions of header, text, and trace, and have a system-oriented header and trace which is usually user transparent. For the typical network situation, the user header, text, and trace can be identified as the user-generated portions of a message or response, while the communications header and tail can be associated with a communication overhead such as SDLC or Packet, which is used to move the information between the specific individual sites.

QUESTIONS

1. What are the three primary segments of a typical message format? What are their typical makeup?

2. What typical functions are required for validating user access to the system?

3. What typical functions are required for addressing purposes, both direct and implied?

4. What typical functions are required to ensure message receipt and validity?

5. What portions of a message format may get generated outside the user's control? What are those segments used for?

9

TERMINAL TYPES

A.

Background

In the terminal world, especially with the proliferation of vendors, there is quite a bit of confusion regarding the definition of the different types of terminals which are available today. Since there is no commonly agreed upon definition, for purposes of this text there will be five major definitions made, each with a different level of capability and also an increasing cost. It should be kept in mind, however, that the definitions presented here are not necessarily those that are presented by vendors when they are selling the hardware to the users, but they do have a definable level of difference which can be evaluated by the user to determine which level of terminal capability the user wants. Once the level of capability has been determined, the user can go through the selection process and determine which of the various vendor products meet the basic criteria defined here.

B.

Uncontrolled

The first level of terminal definition is called *uncontrolled.* An uncontrolled terminal is one which cannot be polled or called; in other words it is on line all the time, and when it is transmitting, the receiver at the other end must also be on line to accept the information, otherwise the message will be lost. Also, when transmitting to the uncontrolled terminal there is usually no way to determine if the message was actually received because a response is usually not provided.

In general, uncontrolled terminals are used in process control type applications where they monitor physical functions. Upon monitoring the functions, the information is sent to some other site where it is collected and used to determine whether some corrective action should be taken, usually through a different path. In this mode of operation, if one of the monitoring messages is lost, it cannot be regenerated. This loss is due to the fact that for the most part, uncontrolled terminals do not have any type of memory which can be used to regenerate and retransmit information. The basic rationale for this mode of operation is that the functions being monitored will not change significantly within the average sampling time, and if a particular segment of data is lost, it is not necessarily critical to the function being monitored. Although there are terminals which are used for monitoring purposes that do have memory and can therefore retransmit information, they are not as widely used, because the memory itself adds a significant cost factor to the terminal.

In the data communications environment, the terminal that most typically represents an uncontrolled terminal is the teletype *keyboard only,* which is on line all the time, and when the operator depresses a key, the character is sent immediately to the other end (therefore there can only be one keyboard on line at any time). From a receiving point of view, the teletype *receive only* printer is the terminal that typifies this uncontrolled mode of operation. The teletype RO will print any character being transmitted to it but does not have the capability of acknowledging receipt of those characters. From an operational point of view the uncontrolled terminal requires human intervention in the event that it is necessary to recover any missing or lost data, if it is even available to be recovered.

C.

Controlled

A *controlled terminal* typically has some form of memory even if this memory is paper tape. The basic difference between the controlled terminal and the uncontrolled terminal, however, is the fact that the controlled terminal can be polled (which is an invitation for the terminal to transmit) and called (which is an invitation for terminal to receive). This polling and calling capability means that there will always be some form of positive and/or negative response to a master site from the terminal to validate whether the terminal is operational and can receive or transmit. In the event of a transmission error, the terminal, because it has a memory, can retransmit a message when necessary. This situation will be slightly different in the event of paper tape storage, in that an operator must reinsert the paper tape to transmit again. In that particular case a separate administrative message must be sent to the terminal so that an operator can be informed that a paper tape transmitted message was received in error.

The terminal which most typifies the controlled terminal is the entire line of teletypes up to the Model 39. Other terminals which fit this category in general are teletype replacements such as the Hazeltine *Glass TTY*. Many other vendors make terminals in this category and they can usually be identified as being at the low end of the vendor's product line.

D.

Semi-Intelligent

The next three levels of terminal are all usually called intelligent terminals by the vendors. For purposes of delineation, however, the intelligent classification has been broken down into three separate segments starting with this level which is called *semi-intelligent*. The semi-intelligent terminal can be polled and called and also has a memory. This memory can be core but is usually semi-conductor, and the significant capability difference that exists at this level is the fact that the vendors will provide firmware for specific predetermined functions. Firmware consists of a read only memory into which specific functions such as screen formats and editing have been stored. These functions are determined and fixed by the vendor and cannot be changed by the user, unless the read only memories into which the firmware instructions have been stored are physically removed and exchanged. In some cases the user can specify specific functions which they want, and the vendor will then put in the necessary firmware to accommodate those requirements. The specified requirements, however, cannot be changed unless they are removed and replaced by a read only memory (ROM) with different functions.

Many different vendors make this type of terminal which will also be at the lower end of the product line. Some of the typical vendors of semi-intelligent terminals are Sycor, Incoterm, ADDS, Four Phase, DataPoint, and Raytheon. There are many others and the ones described here should be looked on only as being typical of the vendors manufacturing this level of terminal and not necessarily as a recommendation of them.

E.

Intelligent

An *intelligent terminal* incorporates all of the functions of the previous terminals including the memory and vendor-supplied firmware, but in this case, an additional feature is provided which gives the intelligent terminal more capability than the three previously described terminals. The intelligent terminal has vendor-supplied software. The vendor-supplied software means that the user can make changes to his terminal functions from the terminal keyboard. These changes can be either the modification or generation of new screen formats, edit criteria, and maybe some transmission format capabilities. At this level of terminal definition the user will begin to see the addition of tape casettes and floppy discs for local storage of functions which were stored in ROMs in the previous terminals. Once the capability for floppy disc storage is available, the capability for adding many additional processing functions exists, and at this particular level of terminal one of the most significant functions that could be performed is the collection of information in a local environment for subsequent transmission to a central site for processing—in other words, a data collection function such as key to disc or key to tape.

Most of the same vendors who make the semi-intelligent terminals also make the intelligent level of terminal. It should be remembered, however, that the vendors themselves do not have any clear-cut definitions as to the capabilities of the various terminals, and therefore will call many different kinds of terminals "intelligent." It will be up to the user to determine the level of capability that he wants and can afford in his particular application.

F.

Programmable

The *programmable level terminal* incorporates all of the functions provided in the previously described terminals but has as its unique feature the capability of incorporating user-provided software. The user-provided software is usually in one of the high level programming languages which can be used locally for the operator to design, develop, and implement particular programs to be used at that remote site. The most common language being used at this time is BASIC. There are many versions of BASIC provided by the different vendors, so if it is desired to use this level of terminal, careful consideration should be paid to the level of capability which is required at that terminal and, in turn, the level of capability of the "BASIC" software.

Once this level of terminal is reached, the probability exists that additional main memory at the terminal will also be required, providing for fairly extensive software capabilities at the remote site. In other words, instead of having just a terminal, what the user really has is a remote processing location, If it had not already been considered at the intelligent level, consideration should definitely be given at the programmable terminal level as to whether this kind of terminal should still exist in a multidrop data communications environment. A stand-alone communications environment using either point-to-point dedicated lines, dial-up lines, or packet can be used for what is really a computer-to-computer communication at this level.

Once additional capabilities exist to generate software in a local environment and peripheral storage is available (some vendors can integrate hard discs and large mag tape units onto the programmable terminal), many other capabilities are now available to the user. The first of these is to write and/or use local applications programs for local processing requirements, thereby reducing or eliminating the need to tie to a central site for processing of locally generated information. These various software applications can be stored on the local peripherals and brought up when required for processing in the local environment.

Another application which can be performed on a programmable level terminal is the access of local data bases. Although the segmentation of data bases is a totally independent subject which has its own advantages and disadvantages, if it can be assumed that the data base can be segmented in the first place, then either entire data bases or portions of data bases can be stored in a local environment for local access. As can be seen, with the additional levels of software capability at a programmable terminal and the availability of local data bases, the requirement for an extensive data communications network is reduced more and more. In actuality this tends to lead towards operation more in a batch mode and could save a considerable amount of money with a network reduction. It should be recognized, however, that the ability to operate in this mode is very much application oriented and must be part of an overall management decision.

At the programmable terminal level the capability for data collection also exists, just the same as it did at the intelligent level, although more data can be stored because of the larger peripherals. This is significant for both types of terminal because the operators can be independent for both the network and the central site CPU. If there are problems with either one, the operator can continue to collect information locally, which can then be transmitted to the CPU when the problem is corrected. Terminal utilization and efficiency can be improved significantly.

One more significant function must be considered at this level of terminal, and that is the incorporation of some form of local diagnostic capability for terminal, peripheral, and entry device check out. This is required because the capability usually exists in most systems to validate the operation of the central site processors and the communications facilities (lines and equipment), but to date very little has been done to diagnose problems which exist in the remote terminal environment. If a particular problem area can be isolated by testing and analyzing from a central site, the appropriate vendor can be summoned to correct the problem, instead of having a situation where the wrong vendor or multiple vendors must be called to resolve problems which cannot be specifically identified. In order to incorporate the terminal diagnostics, the user should evaluate his own capabilities to generate them with or without the vendor in order to improve the probability of specific problem identification.

Finally, although it is not included in the definition list, a word should be said about the device which is called a *batch terminal*. A batch terminal is an application-oriented device with varying levels of capability, but it fits very well into the above definitions of either intelligent or programmable terminal. The level of firmware/software capability and peripheral couplement will determine which level it should be included in. A summary of the capabilities of the five levels of terminal definition is shown in Fig. 9-1.

Types of Terminals (Controllers)

Uncontrolled

Transmits and/or receives directly on line
Usually no memory
Usually no retransmission capability
Utilized for monitoring, telemetry, process control

Controlled

Has some form of memory — could be paper tape
Can be polled and called
Can possibly perform some transmission validation functions

Semi Intelligent

Has buffered memory
Has vendor supplied firmware
Can perform some form, validation and edit functions

Intelligent

Has extended storage capability (cassettes, floppies, etc.)
Has vendor supplied firmware
Has vendor supplied software
Can perform most remote data entry functions
Can "stage" data for later transmission

Programmable

Has all functions of Intelligent Controller but in addition
has user supplied firmware/software
Can perform remote processing functions

Batch

Standard batch entry, transmission, reception, and print of
batch jobs

Figure 9-1. Types of Terminals

G.

Selection

When making a selection for a particular terminal the user is faced with a myriad of decisions. In order to sort them out in a rational form the decisions are broken down into two major categories. First, is the set of application requirements, and second is the mechanism whereby the information will be transmitted to other locations.

When the application requirements are considered, foremost on the evaluation list must be what the user is trying to do at the remote location. This is usually determined by the operational and/or management requirement, and the more functions which must be performed out at the remote sites, the further down in the ladder of terminal definition you will find the appropriate terminal. It is necessary to recognize here that with the additional capability existing at the remote terminals, especially with respect to screen formats and edit criteria, there will be a significantly reduced overhead in communications required between the terminal sites and the central site because of the elimination of the requirement to transmit the screen formats and edit functions back to the terminals. The time used for this overhead takes away from the time available to transmit valid application information; if multidrop lines are used fewer terminals can be connected to them.

The next function at this level which has to be considered is the *response time*. The response time for purposes of this text is defined as the time it takes from the depression of the "enter" key by an operator at a terminal until the time a response begins to display at the operator's terminal. Regardless of the path the message must take and the ultimate destination of the transmission, the operator is waiting all during the time the messages are in transit, and therefore the most reasonable definition for response time is the time that the operator has to wait for response by the network and system. Individual response time numbers for particular pieces of hardware are not significant except for the contribution they make to the overall response time.

Any terminal-oriented system will have significant costs involved with operators. This means the operator response time is a very critical function, because all the time the operator is waiting for a response from the system, that operator is nonproductive. The longer the response time, the more wasted time there will be in the system with the resulting additional overall cost to the user. To give an example, if a typical transaction time is two minutes, and the response times can be reduced and the operator nonproductive time can be reduced by only fifteen seconds, an overall improvement of up to 12½ percent can be realized in productivity. This can go a long ways toward paying for a higher level of intelligence at the terminal, and the added benefit is obtained of less communications being required to the central site. This may even lead to a requirement for less telephone lines.

In the above descriptions of different terminal types it should be noted that the definitions apply to the terminal *controller,* because in a typical environment there are many terminals which have cluster arrangements where a single controller can accommodate up to thirty-two devices (CRTs, keyboards, printers, readers, etc.), but the actual processing, buffering, and intelligence actually reside in the controller itself. For those devices where the controller is built right into the device cabinetry, it appears to the user as a single intelligent device, but in reality the intelligence still resides in a separate functional "black box" which can be identified as the controller. In other words, the controller contains the buffering, the controller contains the read only memories, the controller contains the intelligence, and the controller is the component that handles the required communications interface.

Additional functions which must also be considered in the selection of a terminal are functions such as the capability of operating in just a batch mode, an on-line mode, or both. As soon as the requirement for communication to another site is involved there must be some form of communications interface, and therefore as a minimum the RS232C interface should be established as a standard for interfacing with modem equipments.

The speed of transmission must also be considered, and this is somewhat dependent upon the types of I/O devices connected to the controller, because if the I/O device is connected directly to the line, the line transmission rate is limited to the speed of the device, and no other device can be transmitting at the same time. This also involves the definition of whether the controller is a synchronous or asynchronous device, because the information may be transmitted a character at a time with start and stop bits involved or synchronously in a message-framed environment.

On the negative side of putting more intelligence out at the remote sites we have three major functions to consider. First is the price. As more capabilities are added to a terminal controller, the price obviously goes up. The offset to that price has to be weighed against the improvement in operator efficiency, improvement in line utilization, and the reduction of overhead requirements at the central sites for processing what the operators have been entering. Although price is usually the primary consideration, it must be weighed in the overall system environment, because in many cases, even though the price gets multiplied by the number of terminals which must be supported out in the field, the effective improvement in system utilization may more than outweigh that additional front end cost.

The second potential disadvantage is the requirement to have more capable operators who are required to take advantage of the additional functions which are provided in increasing levels of intelligence at the terminal sites. This may be overcome by better training, but proficiency and operation in a degraded or failure mode requires additional knowledge and capability on the operator's part which usually means additional cost on a per operator basis.

The third major disadvantage involved with improving the intelligence at the remote sites is the addition of more comprehensive and complex maintenance and logistics procedures. Since there are more components at more sites performing more applications, the situation is such that failures or degraded operation will cause more noticeable impacts on system operation when they occur. This means a more comprehensive set of diagnostic procedures and problem correction techniques must be implemented and controlled from the central site. Effective vendor support must be maintained to correct problems faster, and, at the same time, a procedure for interfacing with different vendors for the correction of problems must be implemented and adhered to.

On an overall system design basis, depending heavily upon the applications to be performed, there is usually one specific level of terminal intelligence which fits the bill much better than the others. This obviously is the level of terminal which should be selected, with the exception of one other factor—the requirement for future expansion. Most terminal-oriented systems increase in message traffic volume by a minimum of 100 percent at the end of the first year, due to new applications being performed at those terminals which also may require more remote processing capability. If a user is on an edge between two terminal types, he should then pick the more intelligent level, because within a year's time the probability is that those additional functions will be necessary, and the user will then be spared the trauma of upgrading again within a short period of time. As a corollary to this expansion process, the user should always select a product which is no higher than midway in the vendor's product line and validate that the selected product is upgradable to the higher level with little or no change to existing software. This is necessary, because when expansion comes (requirements rarely, if ever, decrease), the capability to upgrade with minimal cost and operational impact will be available.

QUESTIONS

1. What are the attributes of an uncontrolled terminal?
2. What are the attributes of a controlled terminal?
3. What are the primary capabilities of the three levels of intelligent terminals?
4. What are typical applications for a user of each of the five types of terminals defined?
5. Identify three major considerations in selecting a terminal for system use.
6. What are two disadvantages of putting more intelligence into more remote locations?

10

MULTIPLEXERS

A.

Background

The term *multiplexer* (MUX) is derived from the Latin words *multi* meaning "many" and *plex* meaning "mix." A multiplexer takes multiple low-speed lines and combines their individual data transmission volume requirements in such a way that a specific grouping of them can be transmitted on a single higher speed line. The overall effect is that instead of having a significant quantity of low-speed lines connected from a single transmitting location to the same receiving location, the low-speed lines can be combined at the remote location, and only a single line (at a higher speed) will be required to transmit all of the information to the receiving site and vice versa. This allows for a very significant decrease in overall cost because the quantity of lines will be significantly reduced. At the same time, each of the individual remote locations will still appear to have a direct line access to the central site because the multiplexer is, in fact, transparent to their operation (except during failure modes). For those situations where the user has a multidrop line with response times continually increasing due to heavier and heavier data transmission requirements, the use of multiplexers is one of the primary alternatives to consider. (Implementation will depend greatly on geographic locations of terminal sites.)

B.

Basic Theory

There are two basic kinds of multiplexing techniques. The first is *frequency division multiplexing* (FDM), and the second, *time division multiplexing* (TDM). Most of the FDM units are used to combine very low-speed circuits onto single voice grade lines for transmission to a central site, while the TDMs are used for both low- and high-speed lines for the same purpose. It should be noted that an FDM is an analog device where the inputs are combined to share the same voice grade line, and therefore a modem is not required. A TDM is a digital device, so that a modem is required between the transmit multiplexer and the receive multiplexer (the receive portion of a multiplexer is called a demultiplexer). This will be described in more detail later.

Frequency division multiplexing is also implemented at the voice channel level by the telephone company for long-haul transmission on both coaxial cable systems and microwave radio. This capability allows the telephone company to combine many voice grade lines for long-haul transmission between specific cities using what are known as "wideband" lines. Time division multiplexing is also being used by the common carriers for transmitting data at different speeds as well as to transmit voice using the pulse code modulation techniques which were described in Chap. 5. For a description of the telephone company frequency division multiplexing techniques at the different carrier levels, refer to Chap. 13.

As was described above, a TDM is basically a digital device. Its theory of operation is that the digital bits and bytes will share the time available on a high-speed line, so that each of the low-speed incoming channels will have a dedicated portion of the high-speed outgoing line assigned to it. This will be explained in more detail in Section E of this chapter.

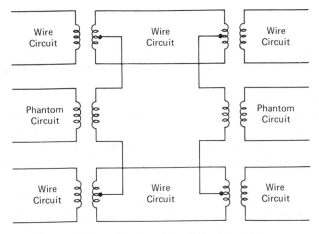

Figure 10-1.   Phantom Circuit Configuration

C.

Phantom Circuit

One of the earliest attempts to transmit more than one channel of information on a particular circuit was the use of the phantom circuit shown in Fig. 10-1. This circuit allows three channels of information to be carried on two circuit facilities. Subsequent developments allowed a more efficient means of "stacking" different frequencies onto the voice grade line for transmission.

D.

Frequency Division Multiplexing

As was described previously the telephone company multiplexes voice channels in order to utilize the capabilities of wideband long-haul facilities more efficiently, but multiplexing at these levels is both transparent and unavailable to typical voice grade line users. What is available to voice grade line users, however, is the capability to multiplex very narrow (low-speed) circuits into the standard voice grade channels utilizing FDM. Figure 10-2 shows a typical subvoice band FDM channel and frequency assignment chart. This specific segmentation follows the standard CCITT recommendations where a nominal guard frequency band separates each channel from the

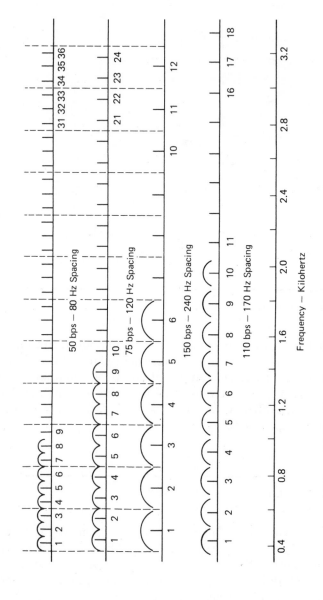

Figure 10-2. Frequency Division Multiplexing Voice Channel Spacing

adjacent one. The filters used for channel isolation normally have a 30-35 db attenuation in the middle of the guard frequency band, and the same mode of segmentation can be used to multiplex low-speed lines of 150, 330, and 600 bit per second transmission lines onto 2400 bit per second voice grade lines.

Frequency division multiplexing is shown diagrammatically on Fig. 10-3, and at the same time compares that with time division multiplexing, which is shown in the lower half of the diagram. FDMs are usually used for low-speed applications (150 bps and 300 bps) and are connected on a full-duplex voice grade line which may have conditioning applied to it.

E.

Time Division Multiplexing

Time division multiplexing has been in use for many years, but it has only been relatively recently, with the advent of less expensive solid state components and increased use of computers, that TDM has become more and more applicable as a means of conserving line efficiency. This is due to the fact that a TDM is a digital device and can therefore select incoming bits digitally and apportion them over a particular higher speed bit stream in the same time interval, so that the transmitting multiplexer will put a bit or a byte from each of the incoming lines in a specifically allocated space, and the demultiplexer at the other end, knowing where the bit or byte from each of the incoming lines is located, can output those bits or bytes on appropriate output lines at appropriate speeds. This is also shown diagrammatically in Fig. 10-3.

TDMs have three basic modes of operation. They are bit multiplexing, byte multiplexing, and block multiplexing. For purposes of this text the byte multiplexing technique will be described although the others are implemented in exactly the same way functionally.

In a byte multiplexing TDM the digital information which comes from the low-speed lines is combined in the form shown at the bottom of Fig. 10-3, so that the sequence starts off with a predetermined sync byte that defines the start of the sequence. This is followed by a byte from line 1, a byte from line 2, a byte from line 3, and so on until a byte from each one of the lines has been transmitted. At that point in time another sync byte is sent, and the sequence is repeated. This

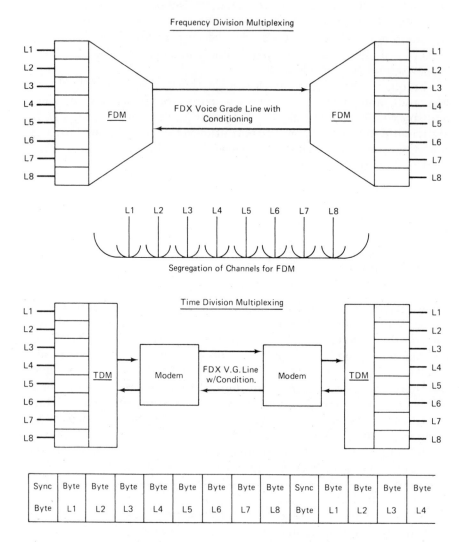

Figure 10-3. Multiplexing Techniques

goes on continuously from end to end, from the multiplexer through the modulator over the voice grade line, to the demodulator, then to the demultiplexer, and then to the specific output line to which the character belongs. To both the remote site and the central site it appears that there is a direct connection between them. In the event there are any errors detected, the messages are sent back and forth as if there were a direct connection at the low-speed transmission rate. The TDM will therefore appear to be transparent to the low-speed line and the central site. If a particular line does not have any data to be transmitted, then it is advisable from a user's point of view to transmit some kind of identifiable characters such as an ASCII sync character to identify that the line is operational. If all zeros or blanks are sent, it is possible for one end of the line to think that the other end is nonoperational. TDMs in general utilize synchronous transmission modes on full-duplex conditioned leased lines.

It should be noted that some TDMs are single ended. This means they will multiplex at the remote end, but at the central site or computer end, the computer itself will do the demultiplexing. The demultiplexing done by the computer may be required because of the nonavailability of communications ports, although it does create a much heavier load on the CPU in that many more CPU cycles are required to do the demultiplexing function. Single-ended FDMs are not available because they are analog devices.

Multiplexers can also accommodate incoming lines with different speeds, as long as the total bit-carrying capacity of the incoming lines does not exceed the bit-carrying capacity of the single outgoing line. In the event that a mixed group of incoming lines is being accepted, a "complex scan" technique is used where the higher speed lines (of the low-speed inputs) are sampled and transmitted more often within a particular sequence between sync bytes than the lower of the low-speed inputs. For example, if one of the low-speed lines is twice as fast as another one, it will have two bytes transmitted in any sequence for each one of the half-speed lines. All of the descriptions here assume that both ends of the multiplexer pair are specified so that each incoming low-speed line at the remote end will be specifically related to an identified line coming out at the demultiplexer end. It should also be noted that when using TDM equipment as opposed to FDM equipment it is much easier to diagnose specific TDM logic problems, because the information is digital and can be measured more accurately with standard test equipment.

FDMs, being analog in nature, have much more complex requirements when performing diagnostics and metering. Various levels are measured, frequencies and distortions which, because they are analog, leave much more of the interpretation of what the problem really is up to the maintenance personnel. On the other hand, the FDMs are in general less expensive on a per line basis and are very reliable for low-speed circuits such as those for teletypes.

F.

Intelligent/Statistical Multiplexers

Along with the newer technological capabilities which are available due to LSI and VLSI (Large Scale Integration and Very Large Scale Integration) components, it has also been recognized by network designers that, in general, most buffered terminals require actual communication line time less than 2 percent of the time they are in use. This means that for 98 percent of actual clock time a buffered terminal will not require line time for transmission or reception of information. (These types of terminals are single device controllers, and if multiple devices on a cluster controller are used required, line utilization may increase.) If it would be possible to identify the terminals which require transmission time and only allocate time slots for them in a particular sequence, then it would be definitely feasible to have many more low-speed lines connected to a multiplexer than would otherwise be capable of being supported if they were all busy at one time.

The device that can take advantage of that capability is called an Intelligent, or Statistical, Multiplexer. This device will arbitrarily select, in a priority sequence, those incoming lines which are busy and allocate slots for them to transmit to the central site. Each of the remote sites which is busy will keep its slot until completion of its transmission, at which time the slot becomes available to another line if required. In the event all of the available slots are filled, and there are more terminals or lines which are connected that require servicing, they will be inhibited from transmitting until a slot becomes available. This inhibition is most often accomplished by not returning a "clear to send" signal response to the terminal's transmission of a "request to send" signal (RS232 defined signals). A diagrammatic representation of a statistical multiplexer is found in Fig. 10-4.

The availability of slots is determined by the transmission speed capability of the voice grade line between the two modems. It should be noted that many statistical multiplexer configurations can take advantage of a lower speed transmission between the modems, such as 2400 bits per second with less conditioning, whereas a set of incoming lines to a regular TDM might require a 9600 bit per second capacity along with more conditioning and, in turn, additional cost. A statistical TDM could get away with a less expensive modem and less conditioning while transmitting at 2400 bits per second. Only in the event that more low-speed lines have to be added would the transmis-

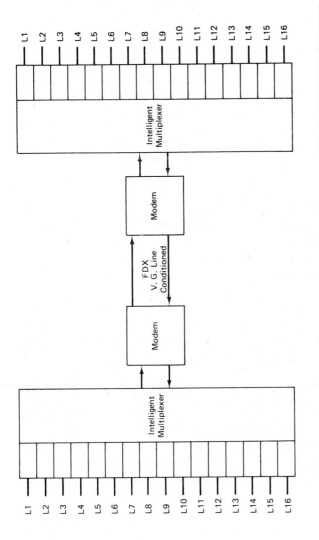

The following table appears within the figure:

Sync	Cont	Byte	Cont	Byte	Byte	Byte	Byte	Byte	Byte	Byte	Byte	Sync	Cont	Cont	Byte	Byte	Byte	Byte	Byte	Byte	Byte	Byte
Byte	Byte	L1	Byte	L5	L6	L9	L11	L13	Byte	L13	Byte	Byte	Byte	L2	L5	L9	L11	L13	L15

Lines L2, L15 and L16 waiting for slot
Lines L1 and L6 complete message in this
block which makes 2 slots available.

Line 16 still waiting for slot to open
Corresponding bit in each control byte
identifies active line.

Figure 10-4. Intelligent/Statistical Multiplexing

sion rate between the statistical TDMs then be increased to accommodate the addition of more lines. This incremental increase in transmission speed (2400 bps, 4800 bps, 9600 bps) would continue until the error rates got to the point where additional TDMs would be desirable instead.

Statistical TDMs are being utilized more and more in those environments where terminals are being added in the remote environment on an incremental basis as user requirements dictate. An important feature to recognize relative to a statistical multiplexer is the fact that it is usually a byte-oriented device just like a regular TDM. And also the intelligence in a statistical TDM is limited to the efficient handling of multiple lines on a byte basis. Therefore, there is relatively limited additional software capability. It is possible, however, to have error detection and control techniques built into a statistical MUX.

Some statistical TDMs are called *concentrators* by vendors, but for this text, and in almost all cases, a concentrator is a store-and-forward device which handles entire messages and will be described in more detail in Chap. 11.

QUESTIONS

1. What is the basic function of a multiplexer?
2. What are the two basic kinds of multiplexing techniques and in what environments are they used?
3. Through what kind of device can active lines be combined for transmission over a high-speed circuit? How is that function performed physically? What happens when more lines are required to be active than available bandwidth to carry them?
4. Which multiplexing technique is analog and which is digital? What difference in hardware is involved when implementing them?
5. Draw a diagram of at least four levels of "piggyback" multiplexing showing input and output transmission rates at each level.

chapter

11

OTHER NETWORK HARDWARE

A.

Background

In the data communications environment there are many items of hardware which are required for the physical movement of information from one site to another, for the logical processing of the information in order to get it ready for transmission and to validate its correct reception at the receive end. Even though this equipment is not identified specifically as performing a communication line function, it is mandatory to complete the process of moving information between two different locations.

At the remote sites there are the various terminal controllers which were described in Chap. 9. Since this remote environment has historically been considered a unique one with only very specific functions to be performed, it is fairly easy for most users to relate to the capabilities provided in those equipments.

At the other end (the central CPU or processing site), the function delineation is not so sharp. Many equipments were developed as special-purpose devices, while others were designed to handle all of the necessary logical functions which were to be performed at the central processing site. To make matters a little worse, some designers took the special-purpose devices and gave them some, but not all, of the additional attributes of the multipurpose machines. So, even though there was at one time a fairly sharp differentiation between the functions of the devices with different names, that is no longer the case.

Therefore, what is described in this chapter are those names of equipments which are most common, with the classical definition of the functions which used to be performed uniquely by those machines. The reader should be aware, however, of the fact that many vendors describe their offerings with names that are not necessarily descriptive of the functions they perform. As such, the user should review the functions which the device performs to see how they meet the user's requirements and not rely on just the name for a description of the functions to be performed.

One specific point to mention here relative to equipment names is that of statistical multiplexers, described in Chap. 10. These are sometimes called *concentrators* by certain vendors when they perform additional buffering or processing functions.

B.

Concentrators

Chapter 10 described the various types and uses of multiplexers. Multiplexers are usually byte-oriented devices with very limited storage capability (one or two characters at a time), and except for intelligent multiplexers, there is very little logic involved in the combination of multiple low-speed lines onto individual high-speed lines. If it is desired to perform some kind of processing function on the information, for purposes such as routing, editing, error detection, etc., the information being transmitted can no longer be handled on an individual character-oriented basis. The information must then be handled on a message basis, and even more so in a store-and-forward mode. Store and forward means the reception of a complete message at a particular location, the validation that the transmission was correct, and then the acknowledgment back to the transmitter that the message was received correctly. On an evolutionary increase in capability basis, the next level of equipment over and above a multiplexer is called a *concentrator*. The concentrator is basically a store-and-forward device which takes information on a message basis from multiple incoming lines, high speed or low speed, and retransmits those messages to a central site for processing. This retransmission to the central site may occur in either a local or a remote environment and can occur on more than one line at a time. In effect, the concentrator acts as a master to all of the remote site terminal locations and, in turn, acts as a terminal site itself to the central site master. In the event the central site master is in the same location (local environment), the concentrator may transmit to that central site in either a serial mode over a communications line or in a parallel mode over a local emulation type interface such as a disc or tape. It is also possible for the serial path to be in a local mode with a direct wire connection at extremely high data rates (megabits per second).

A typical concentrator type configuration is shown at the bottom of Fig. 11-1. Concentrators are usually implemented to relieve the network control overhead from the central site hardware. In that regard, the concentrator will poll and call all of the remote site, bring the information in on a message-oriented basis, and in turn pass that information on to the central site via a master/slave relationship at a higher speed. In a local environment, the probability for transmission errors at the high speeds becomes extremely remote. Concentrators can be looked on as message buffering locations which can also reduce loads on the central site hardware by storing messages on its own peripherals during failure or degraded modes of operation and send the messages on to the central site only when the capability exists to process those messages.

Concentrators can also perform data compression functions, forward error correction, and other network related functions which also take additional overhead off of the central site hardware. For the most part, concentrators will not perform any unique routing functions. They take information from a central site and distribute it to remote sites and take the remote site transmissions and transmit it only to the central site. Terminal-to-terminal communications which require routing are performed in either message-switching equipments or front-end processors, which will be described in Sections B and C. Concentrators are to be considered data processing devices and in most cases are built around minicomputers today.

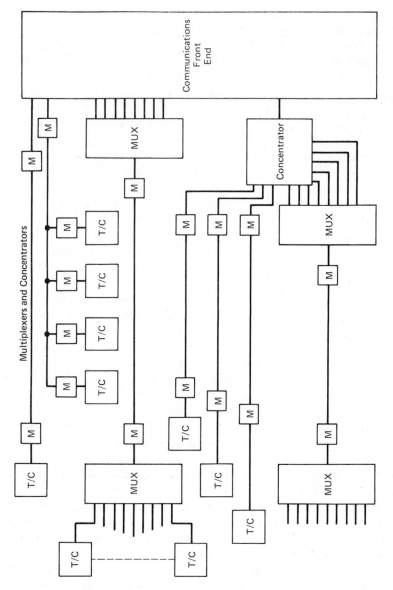

Figure 11-1. Concentrator/Front-End Configuration

C.

Message Switches

A message switch is a store and forward device just like a concentrator and can be considered a complementary type of hardware. Message switches were originally developed for the movement of traffic between terminals located in different parts of a network, and they performed no data processing function other than to route information coming in on one line and going out on another line. The software required for operation of a store-and-forward message switch was extremely complex, however, in that all of the possible combinations and permutations of network problems had to be incorporated in order to accommodate the many and various types of network malfunction. For example, the standard polling and calling arrangement to bring information in from remote terminals, and send it back out, had several possible abnormal situations. The following list includes some of these situations:

1. Terminal down
2. Line down
3. Terminal does not answer
4. Wrong terminal answers
5. Terminal sends garbled information
6. More than 1 terminal transmits at a time
7. Terminal never stops transmitting

Each one of these individual cases had to be handled completely and correctly so as not to impact any other part of the system. In addition, in the event a particular line or terminal was down for a period of time, the store-and-forward message switch had to have the buffering and queue management capability to stack the traffic destined for that site, and send it out in accordance with a predetermined set of guidelines when the terminal and/or line became operational again. These situations cause a significant amount of overhead software to be incorporated in message switches, because when there are very large queues destined for a particular line or terminal, it would be quite possible for a newly received message to be sent out immediately because of some kind of priority situation. This means a store-and-forward message switch would have to have not only a queuing capability, but a priority handling capability by terminal and by line.

In the event there are multiple terminals and multiple priorities, the queue management software would have to be able to go in accurately and open up a particular queue, insert a message, and then close the queue again. Problems will obviously arise if the queue chain gets broken for one reason or another (hardware or software). The tail end of the queue will never come out of the system unless there is software available to go in and find the broken queue chains and determine where the messages must be sent. The queue management mending software may have to be done in an off-line mode because of memory or cycle time limitations, but if it is not done, more and more of the peripheral storage will be taken up with what are in reality *headless queues* which can never be sent (also called *broken chains*). Eventually, the peripheral will be filled with these broken chains, and there will be no room for new traffic, and the system will probably come to a halt.

Along with the queue management software which must be incorporated, the proper criteria must be established for transmission of the queues when a period of time passes before the message can be transmitted. This requirement stems from the fact that many messages are time dependent and therefore have no use or applicability if they are not transmitted within a particular time frame. If one looks at an airline system for a moment, it can be seen that a particular flight manifest must be transmitted to the boarding gate prior to the flight departure, because after the flight departure the manifest will have no meaning at the boarding gate. The necessary software must be incorporated to make this timing determination, usually in the header of each message, if a queue management system is to operate correctly in the store-and-forward switching mode.

Many of the minicomputer networking systems are using store-and-forward techniques, but without any of the large peripheral storage devices. In this mode they use some form of core or semiconductor buffering for the individual messages and are therefore subject to degraded or shut down modes of operation if a particular line is down, and a queue builds up for that line which cannot be transmitted. This in turn uses up all of the available buffer area which does not leave enough buffers for other lines and their applicable queues. Devices which operate in this mode are sometimes called *transaction processors* and will be discussed further under Part D where CPUs used for communications are covered.

There are two basic differences then between a concentrator and a message switch. First, a concentrator passes all of its traffic on to a central site, while a message switch takes in all of the traffic and routes that traffic either to a central site or to other remote sites.

Second, a message switch may or may not be connected to a central site for processing purposes. If it is connected to a central site, that site will have its own unique address and will be treated as a separate line or lines connected to the message switch. A diagram of this configuration is shown at the top of Fig. 11-2.

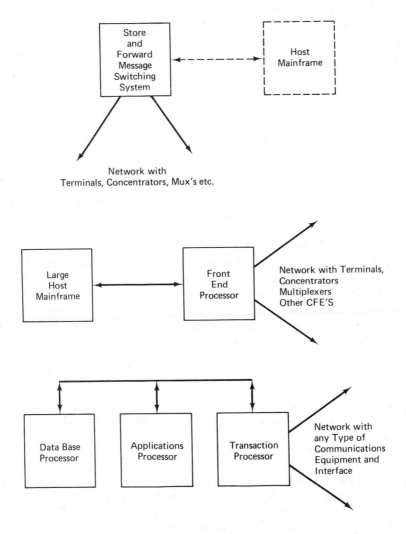

Figure 11-2. Store-and-Forward Message Switch

D.

Front-End Processors

A front-end processor is a device which incorporates the capabilities of both a concentrator and a store-and-forward message switch. In effect, it takes in the information from all remote sites and routes those messages either to the central site CPU for processing or back out to the network for terminal-to-terminal type communications. It has to incorporate all of the features and attributes of both the concentrator and message switch and is therefore a very complex device. Front-end processors also have their own set of peripherals (mag tapes and discs) so that they can store and manage the queues which are involved in the network operation.

In addition to the network and concentration functions, front-end processors may also be designed to perform some kind of data processing function. Most of the time these functions consist of performing error detection and correction, forward error correction, editing validations, and, in some cases, even applications processing with data bases stored on their own peripherals. This last function begins to make the front-end processor look more like an applications type machine, so this type of processing is usually very limited and applicable to specialized situations normally relating to the network operation. Examples of this would be reconfigurations of terminals and lines and temporary storage of information which was sent in from a remote location and stored temporarily on the peripherals of the front-end processor (data collection/batch inputs).

Most front-end processors are either minicomputers or mainframes, and a diagram of how they are connected is shown in the middle Fig. 11-2 and in Fig. 11-3.

E.

CPUs for Communications

As time passed, however, the computer architects found that a totally different instruction set was more efficient for communications processing than for data processing. This is a result of the fact that normal data processing is parallel byte or word oriented, while in the communications world everything is bit and byte serial oriented. The serial orientation, as opposed to the parallel processing, means that a different set of instructions would work more efficiently for one than for the other. Taking this difference into consideration some devices were designed to be communications devices only. In the beginning, most of these equipments were the store-and-forward message switching type because they operated almost entirely in the communications

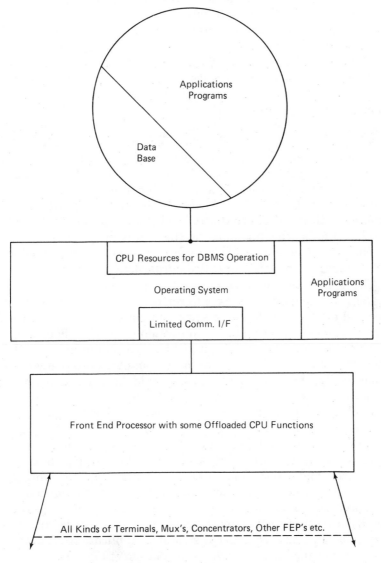

Figure 11-3.   Front-End Processor

environment only; but as the use of intelligent remote terminals grew, along with the requirement to tie them into central processing sites, the communications devices were forced to interface with the data processing device mode of operation. This caused a situation where emulation packages had to be developed to convert the communications transmissions to a format which could then be transmitted to a data processing device. This mode of operation lasted for many years until the late 1960s and early 1970s when a totally different mode of operation began to evolve with the advent of minicomputers.

Minicomputers, because of their limited word size (16 bits usually) and limited main memory capability, started to evolve as special-purpose CPUs. One of these purposes was a communications processor. As time progressed, the movement of more intelligence out into the network gave the terminal environment a capability to operate from a buffered mode where entire messages could be sent and validated, as opposed to previous modes of transmission where separate bits, bytes, or blocks had to be transmitted. As the message mode of operation evolved, a particular minicomputer CPU was designated as the interface device at the central or nodal site for handling both the network control and the reception of all messages. In other words, the functions of the front-end processor, message switch, and processing CPU interface were all incorporated into a single machine which is now called a *transaction processor*.

The transaction processor operates in a message-oriented environment. It transmits messages to remote sites over communications lines and to other CPUs at the same site via a local direct connection usually using some form of communication protocol. When using such a protocol, each of the central site CPUs will communicate with each other in what is in reality a local communication environment. Theoretically this means the CPUs could be separated and could communicate over greater distances with the same software involved, although at a lower speed due to communication line speed limitations. A transaction processor is responsible for control of all of the network lines tied to it (there may be other transaction processors at the same site responsible for other lines), for routing messages between itself and other transaction processors, and also routing messages to the various applications and/or data base management CPUs for appropriate processing by those CPUs. This mode of operation is actually a form of distributed processing, which will be discussed in more detail in Chap. 15 under Distributed Applications. A diagram of this type of connection is shown at the bottom of Fig. 11-2.

QUESTIONS

1. What is the function of a concentrator? How does it differ from a multiplexer?
2. What is the function of a message switch? How does it differ from a concentrator?
3. What is the function of a front-end processor? How does it differ from a concentrator and a message switch?
4. What is the function of a transaction processor?
5. Draw a diagram showing a host processing computer connected to:
   a. concentrator
   b. message switch
   c. front-end processor
   d. transaction processor

DATA TRANSMISSION INTEGRITY

A.

Background

The most significant problem facing the user of data communications today is the fact that the information to be transmitted between two points must go over facilities which were not originally intended to carry digital information. As described in Chap. 5 relative to the modems and the techniques for moving information, and as will be seen in Chap. 13 describing the different kinds of problems which may be encountered on a communications line, the least reliable portion of a communications system is that portion which is identified as the communication line itself. As the data transmission rates in the voice grade environment get higher and higher, the need for more reliable communication capability exists, but in actuality the error rate goes up. It is the mechanisms which we use to treat those errors which will be discussed in this section.

There are three basic modes of operation for detecting and/or correcting errors. The first is the recognition and only flagging the transmission when an error has occurred. This means the receiving unit identifies the fact that an error has been received and provides an output indicating that an error is contained in this particular transmission. This mode of operation is very prevalent in process control type applications where there are uncontrolled terminals with no memories. With no memory, information cannot be retransmitted, and therefore the best a user can do is to flag the fact that an error has occurred. There are also instances where analog information is digitally coded and digitally transmitted where an error cannot be corrected because the original analog information is no longer available. This situation is typical where voice communications are digitally encoded and transmitted to a different location where the voice is reconstituted.

If there is a particular block of information that contains an error, it is not possible to go back and tell the originator to repeat a portion of a word that was being said. What happens here is that if the error is large enough that the human at the receive end cannot understand the word being spoken, then he will request the originator to repeat the original statement. The fact that the digital information had an error which could not be corrected in this case is overridden by the fact that the human can request the retransmission. In general, however, the mode of flagging errors is used when the transmitter cannot regenerate the information so that it can be retransmitted. If a retransmission cannot be made, then it may be possible to establish that there can be specific operational procedures and/or software on an application basis set up to handle the invalid transmission.

The second mode of error correction is where the information has been transmitted from a buffered location and is therefore available for retransmission in the event an error occurs in the initial transmission. When the receiver recognizes an error, it will automatically request the transmitter to retransmit the same information again. The message will be retransmitted and verified again so that the process repeats itself until the information has been received correctly. The user must be aware, however, that there can be cases where the error is being generated by the transmitter every single time, so some form of reasonable limit must be placed on the amount of times a message can be retransmitted before a different course of action must be taken. This may be done in the software of the user's equipment, or it may be done as part of a limit which can be set within the protocol (discussed in Chap. 7). The use of retransmission techniques is the most commonly used alternative for correcting errors in a communication system. The key, however, to the identification and retransmission of information which was received in error is the error detection method itself. Some of the many methods available to do that will be described in this chapter.

As the last mode of providing data transmission integrity, we have the situation where, by adding enough additional information in the original transmission when an error is detected at the receive end, the original transmission can be recreated at the receive end by using this overhead addition of information. This is a forward error correcting mode of data transmission and is implemented in various ways. The basic idea is first to detect the error and then go through some form of mathematical algorithm to create a series of possible bit streams the transmission could have been and determine which of the possible ones is the true one. The most common method of forward error correction in use today is called BCH Code and will be described in Part E of this chapter. So to summarize the three methods of error correction, we have:

1. Flag the error at the receive end
2. Detect and request a retransmission
3. Forward error correction

B.

Echo Checks

One of the earliest modes of automatically detecting and correcting an error was the use of what is called an *echo check*. This particular technique consists of sending a character from one location to another where the receiver sends the character it received back to the originating terminal. In this manner the originating terminal can determine whether the character it sent was the character that was received by the receiver. Even though there are now two different communications paths which must be accommodated (originator to receiver and receiver back to originator) which will double the probability of an error, the closed loop mechanism of this technique ensures that the receiver has detected and stored the correct character. The probability of an error going one direction and being compensated by an error coming back in the other direction is remote and therefore not considered a significant enough problem to be concerned about when this technique is used.

There are a couple of significant limitations in using this particular mode of transmission, because first of all the operator must be on line transmitting a character at a time. With the human being as the slowest user of a system, it means that the available line capacity will be grossly underutilized. The second major limitation is the speed of transfer which is limited to a character at a time. During the time that one operator is on a multidrop line, no other terminal can be operational on that same line. Therefore the other terminals on the same line, if there are any, will have to wait until that operator is through before they can use the line. In general, this is the reason why on-line terminals requiring echo checks are rarely used in today's high-speed communications environment where the availability of buffered terminals, which eliminates the echo check requirement, are now available.

C.

Parity Checks—VRC, LRC, BCC

Of all the possible techniques to determine whether an error has occurred during the transmission of a message, the technique most widely used is what is known as *parity*. Parity consists of the addition of some noninformation-carrying or redundant bits to another specified group of bits, so that a particular mathematical calculation can be made at the receive end to determine whether the group of bits including the parity bit or bits are the same, which will mean the original information was received correctly. The very first type of parity which was used was called character parity or VRC (Vertical Redundancy Checking). VRC is used on a character level to determine that the bits of a particular character were received correctly. During times that information was transmitted one character at a time at relatively low speeds, this was the best and most reliable means of detecting individual character errors. Due to the multibit modulation schemes in use today, the same noise which used to cause an error in a single bit of a character will now cause errors in multiple bits of a character, thereby making this particular scheme not as reliable as it once was because of compensating errors (described later). VRC consists of adding a single bit at the end of a character to create either an "odd" parity or an "even" parity. What this really means is that if you use ASCII code with 7 bits per character the parity bit is added to make the total of "1" bits odd if odd parity is used, and if even parity is used the sum of "1" bits with parity is even. Vertical parity probably got its name from the days when characters were punched out on paper tape, because when looking at a paper tape, the individual characters are in a vertical position. Parity was not used with Baudot code but was used with most 7-bit codes such as ASCII and is also sometimes called vertical redundancy checking (VRC).

Any code can be created so that it can have an odd or an even parity as long as the hardware at the transmit end is generating the same kind of parity that the hardware at the receive end is looking for.

As the speed of data transmission increased in the early 1960s to 2400 bits per second and above, the incidence of errors which could not be detected began to increase, because VRC can only detect an odd number of bit errors in a transmission. If 2 bits within a particular character were reversed, the sum of the bits would still be the same, and the parity bit would still be the same, even though the character is now incorrect. With the advent of 2400 bit per second transmission and the utilization of multibit modulation schemes of 2 bits at a time, the errors that used to cause only single-bit errors were now causing a much higher incidence of 2-bit errors where specific bits were being changed in a compensating manner.

In order to overcome this limitation, an additional level of parity detection was implemented, which was called LRC (longitudinal redundancy checking) or BCC (block check character). Using LRC for a specific block or message, an additional seven bits were added at the end so that an odd or an even parity was created for each longitudinal row of bits. The parity sequence provided for all of the one bits of each character of the message to have a parity bit associated with them, all of the two bits, all of the three bits, etc., until each of the common bits in all characters had a bit at the end, giving either odd or even parity appended to the end of the message. The LRC character itself must contain the same type of parity as is used for the block.

By using an LRC, if there were two compensating errors in a particular character, the character would check out okay, but the block check character would show two errors in it. This mechanism gave a significant amount of additional capability to detect what would have otherwise been an undetected error in a transmission. As an additional capability with the use of LRC characters, some vendors set up a situation where all of the even characters in a block would have their own block check character, and all of the odd numbered characters in a message would have their own block check character. By segregating the odd and even block check characters, the probability of an undetected error was further reduced because transmission errors usually occur in bursts, and if errors were to occur, they would probably be in adjacent characters as opposed to nonadjacent ones. LRC was in use many years until the more common use of higher speed communications (4800 bps and up) made an additional level of parity checking required because of the higher probability of compensating errors occurring in contiguous and noncontiguous characters at those speeds. A diagram of the VRC and LRC parity detection schemes is shown in Fig. 12-1.

Vertical Redundancy Checking

Bit Position #	#1	#2	Information Characters #3	#4	#5
1	0	1	0	0	1
2	1	0	0	0	0
3	0	0	1	1	0
4	0	1	1	1	1
5	0	0	0	0	1
6	0	0	0	0	0
7	1	1	1	1	1
Parity* * Odd	1	0	0	0	1

Longitudinal Redundancy Checking

Bit Position #	#1	#2	Information Characters #3	#4	#5	Block Parity Char.
1	0	1	0	0	1	1
2	1	0	0	0	0	0
3	0	0	1	1	0	1
4	0	1	1	1	1	1
5	0	0	0	0	1	0
6	0	0	0	0	0	1
7	1	1	1	1	1	0
Parity* * Odd	1	0	0	0	1	1

Figure 12-1. VRC and LRC Parity

D.

Block Parities—SRC, Interleaving, CRC

Once the probability of undetected errors increased to an unacceptable level due to burst noise and the modulation methods employed, a new means of reliably detecting errors had to be implemented. The new techniques had to be based on all of the bits transmitted as part of a message or a block, and not just the individual characters in a character orientation. This was even more critical because many of the newer transmission techniques are not character oriented but are bit oriented, which is especially true in the use of graphics.

Two of the earlier techniques which were used to check an entire block of bits were *spiral redundancy checking* (SRC) and *interleaving*. The SRC is the same technique as LRC except that the individual bit positions of the characters are calculated on a diagonal instead of on a straight horizontal. Even if the bits making up the message are not character oriented, they can be set up in sequences of 8, and the spiral checking can take place. At the top of Fig. 12-2 we can see that the bit position 1 of character 1 is combined with bit position 2 of character 2, 3 of 3, 4 of 4, etc., until we get to the eighth bit of character 8, when we go back to the first bit of character 9 and start the sequence over again until we get to the very end. When we get to the very last character in this mode, we can add a single SRC character at the end which provides an odd or an even parity for all of the bits contained in the message. In the event the message is bit oriented and there are not enough bits to fill out the last character, the hardware will "pad out" the last 8-bit sequence so that there is an integral number of 8-bit segments. Due to the fact that only a single character is used as the SRC character, it turns out that mathematically there is only very little improvement over a straight LRC detection. The advantage comes in the probability of errors occurring in bits which are further removed from each other. Because of the extensive mathematical calculation required, SRC is not widely used today.

A second method of attempting to detect compensating burst errors is known as interleaving. Interleaving is shown at the bottom of Fig. 12-2. There are 8 characters of 8 bits each (ASCII type) where all of the 1 bits from each character are put together, all of the 2 bits, all of the 3 bits, etc., until all of the eight bits are put together in an eighth segment to be transmitted. At that point in time the ninth character starts off as if it were the first character again, and the

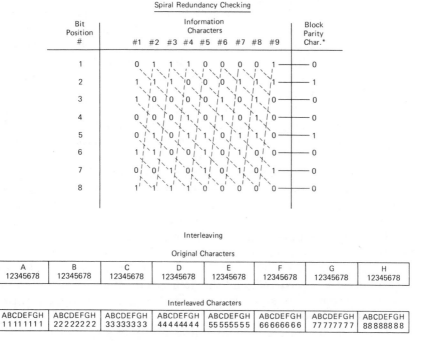

Figure 12-2. SRC and Interleaving

sequence continues for 9 through 16, then 17 through 24, etc. In the event there are not enough characters to complete a full sequence of 8 characters at the end, the additional characters can be padded out by the hardware, or a short interleave can be generated. For this configuration it would take a much more specific set of error conditions to cause compensating errors and therefore is better at detecting compensating errors than the straight block check characters, but again, due to the extensive manipulation of information, and the fact that interleaving is still not that much better than straight block check character detection, it also is not used very often today.

The technique that is used most extensively today for bit oriented checking of errors on a block or message basis is called cyclic redundancy checking (CRC). CRC has been designed to validate transmission of a bit and/or character oriented transmission sequence and is basically done by the use of a unique mathematical polynomial which is known to both the sender and the receiver. This specific polynomial value interacts through a predetermined mathematical algorithm on the data being transmitted and then on the data being received at the receive end to create a remainder, which is transmitted in addition to the data (remainder comes from dividing the polynomial into the transmitted bit stream). If the calculated value at the receive end, using the same algorithm and the same polynomial as the transmit end, is compared and found to be the same, the data is known to have been transmitted correctly.

The most widely used CRC is called CRC/16 and uses a 17-bit generator polynomial* that is based on a Euclidian algorithm. The Euclidian algorithm is itself based on the fact that prime numbers have unique characteristics when being divided into integers. A prime number is a number that can be divided only by itself and the number one without leaving a remainder. Simply stated, if an integer is divided by a prime number, the remainder is unique. In the same manner, when a serial bit stream, regardless of length, is divided by a binary prime number, the remainder has unique properties. If the remainder calculated at the receive end does not match the remainder calculated at the transmit end when they are compared, it is known that an error has occurred, and the appropriate steps according to the operating protocol must be implemented to obtain a retransmitted version of the message.

To get an idea of the estimated probability of an undetected error occurring, CRC redundancy checking utilizing the 17-bit polynomial has been calculated to allow only 1 bit error for every 10^{14} bits transmitted. In the real world that means transmitting at 9600 bits per second, 24 hours a day, 365 days a year; it would take approximately 3000 years for a single bit of undetected error to occur. This becomes even more critical when discussing the higher data rate transmissions which will occur on digital links using satellites where transmission rates may very well be in the 250-kilobit per second rate and multimegabit per second rate. At a 1 megabit per second transmission rate it would still take over thirty years before a single undetected bit error would occur based on statistical probability. It is therefore, by far, the most powerful practical tool today for detecting what would otherwise have been undetectable errors. CRC is so widely used today that some chip manufacturers have implemented the algorithm in chips which can be purchased and implemented by the user independently of any other technique he is now using. Many vendors have even incorporated the CRC method of error detection

---

*Divisor polynomial most often used is $X^{16} + X^{15} + X^2 + 1$ which is 11000000000000101

into their communication protocols, and typical of these are all of the new SDLC type protocol vendors, as well as DEC with their DDCMP. For any application which requires a high reliance on the integrity of the data, and where the data transmission rates will be 2400-bits per second or greater, the CRC method of error detection is by far the best one to implement.

E.

Forward Error Correction—Hamming, BCH

So far in this chapter we have been discussing the means of detecting errors in the transmissions. Without some means of correcting the erroneous messages the detection methods are just academic. Since the flagging technique does not correct any errors but only identifies them, we will not consider them further in this chapter. Also, the error detection schemes described in sections C and D can be implemented within specific protocols to provide appropriate retransmission sequences. What will be considered now are the various methods whereby information which has been received in error can be corrected without retransmission. In discussing the means of correcting errors in data transmissions we have to pay careful attention first to the mode in which the information is being controlled. This is dealt with extensively in Chap. 7 (Protocols) where the sequence of retransmitting blocks or messages in error is identified.

The relationship between the protocol and the method of error correction can be seen when looking at Fig. 12-3, both the top and the bottom segments. We have first, at the top, a block-by-block transmission and, at the bottom, a series of blocks transmitted from one end with acknowledgments coming back during some later point in time while the transmitter is in the process of sending subsequent blocks. The block-by-block transmission method is really a half-duplex mode of transmission. Each block is sent, and another block is not sent until the preceding block has been acknowledged as being received without error. Block 1 will be followed by ack 1, block 2 by ack 2, etc., until there is a block with an error. The error block will be retransmitted as many times as the protocol allows before some other action must be taken if there is a continuous error in that particular block. In the bottom portion of Fig. 12-3, where we have the continuous mode of transmission which really represents a full-duplex protocol, we have a sequence of blocks transmitted, with acknowledgments coming back in the opposite direction. When a particular block

Block by Block Transmission (HDX)

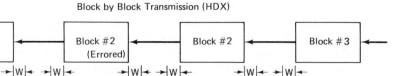

W -- Wait Period Due to Propagation and Turnaround.

FDX Mode Transmission

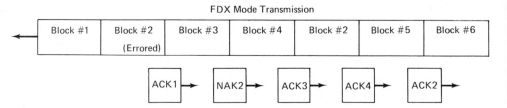

Figure 12-3.   HDX/FDX Transmissions

is received in error, a "NAK" is transmitted back to the originator, and upon completion of the block presently in progress, the error block will be retransmitted.

As can be seen, the line utilization in the block-by-block (HDX) transmission is relatively poor, while the utilization in a FDX sequence is much better. This is not the overriding consideration, however, in that we have other factors which must be considered when deciding on whether to use a block-by-block transmission or a continuous mode of transmission.

Primary of these considerations is the buffer requirements which exist for each of the two cases. In a block-by-block transmission, only one block of information must be stored at a time at either end. Since a particular block must first be received correctly by the other end, there is no necessity to store a second block until the first block has been acknowledged. If there are many different locations and/or many different central sites, the user can come to a predetermined definition of the amount of buffering required to handle this entire system. This is not the case in a continuous mode of transmission where both the remote sites and the central sites must maintain multiple blocks of information, because each of the blocks has to be acknowledged in sequence. If one of the blocks is not received correctly, in all of the standard vendor protocols, all of the subsequent blocks must be stored until that block is received correctly. If one makes the assumption that the same block can be in error more than once, then depending on the transmission rate and the propagation delay (especially considering satellites), many blocks may be stacked up waiting for the arrival of a block which has to be retransmitted. If we take the case of a 50-kilobit transmission, which is standard in satellites, with block sizes of 500 characters (4000 bits) and a satellite propagation delay of approximately one second, we have a situation where just a single block in error will require storage of 12 total blocks of information before the error block can be retransmitted. Since it takes another one-second time frame to acknowledge the error block that was retransmitted, we have a situation where 24 blocks have been stored at both the transmit and the receive end with only one block in error. One can imagine the situation if a protocol allows multiple retransmissions of the same message.

Take for example a standard number of three retransmissions before a different error sequence must be followed. With one error requiring 24 blocks, two errors would require 36 blocks and the third error would require a total of 48 blocks of information to be stored at both ends. Multiply that by the total amount of lines and/or terminals which are available, and it is easy to see how the user, at a central site especially, can run out of buffer space very quickly. This is extremely critical for those systems which have transaction processors utilizing solid state memory for buffers (no disc or tape peripherals). These machines use a buffer pool arrangment and do not have very many spare buffers to begin with. Therefore, it is quite possible for a single line having multiple errors to use up a majority of the buffer pool available, which in turn will slow down or cut off the entire rest of the system communicating with that one CPU. This is by far the biggest reason why many users today are staying with half-duplex protocols for the block at a time transmission, so that they can accurately predict the amount of buffering available. They know they will never have a situation where errors will cause system shut downs due to the queues which would build up. Naturally, most times the system would run relatively error free, but for those few instances when error occurs due to atmospheric conditions or other equipment problems, the impact on the system could be devastating. The network could very well shut down at the most critical time of its utilization, and this could be caused just by a single line.

One of the alternative modes to this particular limitation of the full-duplex protocols is the use of SDLC. SDLC is a full-duplex protocol, but the buffer requirements would be limited to a maximum of 7 for each location, because the protocol definition says that the transmitter must stop sending blocks of information after it has sent 7 blocks, unless an acknowledgment has been received for 1 or more of those 7 blocks of data transmitted. This is more fully described in Chap. 7. Because of the 7 unacknowledged block limitation, where the transmitter will otherwise shut down automatically, the user can accurately plan for the worst case buffer situation in the event of errors in transmission.

The above two methods of retransmission have to do with the recognition of an error and retransmitting the information that was received in error. There are many instances, especially those where long propagation delays are involved (such as satellites), where it may not be feasible to go back to the originator to retransmit information. For these particular situations, the user has at his disposal a capability for adding additional overhead information on top of each message so that if, under specific conditions, an error is recognized, the original bit stream can be recreated without going back to the originator for retransmission. These particular techniques are known as *forward error correcting codes.* Two of the most commonly used are Hamming and BCH (Bose, Chaudhuri, and Hocquengham).

The Hamming method of forward error correction (FEC) is dependent on the length of the information blocks being transmitted. The example to follow is shown in Fig. 12-4, and only an elementary description of the concept will be shown. Hamming code requires the addition of binary bits in a predefined series of locations within the original bit stream to be sent. As can be seen in Fig. 12-4, there is a 10-bit sequence to be transmitted. Bit positions 1, 2, 4, and 8 are reserved for the Hamming bits which will be calculated by the algorithm which we have to go through. If the original bit stream is longer (it will usually be much longer), then the additional locations of 16, 32, 64, 128, 256, etc., must be reserved for the addition of Hamming bits. The Hamming bits are identified by a square with the letter H associated with them. It should be noted at this point in time that Hamming code will allow for the forward error correction of only 1 bit error, while it will be able to recognize errors of more than 1 bit, but will not be able to correct for them.

With the 10 bits of original data required for transmission and then 4 bits set aside for Hamming bits, we have a total of 14 bit positions which will be transmitted. The calculation of what the Hamming bits are supposed to be are calculated as follows. Each of the bit positions which are represented by a 1 bit (5, 11, and 12) are converted to a binary representation of their decimal position, as seen in the calculation section. The bits are then added in a binary mode without carrying. The summation is seen to be 0010. These are the Hamming bits which are to be transmitted in the Hamming code block and will be sent on the communications line. This can be seen

		Bit Positions									
Information Block to be Sent		10	9	8	7	6	5	4	3	2	1
		0	0	1	1	0	0	0	0	1	0

					Bit Positions								
Hamming Code Block	14	13	12	11	10	9	8	7	6	5	4	3	2	1
	0	0	1	1	0	0	H	0	0	1	H	0	H	H

H — Hamming bits

Calculation of Hamming Bits by Sender

$$5_{10} = 0101_2$$
$$11_{10} = 1011_2$$
$$\oplus \quad = 1110_2$$
$$12_{10} = 1100_2$$
$$\oplus H = 0010_2$$

					Bit Positions								
Transmitted Hamming Code Block	14	13	12	11	10	9	8	7	6	5	4	3	2	1
	0	0	1	1	0	0	0	0	0	1	0	0	1	0

					Bit Positions								
Received Hamming Code Block	14	13	12	11	10	9	8	7	6	5	4	3	2	1
	0	0	1	0	0	0	0	0	0	1	0	0	1	0

Check Calculation by Receiver

$$H \quad = 0010_2$$
$$12_{10} \quad = 1100_2$$
$$\oplus \quad = 1110_2$$
$$5_{10} \quad = 0101_2$$
$$\oplus \quad 1011_2 = 11_{10} \text{ (Location of Errored Bit)}$$

Figure 12-4. Hamming Code FEC Example

in the "transmitted Hamming code block" bit position of 8, 4, and 1 which have the 0's, while bit position 2 has the 1 bit.

If we make the assumption that bit position 11 has been changed from a 1 to a 0, we can calculate at the receive end the fact that a single bit has been changed. This is done by taking the Hamming bits and adding them to the binary representation of the received decimal locations where all of the 1 bits have been received (positions 5 and 12) and adding them to the Hamming bits. As can be seen in the check calculation, we have the Hamming bits added to positions 5 and 12 leaving a result of 1011. The 1011 result indicates bit position 11. By definition of the procedure, we now know from this calculation that bit position 11, whatever it is right now, is in error. Therefore, it must be changed at the receive end to a 1. In this mode we have corrected a single bit error in a transmission. If there were no errors in the transmission, the result of adding the Hamming bits along with all of the binary representations of the decimal bit positions would result in a sum of all 0's. By calculating all 0's the receiver would know that there were no errors in the transmission. This has been a gross level representation of the workings of Hamming code, because in the event there is more than one error or the Hamming code bits themselves have been in error, there are additional calculations required to make that determination. These will not be covered in this particular text because, for the most part, errors today occur in multiples (bursts), and therefore, single-bit-error forward error correction is not as feasible or practical to use as multiple bit forward error correction.

The most commonly used method of forward error correction today is the BCH forward error correcting algorithm, which is based on the same type of Euclidian algorithm as was described for CRC error detection. In the case of the BCH code, the remainder is transmitted along with the data and then used by the receiver to recalculate the original data stream.

There are two basic limitations to the BCH method of FEC. First, the most errors which can be corrected for equals one less than the total amount of BCH bits used as a remainder. What this means is that in a particular message with a 16-bit remainder used, up to 15-bit errors can be corrected for. The second limitation is that the errors, regardless of the amount, must occur within a 16-bit contiguous sequence, an example of which is a message where there are two bit errors in one part of the message and two bit errors in another part of the message, separated by more than the length of the BCH remainder. This occurrence cannot be corrected. For both of the limiting cases of BCH capability to forward error correct, the receiver must still go back to the transmitter to request a retransmission.

Even though most transmissions today are based on 8-bit characters, if the data is not character oriented, the same algorithm will work because the hardware will treat the bits as binary stream information. This mode of calculation is transparent to the user.

The method whereby BCH recreates the original bit stream is conceptually as follows. When an error is recognized in the comparison of the remainders, the original length bit stream is generated with all 0's, then changed one bit at a time, and incremented until a specific configuration leaves the BCH remainder. The definition of the algorithm says that there can only be one data sequence to give the unique remainder. Therefore, if only one bit stream out of all bit streams possible is found to give the unique remainder, that, by definition, was the original transmitted bit stream.

If more than one bit stream gives the unique remainder, it means that either the remainder is in error or the amount of errors has exceeded the remainder length, or the errors have occurred outside the contiguous length of the BCH remainder. A very limited portion of BCH operation (error detection phase) is shown in Fig. 12-5 for a 9-bit sequence. The original block being transmitted and the binary prime are shown along with the division and the remainder. The remainder is appended to the transmission, and a single bit error (seventh bit) is shown. At the receive end, the same binary prime number is divided into the data stream (both ends use the same binary prime and therefore know how many remainder bits there should be). Since the remainders do not compare, the original bit stream must be changed mathematically in hardware/software or firmware or a combination of these methods one bit at a time until the unique remainder is found (not shown), and that is the originally transmitted bit stream.

With very long data streams the number of calculations which are necessary to determine the original bit stream when an error occurs is very extensive. Due to this fact, BCH has been implemented in what is effectively a microprocessor. The microprocessor contains all of the necessary coding and firmware and will therefore perform the same operation, at each end, the same way every time. It is also possible to build chips which will contain all of the necessary calculating capability. These chips are available today and can be installed by the user if he wants a forward error correcting code in his system on any given link.

There are other factors to consider in forward error correction, such as what to do when the FEC cannot recalculate the original bit stream and information has to be retransmitted. If the propagation delays are very long (which is one of the primary reasons for putting in FEC in the first place), it may not be feasible to go all the way back to the transmitter to retransmit the block. The user must analyze in detail the alternatives which are acceptable if messages with FEC cannot be retransmitted. Store and forward techniques along the path

		Bit Positions									
		9	8	7	6	5	4	3	2	1	0
Information Block to be Sent		1	0	0	1	0	0	0	1	1	1

Expressed as General Number

$$x^9 + x^6 + x^2 + x + 1$$

Times x^4 (4 Redundant Bits to be Added)

$$x^{13} + x^{10} + x^6 + x^5 + x^4$$

Division by Binary Prime

$$
\begin{array}{r}
x^9 + x^5 + 1 \\
x^4 + x + 1 \,) \, \overline{x^{13} + x^{10} + x^6 + x^5 + x^4} \\
\underline{x^{13} + x^{10} + x^9} \\
x^9 + x^6 + x^5 \\
\underline{x^9 + x^6 + x^5} \\
x^4 \\
\underline{x^4 + x + 1} \\
\end{array}
$$

Remainder = $x + 1 = 0011_2$

	13	12	11	10	9	8	7	6	5	4	3	2	1	0
Transmitted Block	1	0	0	1	0	0	0	1	1	1	[0]	[0]	[1]	[1]

	13	12	11	10	9	8	7	6	5	4	3	2	1	0
Received Block	1	0	0	0	0	0	0	1	1	1	[0]	[0]	[1]	[1]

Division by Same Binary Prime

$$
\begin{array}{r}
x^9 + x^6 + x^5 + x^3 + x^2 \\
x^4 + x + 1 \,) \, \overline{x^{13} + x^6 + x^5 + x^4}
\end{array}
$$

Remainder = $x^0 = 0001_2$

Comparing Remainders

$$
\begin{array}{l}
0011 \\
\underline{0001} \\
0010 = \text{Non Zero} = \text{Error}
\end{array}
$$

Figure 12-5. BCH Code Error Detection Portion Example

of the message may be used to reduce the total propagation delay from a transmitter to a receiver when multiple links are involved, but further definition and description of the alternatives are dependent on the particular application because of the uniqueness of each application.

F.

Data Compression Techniques

As data transmission rates increase, and the distances over which they must be transmitted also increase, there is a much higher probability of errors occurring, so that the time frame for correcting those errors requires extensive buffering at the transmit and receive end of the communications path. As was stated previously in this chapter, store-and-forward techniques for individual segments of the communications path can be utilized to decrease the total propagation delay before an acknowledgment or negative acknowledgment will reach the individual transmitter, and this is very significant on those links where satellite transmissions and multiple satellite links in a single path are involved.

With the use of forward error correcting codes we have a mechanism whereby requirements for retransmissions are substantially reduced. However, there is another technique which can be used to further improve the probability of a successful transmission when long block lengths are involved. That technique is called *data compression*. Data compression means the elimination of specific bits of information without changing the total information content. There are various techniques for implementing data compression, and they will be described in this section.

One of the simplest modes of compression applies to the technique using punched cards. If there are only 60 columns in an 80 column punched card which have information, then only 60 characters worth of information should be transmitted. This also applies to output devices, such as a typical computer printer where there are 132 columns. If only 75 valid characters are to be printed, only those characters should be transmitted. These techniques do not require any particular kind of coding technique other than to identify via control characters that the end of a particular line or block has been transmitted.

Other relatively simple forms of data compression are to delete fixed information from a form, that is, to identify a format at both the receive and transmit end and then transmit only the variable information along with a definition of the format which was used, so that the receiver can apply the information it detects to the appropriate fields of the previously identified form.

Redundant characters can be coded so that after identifying the coding technique, a long alpha sequence can be compressed with an alpha numeric transmission. For example, if there are 5 of the same ASCII characters to be sent, then the transmission would be changed to have a numeric ASCII 5 and then the character transmitted. This sequence would have to follow a control code identifying to the receiver that an alpha numeric representation is being provided for a sequence of alpha characters. Three characters (control, quantity, alpha) will represent the original 5 characters. This too has only very specific and unique applications and therefore is used only in limited cases.

One of the most often used methods of data compression is the binary coded decimal representation of ASCII numeric characters. If there are transmissions which involve many numbers of large orders of magnitude, it will be much more efficient to transmit them in binary form. Since each ASCII character is represented by 8 bits, up to a numeric 256 can be described within that 8-bit sequence. For a 16-bit sequence, a numeric value up to 65536 is represented, so instead of sending 8 bits for each numeric character there can be a very significant reduction in the total amount of bits being transmitted if the numerics are coded in binary. This technique is especially applicable where there are many numerics to be sent, although, depending on the application, alpha characters can also be included as long as the overhead of going back and forth between the alpha representation and the BCD representation does not exceed the quantity of data compression realized by implementing the BCD.

For those applications where program development is being undertaken and many computer dumps must be transmitted over a communication line for debug purposes, hexadecimal code can be used where 4 bits will represent all of the numerics to be transmitted as well as the alpha characters A through F. This of course is a very specific application, although in a distributed type system where development is going on at different locations, it can be a highly effective means of allowing multiple users to interact and debug the same problem at different locations.

The techniques described above are known as "brute force" types of data compression. There is another area of data compression techniques which are based on mathematical algorithms, which are designed to work on the probability of specific sequences occurring and taking those specific sequences and coding them with a shorter sequence of bits. In other words, those sequences of fixed length which are used most often would be represented by a sequence of bits that is much shorter. The less often a particular sequence occurs, the more bits it may take to define that particular sequence, but in an overall situation the quantity of bits being transmitted is significantly reduced.

One of the techniques which assigns shorter bit sequences to frequently occurring symbols and longer bit sequences to less frequent symbols is called *Huffman Coding*. The technique is very much like the one which Samuel Morse used when he developed the Morse Code, that is, the most often used characters in the English language were represented by the least amount of dots and dashes. In the Huffman Code, the probability distribution of the source information must be known, and from this a code sequence can be defined using a method known as the *tree method*. An example of this is shown in Fig. 12-6. For a given set of symbols (6), a probability factor is worked out (shown in column two). The tree is then developed which will give a unique set of codes which identify the specific probability of the information being transmitted.

In referring to the figure we can see that the tree combines the two lowest probabilities, .09 and .04, of symbols S5 and S6, into a node which represents the combined probability of that pair, .13.

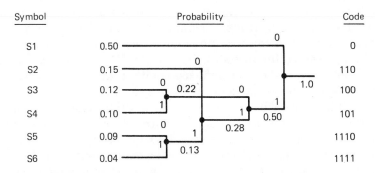

After constructing the tree, by combining successive lowest probability pairs into nodes, 0 and 1 binary values are assigned to each branch. The code is derived by tracing from the 1.0 probability node to each source symbol, identifying the "1's" and "0's" which are encountered.

Figure 12-6.   Huffman Code Tree

Then the next pair of low probabilities, in this case those of symbols S3 and S4, are combined into a node of .22. The next two lowest probability numbers are .13 (the combined S5 and S6 nodes) and .15, the probability of S2. This pair then joins into a node with a combined probability of .28* The tree is then completed by combining S1 and the last node, which results in a combined probability of 1. Next, 0 and 1 binary symbols are assigned to each branch of each node. The bit sequences representing each symbol can now be constructed by moving from the 1 probability node down the most direct path and writing down from left to right 0's and 1's encountered along the way.

In essence, this algorithm reduces the original source alpha bits into "super symbols" of a combined probability. At the 1 node, there are only two super symbols, 0 and the 1 respectively. By working backward, it is easy to break down and assign the 0's and 1's at each branch until the original sequence source symbols are reached. This can also be done dynamically because once a 0 is recognized as the first bit of the super symbol, we know that symbol S1 is represented uniquely. When a 1 bit is recognized we see that it is necessary to look at at least two more bits to determine the particular code sequence. If three 1 bits in a row are recognized, we must look at a fourth bit to determine the original symbol. If each of the original symbols was a four-bit sequence, we see that in half the cases the 4 bits can be reduced to 1 bit for transmission purposes (S1 occurs 50% of the time), for 37 percent of the cases (S2, S3, and S4) 3 bits can be used to transmit the data instead of 4, whereas only 13% of the time (S5 and S6) will a full 4 bits be required to transmit the original symbols. By carrying this technique to the extreme, any specific character length definition can be reduced to a Huffman code in such a way that the total transmission of bits can be reduced by a significant amount. Typical compaction ratios of 2:1 to 4:1 are common using these Huffman codes. Huffman is also a straightforward code to implement and can be done using either hardware or software, and it is also possible to get some of these codes in chips.

The method described earlier where multiple characters of the same type can be transmitted using a control character with an alpha and a numeric representation is called *string coding,* which can also realize compaction ratios of 4:1 or more depending on the application. The applications where string coding is used extensively are in graphic or analog type information. It should be noted that string coding is effective only when the strings exceed a length of four

---

*Following this, the .28 combination is joined with the .22 combination which gives a probability of .5 occurrence.

repetitive characters, and also note that when there are applications with multiple string sequences, a Huffman code type of algorithm can be applied to the string sequences to provide an even greater amount of data compression.

There are also other exotic techniques which are used for coding English text based on the probability of character occurrence as well as the occurrence after other characters (the character Z would not follow the letter H, and that particular sequence would therefore have a probability code of 0). This kind of technique is called a *Markov source,* but due to the fact that it will have very little practical application for most users, a detailed analysis of the Markov technique will not be described and is mentioned here so that the user is aware of the availability of such a technique if it is ever required in the future.

QUESTIONS

1. What are the three basic methodologies for detecting and/or correcting transmission errors?
2. What is meant by "echo checking?"
3. Functionally describe:
   a. vertical redundancy check
   b. horizontal redundancy check
4. What is meant by "odd" and "even" parity?
5. How is a cyclic redundancy check implemented?
6. What is the functional capability identified as forward error correction? Give an example of its use.
7. Describe the implications of buffer usage with HDX and FDX transmissions.
8. Give two examples of a forward error correcting code. What are their advantages and disadvantages?
9. Describe three types of data compression techniques.

TRANSMISSION BANDWIDTHS AND IMPAIRMENTS

A.

Background

The bandwidth of a communications channel is one of the parameters which establishes the volume of information that it can support, and in the absolute best case, according to Shannon, the maximum amount of information that can be transmitted is twice the frequency of the transmitted signal. Therefore, in a voice grade line which is 3000 cycles in width (300 Hz to 3300 Hz), even if the 3300 Hz signal could be used (which it can't because of the attenuation and distortion at that frequency), the absolute maximum data transmission rate on a voice grade line would be 6600 bits per second. In actuality most modems today require a full cycle for information to be detected (see Chap. 5—Modems), and this means a maximum practical signaling rate of approximately 2400 signal changes per second. As was described in Chap. 5, multibit modulation schemes will be used to increase the actual bit per second information transmission rate, but for purposes of describing the bandwidth and signaling rate we must limit ourselves to describing the frequencies which are being transmitted on the voice grade line.

B.

Channel Bandwidth and Frequencies

To get an idea of the total frequency spectrum, Fig. 13-1 describes various frequency ranges all the way from the low end audible range to the cosmic ray range where wave lengths are described in fractions of a micron, which is $1/1{,}000{,}000$ of a meter. As can be seen, the audible range extends to at least 20 kHz, and since telephones were required to transmit audible frequencies they were designed within that range. The audible bandwidth spectrum is shown in the upper half of Fig. 13-2, where we have human hearing, human speech, and the telephone channel all superimposed on a logarithmic scale and below it the specific band pass of the telephone line itself. This lower diagram describes all voice grade line channels and consists of a total of 4.2 kHz bandwidth of which 0 to 300 Hz is reserved for nonvoice use (used for low-speed teletype traffic), and the high end of 3.3 kHz to 4.2 kHz is used for circuit establishment in the DDD network (Direct Distance Dial). This leaves the band of 300-3300 Hz for actual transmission of voice and/or data. It is this specific band which carries all information in the voice grade telephone network. It is up to the user as to whether voice or data or both are to be transmitted, and it is also up to the various equipment vendors who design their systems to interface with this specific bandwidth capability.

C.

Transmission Impairments

Assuming the user has predominantly voice grade lines, this section contains descriptions of the principal impairments to data transmis-

Band Designation	From		To	
	Frequency	Wavelength	Frequency	Wavelength
Audible	20 Hz	–	20 KHz	–
Bass Viol	40 Hz	–	200 Hz	–
Trombone	70 Hz	–	500 Hz	–
Human Voice	100 Hz	–	1100 Hz	–
Trumpet	200 Hz	–	900 Hz	–
Violin	200 Hz	–	3 KHz	–
Flute	260 Hz	–	2.1 KHz	–
Piccolo	500 Hz	–	4.2 KHz	–
Radio (CCIR)	3 KHz	100 Km	3000 GHz	0.1 mm
Very Low Frequency VLF	3 KHz	100 Km	30 KHz	10 Km
Low Frequency LF	30 KHz	10 Km	300 KHz	1 Km
Medium Frequency MF	300 KHz	1 Km	3 MHz	100 m
High Frequency HF	3 MHz	100 m	30 MHz	10 m
Very-High Frequency VHF	30 MHz	10 m	300 MHz	1 m
Ultra-High Frequency UHF	300 MHz	1 m	3 GHz	10 cm
Super-High Frequency SHF	3 GHz	10 cm	30 GHz	1 cm
Extremely-High Frequency EHF	30 GHz	1 cm	300 GHz	0.1 cm
	300 GHz	0.1 cm	3000 GHz	0.1 mm
Infared	1000 GHz	$300\,\mu$	10^5 GHz	$3\,\mu$
Visible	–	$1\,\mu$	–	$0.3\,\mu$
Red	–	$1\,\mu$	–	$0.69\,\mu$
Orange	–	$0.69\,\mu$	–	$0.62\,\mu$
Yellow	–	$0.62\,\mu$	–	$0.57\,\mu$
Green	–	$0.57\,\mu$	–	$0.52\,\mu$
Blue	–	$0.52\,\mu$	–	$0.47\,\mu$
Violet	–	$0.47\,\mu$	–	$0.3\,\mu$
Ultraviolet	–	$0.3\,\mu$	–	$10^5\,\mu$
X-Rays	–	$10^3\,\mu$	–	$10^7\,\mu$
Soft	–	$10^3\,\mu$	–	$10^5\,\mu$
Hard	–	$10^5\,\mu$	–	$10^7\,\mu$
Gamma Rays	–	$10^6\,\mu$	–	$10^7\,\mu$
Cosmic Rays	–	$10^7\,\mu$	–	$< 10^7\,\mu$

K = Kilo = 1000   c = centi = 1/100
M = Mega = 1,000,000   m = milli = 1/1000
G = Giga = 1,000,000,000 μ = micron = 1/1,000,000

Figure 13-1. Frequency Spectrum

sion and some of the steps taken to overcome them. There is a unique set of these impairments inherent in both analog and digital transmission techniques but the specific items discussed here are only the voice band parameters which will most affect data communications on voice grade lines.

In order to understand better what each one of these terms means and how they affect the line, one must recognize and understand the key parameters relevant to the impairments themselves, and the techniques which are used to analyze them. One of the first definitions which must be made is the decibel (dB). This is a unit which is defined as the ratio of output signal power to input signal power. The formula is described as follows:

$$dB = 10 \log_{10} \frac{\text{output power}}{\text{input power}}$$

Logarithms are used because a signal level in dB can be easily added and subtracted and because the human ear naturally responds to signal levels in an approximately logarithmic manner. It should be

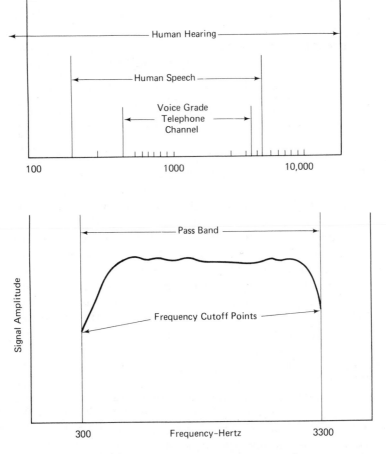

Figure 13-2. Telephone Channel Frequency Spectrum

noted that if the output power is less than the input power the logarithmic result is negative and the line is said to have a loss of that many dB. For reference purposes, the individual output and input signal power is related to a specific level called a dBm, where zero dBm (Log 1 = 0) equals 1 milliwatt which is terminated in 600 ohms impedance. For most circuits the reference frequency used is 1004 Hz. Any measurements made relative to a reference frequency are expressed in decibels relative to 1 milliwatt (dBm) where:

$$dBm = 10 \log_{10} \frac{\text{signal power in milliwatts}}{1 \text{ milliwatt}}$$

Therefore zero dBm means 1 milliwatt and absolute power levels may be expressed as so many dBm.

There can be other test tones which would be used at 1004 Hz, but these test tones would be at different levels. In order to reference measurements back to the original test tone level, another unit of measurement is used. This new level is signal decibel level relative to 1 milliwatt with respect to test tone level (dBm 0) and is defined as:

$$dBrn = \text{signal level dBm} - \text{test tone level in dBm}$$

In this relationship information is normally transmitted at a level which is 13 dB below the test tone level and therefore the data level is 13 dBm0.

It should be noted that the data transmission line measurements for all impairment testing is made with the 1004 Hz tone, which is also called a *holding tone*. The testing is made at the data signal level, not with the test tone level. (This reference frequency testing does not necessarily describe the dB loss at other frequencies.)

According to communication line theory, noise is the primary limiting factor for data transmission. The noise itself does not cause a significant amount of errors in low-speed transmission up to 2400 bps, but for transmission rates above that the effects of other impairments, along with the noise, make the actual noise encountered a significant contributing factor. Other names for this noise, which is an audible hiss on a telephone line, are message circuit noise, background noise, Gaussian noise, white noise, and hiss. The noise is measured in decibels, also above some reference, which is assumed to be −90 dBm. The −90 dBm is an arbitrary level that represents the lowest noise level which is audible to the average human ear. Therefore, the reference noise level which is defined as 0 dB rn is −90 dBm. Other than background noise there is another type of noise called "transient noise." Names typically used for transient noise are impulse noise, fortuitous noise, burst noise, and clicks.

The sources of noise in the data communications channel are crosstalk on adjacent channels, switching, power fluctuations, component failures, impedance mismatches, atmospheric conditions, interface mismatches, and inherent designs of the equipment being used. The primary effect of noise on the actual data which is being transmitted is that the signals are distorted so that the original bit value is modified or lost.

In order to analyze the noise relative to its impact on the telephone, a filter which is based on the response of the telephone, called a *C-Message Filter,* is used as a matching device with a level meter in order to give a representative noise measurement. (C Message Filters simulate the telephone response.) Even though this is primarily a voice type measurement, it is also used for data transmission purposes, and when such a C-Message Filter is used, the units measured are called *decibels above reference noise, C-Message weighted* (dBrnc).

Since noise on a telephone line is also signal dependent, an increase in signal level will cause a corresponding increase in noise. To simulate and then measure these conditions, the 1004 Hz test tone at the data level is transmitted on the line, and at the receiving end another filter is used to remove the test tone. The filter which removes the test tone and allows measurement of the noise, is called a *notch filter,* and testing in this mode is defined as C-Notched Noise Measurement. A circuit configuration which shows the various filters on the line is shown in Fig. 13-3.

Independent of the noise effects, the primary impairment on a telephone line is the loss of energy at each of the individual frequencies, which may be different at each of those frequencies. Because the frequency band we are interested in extends from 300 to 3300 Hz, the amplitude loss at each of the frequencies is referenced to the loss at one kHz. This relationship describes a curve which is known as amplitude response, or attenuation distortion, of a transmission channel and is shown in Fig. 13-4 for a standard voice grade line.

The second primary source of distortion is that caused by the fact that different frequencies move down the telephone line at different rates. What this means is that even though all of the frequencies are transmitted at the same time from the transmit end, they will be

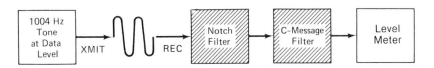

Figure 13-3. Noise Measurement

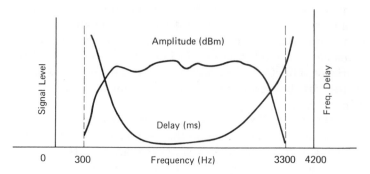

Figure 13-4. Amplitude and Delay Response

received at the other end of the line at slightly different times. This difference is known as *envelope delay* and may be expressed in either microseconds or milliseconds of delay. The absolute delay cannot be determined because the length of the path varies, and besides only the relative difference between the frequencies is important anyway. The differences at the receive end can be measured, and is known as *envelope delay distortion at a given frequency*. It is measured as the difference in microseconds when compared with the delay experienced by a reference tone at 1800 Hz. (The 1 kHz tone is not used in this case.) Actual methods used to measure envelope delay distortion are very sophisticated due to the complexity of making accurate frequency determinations, but for descriptive purposes the relationships are shown in Fig. 13-4.

The next level of distortion is caused by the power line harmonics, especially in telephone carrier multiplexed systems, which creates a forward and backward movement of the zero crossings of the individual frequency, and this is known as *jitter*. The jitter is actually instantaneous phase changes crossing the zero level and is measured by looking at the zero crossing point of a particular test tone (1004 Hz). Noise, because it also affects the zero crossings, can heavily influence the measure of jitter, and therefore, to make accurate measurements, the holding tone should be at the data level. In addition the notched noise measurements should be made in conjunction with the phase jitter measurements because this will help to determine what is actually being experienced—true phase jitter or just the effects of a high noise level.

For low-speed data transmissions, phase jitter is rarely noticeable over the effects of amplitude response distortion, envelope delay distortion, and transient errors which will be discussed in more detail later. Since the telephone channel may be made up of many active components such as diodes, transistors, LSI circuitry, and passive components such as coils, capacitors, and resistors, there is another mode of distortion called nonlinear distortion, which is caused by the specific nonlinear characteristics of the components themselves. These components will distort a data signal, because they cause the generation of unwanted harmonics which add to the information signal in a detrimental manner. Figure 13-5 shows what the effects of nonlinear distortion are. It is known as *clipping*. Although this figure

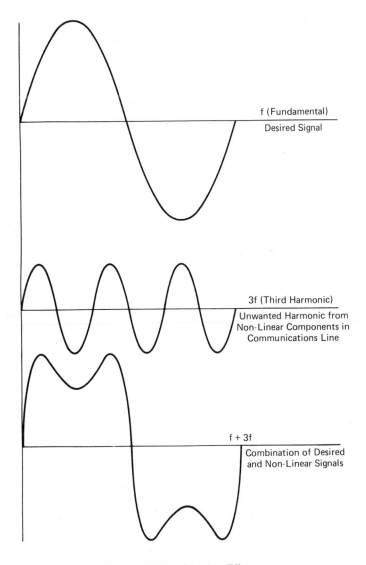

Figure 13-5. Clipping Effects.

is an exaggeration as to the effect, there are many harmonics which will result in this type of distortion.

Nonlinear distortion is measured today on specific test equipment where two sets of very closely paired frequencies are used. Their harmonics and cross harmonics are measured to determine the total amount of nonlinear distortion, and this type of degradation is called either *intermodulation distortion* or *harmonic distortion.*

Line conditioning and equalization (described in section D of this chapter) correct many of the effects of amplitude distortion, delay distortion, and nonlinear distortion, but there are still limits as to how much of those impairments can be compensated for on any given facility.

Another kind of transmission error, the transient type, is also called "line hits" and is the primary source of errors in low-speed transmissions. The reason why line hits cause the errors is that they totally destroy or significantly modify the specific bits being transmitted. These transient distortions are divided into three general categories:

- Drop Out   A sudden large reduction in signal level which lasts more than several milliseconds.
- Phase Hit   A sudden uncontrolled change in phase of the receive signal.
- Gain Hit   A sudden "spike" of noise of very short duration which, as described previously, sounds like "clicks" on the telephone line.

Depending on the particular vendor, and sometimes the users themselves, the names of the different types of distortion are not used exactly the same way and, in some cases, are even given different names. Regardless of the name, however, the user should always relate back to the specific type of distortion he is trying to identify and measure and then relate that back to the terms described in this section. Then the specific measurement methods can be established and accurate readings made.

One other type of distortion warrants discussion here, and that is what is known as *echo.* Echo is also caused by some of the network elements, one of which is called a *hybrid.* A hybrid is a converting coil which takes a two-wire local loop and converts it to a four-wire circuit for long distance transmission. Another hybrid at the other end of the line will take the four-wire connection and convert it back to two wires for the two-wire termination at the other end. These hybrid coils cause a change in what is called the *characteristic impedance* of the telephone lines. In practical use, this means that all of the energy transmitted in one direction will not be absorbed by the receive end, and some of it will actually be reflected back towards the transmitter. This reflection of energy, which can be recognized by the transmitter, is what is known as echo and exists primarily on dial-up lines. In order to eliminate echos from circuits, the telephone company has installed either hybrids or what are known as "echo suppressors" which in effect cause a unidirectional transmission. Hybrids allow for unidirectional transmission on each of the long distance pairs of wires while echo suppressors allow unidirectional transmission on the one circuit one way at a time. Failures of echo suppressors can mean either the echo coming back with enough energy to distort the transmitted signal, or not dropping out fast enough to prevent the loss of the initial bits each time the direction of the transmission changes. (Results in another form of clipping.)

Under most conditions, after a data call is established on a two-wire circuit, the modems will maintain a signal level on the line in a continuous manner so that the echo suppressor, unless it is defective, will not cause any clipping. To eliminate passive echo suppressor problems, the phone company has developed an "active" echo suppressor which dynamically simulates a filter in the opposite direction for transmissions in the primary direction. Because it is adaptive in nature, it eliminates only the echo while at the same time allowing other signals to propagate in the opposite direction. For full-duplex circuits, which are leased lines, the telephone company can enable the echo suppressor on each line in one direction perma- nently so that it does not interfere with unidirectional transmissions. For those circuits where reverse channel modulation techniques are used (transmission in both directions at the same time), the echo suppression circuitry must be disabled.

As a corollary to echoes, it is possible to insert too much power from the transmit end on to the communication line, and this condi- tion causes what is known as *singing*. Singing is normally controlled by decreasing the power output of the transmitting modem, but if it is caused just by the carrier, it can be compensated for by inserting extra losses in the line. In either event, the modem output signal must be within the specifications of the voice grade line specification.

D.

Error Rates and Their Measurement

The most often used measure of the quality of, or the degree of impairment of a communications channel used for data transmission, is the *error rate test.* The error rate is established by using test equipments which generate specific sets of bits and/or blocks of data and then compare the receive information with what was transmitted. The difference between the receive bits and the transmitted bits is known as the *Bit Error Rate* (BER). The sequences of bits which are transmitted are known as *patterns* and can range from the gross test of all 1's (all mark) and alternate mark-space patterns to extremely complex patterns that will not repeat themselves for many millions of bits transmitted. Common pattern lengths, however, are usually in the range of 63, 511, and 2047 bits with the worst case pattern being the 2047-bit sequence as established by the CCITT (Consultive Committee for International Telephone and Telegraph). Because a larger pattern can encompass many more combinations of bits, it is more likely to isolate an otherwise elusive channel problem. The major problem, however, is the fact that the receiving unit must be able to interpret the pattern sent by the transmitting unit, and therefore it will almost always have to be from the same vendor.

The BER, however, is not the best measure for determining the effective information throughput of the transmission line. This is because on communication lines, interference, errors, noise, etc., of a significant level to cause errors usually come in a burst mode. The burst mode may cause multiple bits within a particular block to be in error, while if the same amount of bits in error were distributed equally among all the bits transmitted, there would obviously be a very high block error rate. For this reason the user must also take into account the specific block length being measured or perform block error testing to get a more accurate indication of what the actual line performance will be.

In general, testing will take place with a pattern length which most closely matches the block size which is expected to be transmitted. Once the block error rates are within the user's established limits, the bit error rate testing can be used to fine tune the line.

The Block Error Rate (BLER) is most closely related to the definition of Effective Information Throughput. If the BLER is specified as being 1 percent, then for every 100 blocks of information at the test length, there would be 1 in error for which a single block would have to be retransmitted. This is significant for all modes of transmission, but especially those protocols which use the *go back N* technique and are described in Chap. 4. The *go back N* technique requires the retransmission of any block that is received in error, in addition to all blocks which were transmitted after the block in error.

Another term which is used when describing the various error rates is called the *Error-Free-Second* (EFS). The EFS is very similar to the BLER except that it describes the probability of success for getting a one second long block through correctly, as opposed to the probability of failure which is described by the BLER. Even though errors do not occur for an entire second, a gross level probability of determining how much data can be throughput can be determined, because the second can be related directly to the amount of bits being transmitted. For example, with a 2400-bit per second transmission, a typical 1-second block would contain 2400 bits or 300 characters. If the block size is in the range of 300 characters, then a direct correlation can be made as to the probability of success for individual blocks. Since most communication lines have error rates specified as a typical line, it is relatively simple for the user to determine what the particular line, at a particular transmission rate, is expected to experience, relative to errors and retransmissions.

In reviewing all of these error-rate parameters, we can see that the block size is a critical factor in the effective data throughput. On an intuitive level we can visualize extremely short blocks getting through with a very high degree of probability but the effective throughput is limited by the fact that the network overhead must be accommodated for each individual transmission. That means that as the block length gets longer, the effective throughput will also become greater. This increase is only good up to a certain level, because as the block gets longer it will eventually get to a length where you are just about guaranteed that an error will occur because of its length. What this means is that there is an optimum block-size definition for each individual line with a particular error rate.

Based on an analysis provided by the telephone company for typical voice grade lines without conditioning, optimum block sizes range from about 100 plus characters at 9600 bits per second up to approximately 520 characters for transmissions at 1200 bits per second. For conditioning levels which approximate one-half of the errors being detected, we go from an optimum block size of approximately 200 characters at 9600 bits per second to an optimum block size of around 650 characters for 1200 and 2400 bits per second. This means that for most applications on voice grade lines block sizes, where practical, should be limited to a maximum of between 500 and 600 characters, while the minimum block size should be 100 characters if the user would like the most effective throughput rate for a given line. Each application and each line must be considered separately because it is not uncommon to have lines which are much worse and others which are much better.

One other factor to consider in this environment is that the increase in transmission speed does not give a proportionate increase in effective throughput. For example, a transmission rate at 2400 bits per second will not give twice the throughput at 1200 bits per second, although it closely approximates that. At 4800 bits per second there is an effective increase in throughput of about 1.6 to 1.7 over the throughput at 2400 bits per second.

At 9600 bits per second, however, the effective throughput, even using the optimum block sizes for both 9600 and 4800, may only give an increase in throughput of 1.2 to 1.3 of the throughput at 4800 bits per second. It should be recognized that these numbers relate to a typical voice grade line where long distances are involved (500 miles or more) and is not indicative of those connections where there is direct computer-to-computer transmission on high-quality or conditioned lines. Also, any particular location may have lines which are better or worse than a typical voice grade line and therefore have better or worse experience than the average. What the user can expect in his own specific environment can only be identified with any degree of confidence by specific operation and tests utilizing the equipment and facilities which are to be installed.

What the user should get out of this error rate description is the idea that prior to initial design, he should recognize that 9600 bits per second is not always the most effective means of high data rate transfers, and it is quite possible for a 4800 bps or 7200 bps transmission rate to actually have a better effective information throughput than a 9600 bps transmission rate.

One last point in this description is that the 9600 bits per second is almost never used on a multidrop line today, not only because of the errors, but also because of the polling/calling, networking overhead, and especially synchronization sequences, which effectively lowers the throughput on the multidrop line to something equal to or less than what would be expected on a 4800 bit per second line. It is quite possible that in the future, with improved hardware, and improved line parameters, this can be improved, but at this point in time, 9600 bits per second should never be considered for a multidrop environment.

E.

Line Conditioning and Equalization

Of all of the potential improvements which could be made to the voice grade communication line, it is usually up to the carrier to provide the majority of them because the carrier has controls over most of the facilities. For dial-up circuits, which change from call to call, the idea of conditioning lines for data transmission is not practical for the carrier, because the transmissions will take a different path on each separate call. Therefore, some of the modem manufacturers other than AT&T, provide what are known as *Automatic Equalization Modems* which will correct for some circuit-induced signal distortions on both dial-up and multidrop circuits. There are two types of modems which provide equalization. The first of these is the fixed variety (sometimes called statistical). With fixed equalization it is assumed that the voice grade line has a typical set of characteristics (which it usually does), so fixed equalization parameters can be applied at each end. If by chance, the line does not meet the standard specifications, or if it is close to the edge of those specifications, it is quite possible for fixed conditioning to make the line worse than it was to begin with for data transmission. Some of these modems, however, may have a limited range of equalization adjustment to better match the line.

The second type of automatic equalization is that equalization which, after a call has been initiated, is established by first sending signals down the line to determine the line's characteristics and then applying the appropriate equalization parameters. This normally takes time between the time the circuit connection is completed and the time that data can be transmitted. Therefore, this type of conditioning increases the amount of time for which a call must be maintained. The modems are also more expensive because of the additional circuitry and logic.

Even with telephone company line conditioning we have a choice. The choice is not only with the amount of conditioning which is provided, but also the type of conditioning. C type conditioning has been provided for many years and comes in five different levels, of which only three (C1, C2, C4) are available to leased line users of the DDD network. Conditioning now also comes in what is known as D type, which provides for additional improvement on the line for two areas which were not covered at all with C type conditioning.

It is not really hard to understand the difference between the two types of conditioning and when and where they will help a transmission line's performance. Previously in this chapter the various kinds of line impairments were covered and of them there are eleven which can be adequately described. Four of them can be controlled by the telephone company so that they are maintained within the limits described in FCC tariff number 260, and four more can be controlled by the carriers to their own established limits. All of these are shown in Table 13-1. Of these, attenuation distortion and envelope delay

TABLE 13-1

CONDITIONING AREAS AND COSTS

	BASIC AT&T INTERNAL CONTROL	AREAS OF C-CONDITION CONTROL	AREAS OF D-CONDITION CONTROL
Attenuation Distortion	X	X	SAME AS
Envelope Delay Distortion	X	X	BASIC
Signal to Noise Ratio	X	SAME AS	X
Harmonic Distortion	X	BASIC	X
Impulse Noise	X	SAME	
Frequency Shift	X	AS	
Phase Jitter	X	BASIC	
Echo	X	3002	
Phase Hits Gain Hits Dropouts		NOT CONTROLLED	

Typical Costs (Interstate)

CONDITION LEVEL	COSTS PER POINT PER MONTH
C1 Point to Point	5.25
C1 Multipoint	10.50
C2 Point to Point	19.95
C2 Multipoint	29.45
C4 Point to Point	31.55
C4 Multipoint	37.85
D1 Point to Point	14.20 + $170.00 INST.
D2 2 or 3 Point	47.50 + $162.00 INST.

NOTE   Costs are for reference purposes only and must be validated as to current rates when implementing a particular network configuration.

distortion are controlled through C type conditioning, while signal-to-noise ratio and harmonic distortion are controlled through the D level type conditioning. Each type of conditioning within both C and D type levels are tariffed separately and can be obtained on any leased line either independently or together. They are not mutually exclusive offerings.

The second major group of impairment parameters are impulse noise, frequency shift, phase jitter, and echo. Because the telephone company knows what is intended to be transmitted over those lines, it tends to maintain them within certain limits which are internally set, even though they are not obligated by tariff to do so. The three remaining kinds of impairments—phase hits, gain hits, and drop outs—are not controlled at present because they are transient electrical occurrences (see Section F) and therefore cannot be compensated for as a permanent condition.

C type conditioning is the term which is given to the capability provided by the telephone company to make voice grade lines meet more restrictive specifications for attenuation distortion and envelope delay distortion. Included in these provisions is the attachment of loading coils and other filter arrangements to the line.

The C type conditioning which is available in five varieties, C1 through C5, applies to voice grade lines. C1, C2, and C4 apply to voice grade private lines between user sites, while C3 and C5 apply to lines which are part of some large dedicated network such as the military AUTOVON, CCSA (Common Control Switching Arrangements) and some international links.

By referring to Fig. 13-6, Sections II, III, and IV, the heavy lines refer to the attenuation distortion and envelope delay limits for C1, C2, and C4 conditioning. The thinner lines represent a typical line characteristic which meets these limits. The greater the degree of C type conditioning, the more the attenuation distortion and delay distortion are reduced at both ends of the frequency band.

C1, C2, and C4 conditioning can be provided for any point-to-point 3002 line while C1 and C2 conditioning can be provided on any multipoint 3002 line without restriction as to number of points. C4 conditioning, however, is not provided on multipoint lines with more than one central and three remote points. Charges are made on the basis of a one-time installation charge and a monthly rate for each point on the line whether point-to-point or multipoint circuits are conditioned. More than 50 percent of the conditioning which is provided by the carriers is C2.

D type conditioning is an option which was developed primarily for 9600 bit per second operation on a 3002 line. The standard 3002 specification requires a signal-to-noise ratio of not less than 24 dB, a second harmonic distortion of not more than -25 dB, and a third harmonic distortion of not more than -30 dB. For D type conditioning we have a signal-to-noise ratio specification of 28 dB, a signal to second harmonic distortion ratio of 35 dB, and a signal to third harmonic distortion of 40 dB.

The harmonic, or nonlinear, distortion occurs because attenuation varies with signal amplitude, and a sine wave sent through such a channel will be flattened at the peaks (clipping). This is the same as

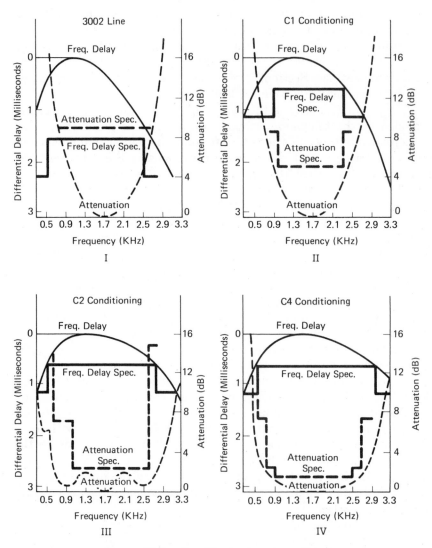

Figure 13-6. Conditioning Levels and Limits

would result from adding harmonics of low amplitude to the signal in the first place. Therefore, this form of distortion (harmonic distortion) is measured in terms of the amount of second and third harmonic content that would cause the same amount of flattening. Noise and nonlinear distortion are critical to data transmission because they interfere with the accurate reproduction of the transmitted wave forms at the receiver. In contrast with the problems caused by delay distortion, their effect cannot be reversed. No amount of hardware sophistication in the receiving modem can recreate the original signal shape once it has been changed by harmonic distortion. The only protection against harmonic distortion is to make the signal less susceptible to it, and the way to do that is to maximize the difference between the unique wave shapes that have to be distinguished by the demodulator. The D type conditioning provides just such an improvement by specifying a lower allowable harmonic content to exist.

D1 conditioning is offered for point-to-point circuits, while D2 is offered for two- or three-point circuits. Charges are also based on a one-time installation charge, plus a monthly rate for each point on the line. Also, D type conditioning is not necessarily available at all locations throughout the country and therefore must be implemented on a location-by-location basis.

QUESTIONS

1. What is the primary factor which limits the ability to transmit data on a communication line? What are four different names for this impairment?
2. What are five sources of line impairments?
3. What are the two primary effects on the transmitted signal which have the most impact on transmission of data?
4. What is an echo? How is it eliminated?
5. What are three types of measurements which can be used to identify levels of errors encountered?
6. Describe the effects of block size on effective information throughput.
7. What line impairments are compensated for with C type conditioning?
8. What line impairments are compensated for with D type conditioning?

14

MANAGEMENT AND CONTROL

A.

Background

It would appear that, based on past experience, the primary concentration of design effort has been the development of a communications network which would provide the necessary paths for the user to move his data most efficiently. More recently, however, it has become increasingly apparent that an even more critical area to consider is the operation and maintenance of the network once it has been installed.

If the user considers what is referred to as the "life cycle cost" of a complete system which includes a network, he will find that the two most significant costs involved are the labor costs for the people to operate the system and the maintenance costs of the network. The network is the most error prone of the system components, there are usually multiple vendors involved, and there are nowhere near enough qualified personnel available to support all the networks which are implemented today.

Since maintenance is such a significant part of the success of a network, this chapter, which deals with the subject is longer than the others, but it should be recognized that there are entire texts which deal with the subject in depth, so this chapter only provides an overview of the common carrier environments which are encountered and typical types of test equipments and procedures. Relatively simple examples are used to provide a feeling for the problems involved, so the reader should keep in mind the fact that actual testing and the isolation of the specific problem causing the encountered errors really involves the use of specialized test equipment by experienced and specially trained network maintenance personnel.

B.

Telephone Company Central Office Types

In the telephone company hierarchy of central offices there are five different classifications, and Fig. 14-1 shows how the various classes are interrelated. Of them, there are today twelve Class I or Regional Center Offices in the U.S./Canada area and approximately 19,000 Class 5 or End Offices to which individual subscriber telephones are connected. A local call from one home to another within the same office (in other words the same exchange number or prefix) is made totally within one of these end offices. A call from one city to another, however, cannot be connected directly from the same end office or two adjacent end offices and therefore may be treated in a number of different ways.

If the two locations are close enough together or if there are many calls between the two, there may be direct circuits from one end office to the other. Such a group of circuits is called a *high usage group*. If these circuits are busy or do not exist in the first place, the call is "route advanced" to the specific Class 4 office associated with the Class 5 (end) office for which the call is destined. Even though all combinations are not necessarily attempted on an actual call, Fig. 14-1 shows some numbers in parentheses which may indicate possible methods used to attempt to place a call from one end office to another. In the absolute longest case the routing goes through nine separate

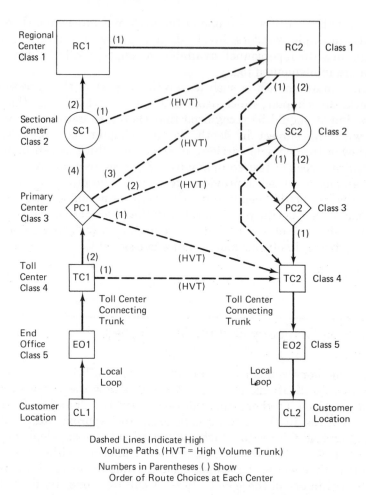

Dashed Lines Indicate High
Volume Paths (HVT = High Volume Trunk)

Numbers in Parentheses ( ) Show
Order of Route Choices at Each Center

Figure 14-1. Telephone Company Central Office Hierarchy

links from the initiating end office through Class 4, 3, 2, 1 office to the alternate Class 1 office, and then 2, 3, 4, and then the fifth level end office, at which point the final connection is made.

It should be noted that the next call may or may not take the same general route, and in all probability (approximately 100 percent) will have a different physical circuit to travel over, even between the same two service offices. For this reason the network user must always assume that for dial-up purposes, each time a call is initiated it will travel over a different circuit. The only time this may not be true is the initial case of two locations connected to the same end office where only the switching equipment is required to interface them. For this particular application the use of short-haul modems as described in Chap. 4 may be implemented.

It should also be recognized that the common carriers, in conjunction with each other, use a technique which is known as *network management* to maximize the utilization of facilities. This is required because of the time differences across the United States. Since a north/south geographic orientation has the same time of day, it may be to the carrier's advantage (AT&T) to route calls between Boston and Miami through Los Angeles during the morning hours because of the low utilization of circuits in Los Angeles at that time. The same idea applies to making calls on the West Coast through eastern cities during the evening hours. These circuits are normally available at those times because the subscriber cross-country calls would not normally be taking place at those times. It is also for this reason (lower utilization) that the telephone company offers reduced rates for calling after 5:00 PM and before 8:00 AM.

C.

Telephone Company Equipments and Interfaces

The telephone company, as well as many of the other carriers, provides communication equipment of all kinds. It would be impossible to list all of the different types of equipment and their uses in this particular text, so just a brief description of the more significant hardware items will be provided. A more detailed listing of the specific modems will be provided because of the magnitude of their impact on users. The types of equipment that the telephone company provide are:

Modems Convert digital to analog information and back again for communication on voice grade telephone lines.

Multiplexers Combine capabilities of multiple low-speed lines for transmission on a single high-speed line.

PBX Private Branch Exchange Equipment for in-house routing of telephone calls.

PABX Private Automatic Branch Exchange Same as a PBX except for many automated features which simplify the internal routing of calls and also provide for interconnection to many different kinds of external lines.

IDF/MDF Blocks Distribution frames for connection of telephone company local loops to in-house wires.

Terminals Typically TTY and Data Speed type terminals. By tariff the telephone company is not allowed to provide data processing terminals although the Data Speed 40 has the full capabilities of any programmable terminal.

Line Monitor Equipment For monitoring performance of communication lines.

Line Test Equipment For testing line parameters to determine where problems exist.

Tech Control Facilities These are facilities which are provided for in-house monitoring and testing of network facilities which are provided by the carrier.

ACD Automatic Call Director A hardware device for monitoring and controlling incoming calls when there are not always enough positions to answer all the calls coming in. Typically, airline reservations agents utilize these equipments.

Communication Facilities These are the total facilities between the modems which move data from one point to another (could also be voice). It includes all of the office type equipment, central office type equipment, cabling, microwave, computers, etc. In other words, it is all the carrier's capabilities to move information between modems or including the modems if not provided by the user.

Standard Interfaces These are the interfaces which are described in the next section to which the telephone company has either designed its equipment or is capable of interfacing with.

When discussing interfaces there are many different types which are recognized by groups around the world. For purposes of this text there will be three types described. The first will be the Electronic Industries Association (EIA) specifications which are always preceded by the letters RS (Recommended Standard). The second set will be the CCITT standard interface specifications which are always preceded by the letter V. The third series of specifications were also established by the CCITT and these are always preceded by the letter X.

RS-232-C Interface between data terminal equipment and data communication equipment employing serial binary data interchange (August 1969).

RS-269-B Synchronous signaling rates for data transmission (January 1976; identical to ANSI X3.1-1976).

RS-334   Signal quality at interface between data processing terminal equipment and synchronous data communication equipment for serial data transmission. (Also adopted as ANSI X3.24-1967; new revision being balloted.)

RS-357   Interface between facsimile terminal equipment and voice frequency data communication terminal equipment (June 1968).

RS-363   Standard for specifying signal quality for transmitting and receiving data processing terminal equipment using serial data transmission at the interface with nonsynchronous data communication equipment (May 1969).

RS-366   Interface between data terminal equipment and automatic calling equipment for data communication (August 1969).

RS-404   Standard for start/stop signal quality between data terminal equipment and nonsynchronous data communication equipment (March 1973).

RS-410   Standard for electrical characteristics of Class A closure interchange circuits (April 1974).

RS-422   Electrical characteristics of balanced voltage digital interface circuits (April 1975).

RS-423   Electrical characteristics of unbalanced voltage digital interface circuits (April 1975).

RS-449   General purpose 37 position and a position interface for data terminal equipment and data circuit terminating equipment employing serial-binary data interchange.

V.   CCITT code designation.

V.1   Equivalence between notation symbols and the significant conditions of a two-condition code.

V.2   Power levels for data transmission over telephone lines.

V.3   International alphabet No. 5

V.4   General structure of signals of international alphabet No. 5 code for data transmission over public telephone network.

V.5   Standardization of data-signaling rates for synchronous data transmission in the general switched telephone network.

V.6   Standardization of data-signaling rates for synchronous data transmission of leased telephone-type circuits.

V.10(X.26)   Electrical characteristics for unbalanced double-current interchange circuits for general use with integrated circuit equipment in the field of data communications (and provisional amendments, May 1977).

V.11(X.27)   Electrical characteristics for balanced double-current interchange circuits for general use with integrated circuit equipment in the field of data communications (and provisional amendments, May 1977).

V.15   Use of acoustic coupling for data transmission.

V.19   Modems for parallel data transmission using telephone signaling frequencies.

V.20   Parallel data transmission modems standardized for universal use in general switched telephone network.

V.21   200-bit/s modem standardized for use in the general switched telephone network.

V.22   Standardization of data signaling rates for synchronous data transmission in the general switched telephone network.

V.22bis   Standardization of data signaling rates for synchronous data transmission on leased telephone-type circuits.

V.23   600/1.2K bit/s modem standardized for use in the general switched telephone network.

V.24   List of definitions for interchange circuits between data terminal equipment and data circuit terminating equipment (and provisional amendments, May 1977).

V.25   Automatic calling and/or answering equipment on the general switched telephone network, including disabling of echo suppressors on manually established calls.

V.26   2.4K/1.2K bit/s modem standardized for use on four-wire leased circuits.

V.26bis   2.4K/1.2K bit/s modem standardized for use in the general switched telephone network.

V.27   4.8 kbit/s modem standardized for use on leased circuits.

V.27bis   4.8 kbit/s modem with automatic equalizer standardized for use on the on leased circuits.

V.27ter   4.8K/2.4K bit/s modem standardized for use in the general switched telephone network.

V.28   Electrical characteristics for unbalanced double-current interchange circuits.

V.29   96 kbit/s modem for use on leased circuits.

V.31   Electrical characteristics for single-current interchange circuits controlled by contact closure.

V.35   Data transmission at 48 kbit/s using 60-to-108 kHz group-bit/s circuits.

V.36   Modems for synchronous data transmission using 60-to-108 kHz group bit/s circuits.

V.41 Code independent control system.

V.54 Loop test devices for modems (and provisional amendments, May 1977).

X. CCITT recommendation designation.

X.1 International user classes of service in public data networks.

X.2 International user facilities in public data networks.

X.3 Packet assembly/disassembly facility (PAD) in a public data network.

X.4 General structure of signals of international alphabet No. 5 code for data transmission over public data networks.

X.20 Interface between data terminal equipment and data circuit-terminating equipment for start/stop transmission services on public data networks.

X.20bis(V.21) Compatible interface between data terminal equipment and data circuit-terminating equipment for start/stop transmission services on public data networks.

X.21 General purpose interface between data terminal equipment and data circuit-terminating equipment for synchronous operation on public data networks.

X.21bis Use on public data networks of data terminal equipment which is designed for interfacing to synchronous V-series modems.

X.24 List of definitions of interchange circuits between data terminal equipment and data circuit-terminating equipment on public data networks.

X.25 Interface between data terminal equipment and data circuit-terminating equipment for terminals operating in the packet mode on public data networks (and provisional amendment, April 1977).

X.26 Electrical characteristics for unbalanced double-current interchange circuits for general use with integrated circuit equipment in the field of data communications (identical to V.10).

X.27 Electrical characteristics for balanced double-current interchange circuits for general use with integrated circuit equipment in the field of data communications (identical to V.11).

X.28 DTE/DCE interface for start/stop mode data terminal equipment accessing the packet assembly/disassembly facility (PAD) on a public network situated in the same country.

X.29 Procedures for exchange of control information and user data between a packet-mode DTE and a packet assembly/disassembly facility (PAD).

X.30   Standardization of basic model page-printing machine in accordance with international alphabet No. 5.

X.31   Characteristics, from the transmission point of view, at the interchange point between data terminal equipment and data circuit-terminating equipment in a 200 bit/s start/stop data terminal.

X.32   Answer-back units for 200 bit/s start/stop machines in accordance with international alphabet No. 5.

X.33   Standardization of an international text for the measurement of the margin of start/stop machines in accordance with international alphabet No. 5.

X.92   Hypothetical reference connections for public synchronous data networks.

X.95   Network parameters in public data networks.

X.96   Call progress signals in public data networks.

X3.1-1976   Synchronous signaling rates for data transmission.

X3.4-1976   Code of information interchange.

X3.15-1976   Bit sequencing of the American National Standard Code for Information Interchange in serial-by-bit transmission.

X3.16-1976   Character structure and character parity sense for serial-by-bit data communication in the American National Standard Code for Information Interchange.

X3.24-1976   Signal quality at interface between data processing technical equipment for synchronous data transmission.

X3.25-1976   Character structure and character parity sense for parallel-by-bit communication in the American National Standard Code for Information Interchange.

X3.28-1976   Procedures for the use of communication control characters of American National Standard Code for Information Interchange in specified data communications links.

X3.36-1977   Synchronous high-speed data signaling rates between data terminal equipment and data communication equipment.

X3.41-1977   Code extension techniques for use with 7-bit coded character set of American National Standard Code for Information Interchange.

X3.44-1977   Determination of the performance of data communication systems.

X3.57-1977   Message heading formats for information interchange using ASCII for data communication system control.

With respect to equipment which is available from the telephone company the modems are listed in Table 14-1. The designations are AT&T defined, and the units are called either Bell Modems or Bell Data Sets.

D.

Access Equipment

In order to be effective as a network operational tool, test equipment must be attached to the line which is to be tested in some manner, if it is not otherwise permanently built into the line circuitry. Table 14-2 is a list of the major access and interface equipments used to provide this line attachment.

One of the most effective lines-access units is the jack and plug concept. Analog jacks are usually placed in the analog line circuit to provide both a parallel and a serial access to the line as shown in Fig. 14-2. The parallel access is used for the monitoring function by attaching the test equipment via a plug to the line circuit to be monitored, while not interrupting the circuit path from the line to the equipment (modem in this example). Attaching the monitor equipment should be done with the monitor connected to the plug cord first and then the plug inserted in the monitor jack last. In addition, the monitor equipment must have a high electrical impedance to the circuit so that it will not appreciably affect the line's operation once it is connected.

Serial or series-access jacks are connected so that the circuit (line) passes through the jack. This way the circuit may be interrupted and carried through the plug and cord to a different line interface unit (modem in the example). An arrangement like this allows a faulty modem to be patched in its place. Electrical contact is made between the upper normal jack contacts for the line circuit and continues through the plug and cord to the spare modem. A corresponding set of digital jacks on the other side of the two modems allows the spare modem to be connected to the user's interface (DTE) through the middle normal jack contacts. As the contact is made between the line and cord plug, the regular or normal modem is isolated from the circuit on the analog side and similarly isolated from the DTE on the digital side by the digital plug insertion. Since the digital interface to a modem will usually be the 25-wire RS232C standard, digital jacks to be used here must be 25-circuit units rather than the 2-circuit units used for analog jacks. The two jack and plug combinations

TABLE 14-1

BELL DATA SETS

Bell Data-Phone Data Sets

TYPE	SPEED	LINE
103A	Up to 300 bps Transmit or Receive	Direct Distance Dial
103F	Up to 300 bps Transmit or Receive	Private Line
113A	Up to 300 bps Orig. Only	Direct Distance Dial
113B	Up to 300 bps Auto Ans. Only	Private Line
201A	2000 bps Transmit or Rec.	Direct Distance Dial
201B	2400 bps Transmit or Rec.	Private Line
202C	1200 bps Transmit or Rec.	DDD & Private Line Includes Telephone
202D	1800 bps Transmit or Rec.	Private Line
202E	600 bps Transmit, with 5 bps Receive	Telephone Powered
202G2	600 bps with 5 bps Rev. Channel Transmit or Rec.	Acoustic Coupled
203A	1800 bps with 150 bps Rev. Channel Transmit and Rec.	Private Line
203B	2400 bps with 150 bps Rev. Channel Transmit or Rec.	Private Line
203C	3600 bps with 150 bps Rev. Channel Transmit or Rec.	Private Line
205C2	1200/2400 bps Transmit or Receive	DDD & Private Line
207	150/300/600/1200 bps Transmit or Receive	DDD & Private Line
208A	4800/5400/7200 bps Transmit or Receive	Private Line with C-2 Conditioning
209	9600 bps Transmit or Rec.	Private Line with D-1 Conditioning
301B	40.8 kbps FDX	Basegroup Channel
303B	19.2 kbps FDX	Halfgroup Channel
303C	50 kbps FDX	Basegroup Channel
303D	230.4 kbps FDX	Supergroup Channel
401A	Up to 20 cps Transmit 2-out-of-8 code	DDD & Private Line
401B	Up to 20 cps Receive 2-out-of-8 code	DDD & Private Line
401E	Up to 20 cps Transmit 3-out-of-14 code	DDD & Private Line
401H	20 cps & 200 bps Transmit	DDD & Private Line
401J	20 cps Receive	DDD & Private Line
402A	75 cps Transmit 8-bit parallel code	DDD & Private Line
402C	75 cps Transmit with Reverse Channel	DDD & Private Line
402D	75 cps Receive with Reverse Channel	DDD & Private Line

TABLE 14-1 (Cont.)

TYPE	SPEED	LINE
403A	10 cps Transmit	Touchtone Telephone
403B	10 cps Transmit	Touchtone Telephone
403C	10 cps Transmit	Touchtone Telephone
601A	Handwriting	DDD & Private Line
601B	Handwriting	DDD & Private Line
602C	Facsimile & Slow Scan Television	DDD & Private Line
603A	EKG Transmit	DDD & Private Line
603B	EKG Receive	DDD & Private Line
603D	EKG Portable	DDD & Private Line
801A	Dial Pulse Automatic Calling Unit	DDD
801C	Touchtone Automatic Calling Unit	DDD

drawn on Fig. 14-2 would be arranged in line, equipment, and monitor connections similar to the 2-wire analog jacks at the top. The names *tip* and *ring* for the analog circuits come from the tip and ring contacts on the plug.

Switches and relays are used to provide monitor and patching capability through activation of circuit contacts as shown in Fig. 14-3. In addition to the patching example used above for jack and plug

TABLE 14-2

ACCESS AND INTERFACE EQUIPMENT

A. JACKS
   1. Analog
      a—Monitor
      b—Patch
   2. Digital
      a—Monitor
      b—Patch
B. SWITCHES
C. RELAYS
   1. Manually Operated
   2. Automatic
D. CROSSBARS
   1. Manually Dialed
   2. Automatic
E. BRIDGES

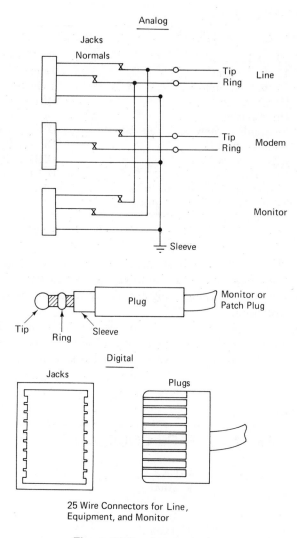

Figure 14-2. Access Jacks

operation, looping back a signal (signal output from specific equipment connected directly back to signal input connection of same equipment) can be done manually with either of the two types of units. The electrical continuity of either jack contacts or switch contacts is critical because a problem in the normal operation path must be avoided.

Both of the above access units, when used, are manually acti-

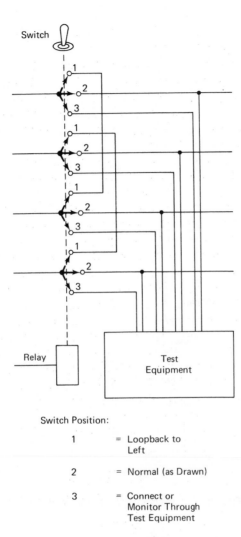

Switch Position:

1   = Loopback to
             Left

2   = Normal (as Drawn)

3   = Connect or
             Monitor Through
             Test Equipment

Figure 14-3. Access Switches and Relays

vated. The first step toward automation is frequently the use of crossbar relay contacts to connect monitor equipments as is shown in Fig. 14-4. Care is taken in the design of the crossbar control unit so that it will not become another source of trouble when trying to isolate the problem. On analog circuits, an analog bridge is hardwired into the normal circuit to allow attaching a third conductor to the normal path. Bridges are usually made with passive devices like the

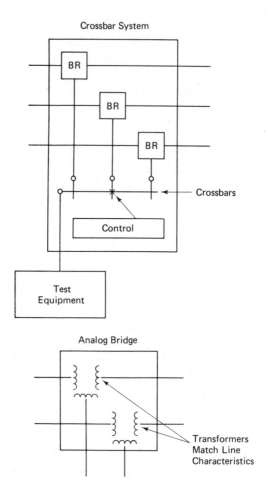

Figure 14-4.   Access Crossbars and Bridges

transformers, as opposed to active devices such as transistors to minimize potential additional troubles.

Digital bridges are frequently made with passive resistors connected in a delta circuit arrangement to provide a three-port circuit of high quality. Both the analog and digital bridges could be wired into the data circuit path by the carrier to allow the monitoring and patching functions. They could also be installed by the user in his own Tech Control equipment environment.

The majority of data access equipments have been designed for human action. Automation, to the extent that little or no human interaction is necessary, can be done by application of computer programs in small, self-contained computer systems for network operational purposes and will be covered in the following paragraphs.

E.

Line Monitors

Line monitors are classified by how they are used, what they monitor, and where they are located. Table 14-3 lists hardware monitors which continually monitor line activity by use of control signals from the modem.

Two common signals used for continuous monitoring are *receive line signal detect,* which is found on Pin CF at the RS232C interface from a modem, and the *Data Quality Monitor* (DQM).

The DQM can be located inside the modem and can use the CG circuit wire to indicate that the preset threshold of bias distortion has been reached, or the DQM can be located in a separate unit attached to the BB circuit for indication purposes as it delivers the receive data to the DTE. Logically, the DQM unit can be installed at either end of the line, the terminal modem interface or the DTE at the DP center (usual location). The alarm mechanism can be activated by either of the above events and can display an indicator for human action or it can send the same signal to a diagnostic program for automatic action. Figure 14-5 presents a graphic display of the location and operation of the DQM in response to the data distortion it monitors,

TABLE 14-3

LINE MONITORS

A. CONTINUOUS
   1. Carrier Failure
   2. Data Quality Monitors
B. BLOCK
   1. Transmission Block Synchronized
   2. Transaction Synchronized
C. MANUAL
D. AUTOMATIC
E. TERMINAL
F. DP CENTER

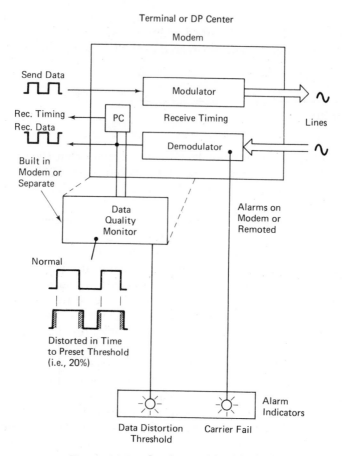

Figure 14-5.   Continuous Line Monitoring

while Figs. 14-6 and 14-7 show practical continuous monitor installations at the terminal DP center DTE respectively.

Block monitor equipment can be attached to the data line at the digital modem interface on either circuit end and be synchronized to monitor and display transmission blocks or entire transactions (messages). This synchronization involves transmission block or message framing character detection for recording or display purposes. Most users of block monitors attach the unit to a line known or suspected to have a trouble, observing the data on the monitor, and directing repair activity to the apparent trouble source. Again, as in the above continuous monitor case, the block monitor may be logically located either at the terminal or at the DP center. Figure 14-8 shows a monitor at the Tech Control area of the central site to utilize a single unit on all the lines from the DP center to many terminal locations.

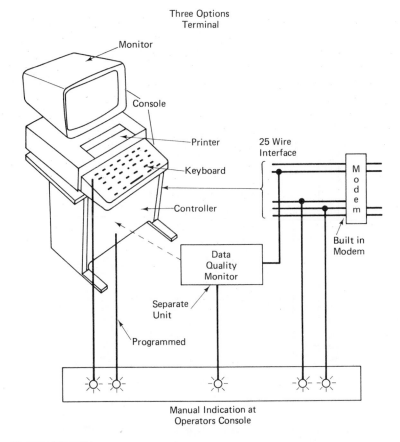

Figure 14-6.   Manual Line Monitoring at Terminals

F.

Manual Test Equipment

There are two basic classes of manual test equipment used in network operations which employ analog lines and modems—analog line test sets and digital test sets. Table 14-4 is a list of typically used analog and digital test equipments which are named after the basic function that each performs.

Analog line test sets are composed of a test signal generator and a signal analyzer to measure the results of passing the signal onto or over the analog line. There are a set of industry-accepted standards for the measurement of a data line using telephone-type circuits.

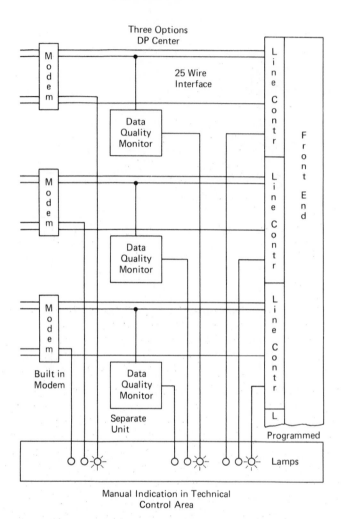

Figure 14-7.   Manual Line Monitoring at DP Center

These standards are designed to compare the performance of the line with a line specification requirement on a "go-no go" basis. The basic set of line performance criteria is signal level, signal frequency, and signal deterioration due to the line impairments at the time of the performance measurement. The units of measurement are those established by common carriers over the years, primarily to the needs of the telephone industry. As discussed earlier, the basic line impairment causing signal deterioration is noise. Therefore, the standards for analog line performance include several tests that involve noise

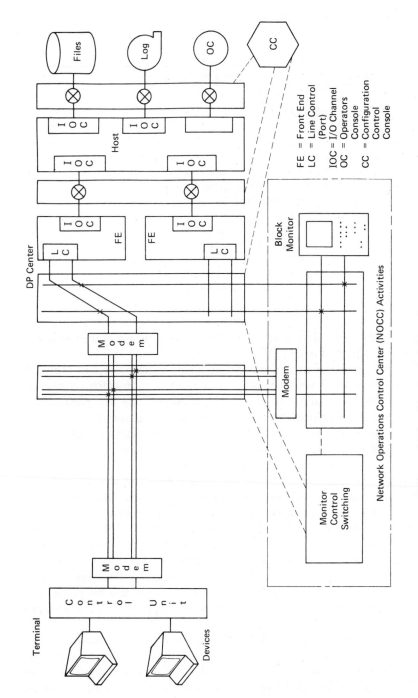

Figure 14-8. Monitor in Tech Control Area

FE = Front End
LC = Line Control (Port)
IOC = I/O Channel
OC = Operators Console
CC = Configuration Control Console

Network Operations Control Center (NOCC) Activities

231

TABLE 14-4

ANALOG AND DIGITAL TEST EQUIPMENT

A. ANALOG
   1. Line Test Set
B. DIGITAL
   1. BERT (Bit Error Rate Testers)
   2. CERT (Character Error Rate Tester)
   3. BLERT (Block Error Rate Tester)
   4. Terminal Test Sets
      a. Block Testers
      b. Terminal Duplicators
      c. System Duplicators
   5. Line Monitors
      a. Data Quality Detectors
      b. Carrier Fail Detectors

measurement. Also circuit or channel conditioning measurements are an important part of analog line test set use.

The modification of communication line characteristics through adjustments of the line operating equipment is performed by carrier company line test and repair personnel, to correct the line parameters back to within specification limits, once an impairment is found by the measurements. User operations control personnel can effectively assist the repair force in isolating the impairment by performing similar tests near the modem (see Fig. 14-9).

Digital test sets are utilized on analog lines on the digital side (RS232 Interface) of the modems attached to each end of the line (usually done at central site only), and they measure the digital output of the communication line. The family of digital test sets are named for the degree of data testing they perform. Again, as discussed in Chap. 13, BERT sets perform a test by bit matching of data patterns, with the intent to verify that the line should be able to carry live data if it successfully performs the test. Since the bit pattern is not exactly the format of the data transmission, there is some margin for error in bit error rate testing.

Figure 14-10 depicts a BERT set which has been carried to the terminal location in response to a trouble call. The opposite approach to the figure would be to place the BERT set on the digital input of the DP center modem and loop the line back at the terminal modem. This latter location would allow a single set to service all the lines emanating from the DP center.

As shown in Fig. 14-11, the BERT set may be replaced by a CERT

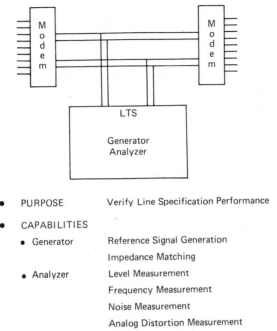

- PURPOSE   Verify Line Specification Performance

- CAPABILITIES
  - Generator   Reference Signal Generation
                   Impedance Matching
  - Analyzer   Level Measurement
                   Frequency Measurement
                   Noise Measurement
                   Analog Distortion Measurement
                   Circuit Conditioning Measurement
                   (Equalization)
- LIMITATIONS   Line is Out of Service

Figure 14-9. Testing with Line Test Set

set to perform additional digital verification tests. The advantage of the CERT testing over BERT testing is that the users actual code set can be used, and also rudimentary line data blocks can be sent using some of these units. In either case, the error performance of the data line is remeasured with "live" traffic (but not live user traffic) and in the environment present at the time of the test.

The next higher level of digital test sets is a family of data transmission block testing units. These have been named BLERT sets in a similar way that BERT and CERT were named. If a block or test message set is used for terminal checkout as is shown in Fig. 14-12 it is generally called a terminal test set. It does, however, work on the principle of a block or message tester. The advantage of block testing is that most of the operating parameters of live traffic are duplicated in the test. The optional approach here is the same as for the other sets, i.e., a single unit at the DP center. One additional advantage to these BLERT units is the monitoring function they can perform while live traffic is flowing on the line under test.

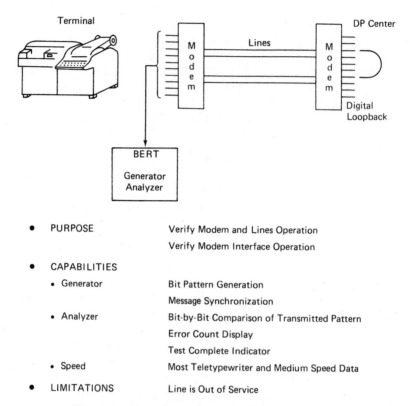

- PURPOSE   Verify Modem and Lines Operation
                            Verify Modem Interface Operation

- CAPABILITIES
  - Generator   Bit Pattern Generation
                            Message Synchronization
  - Analyzer   Bit-by-Bit Comparison of Transmitted Pattern
                            Error Count Display
                            Test Complete Indicator
  - Speed   Most Teletypewriter and Medium Speed Data

- LIMITATIONS   Line is Out of Service

Figure 14-10.   BERT Testing at Terminal Location

G.

Knowledge of the Trouble and Isolation Procedures

This section covers the general types of troubles as to extent and general location of the fault causing the trouble. The three primary areas of concern are the user terminal location, the line between the user locations, and the DP center proper.

Figure 14-13 shows the network trouble isolation environment. Initial knowledge of what the specific trouble is depends on the facility configuration and the availability of either user inputs and/or status indications from monitoring and diagnostic equipments. It is assumed at this point that the user has some form of Network Control capability (called Tech Control or Tech Control Center). Once a network has at least eight communications lines emanating from a single location, it becomes almost mandatory to provide some form of

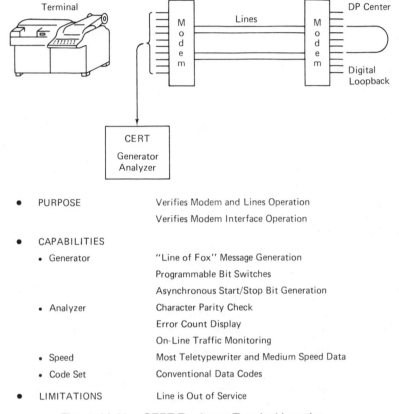

- • PURPOSE   Verifies Modem and Lines Operation
                              Verifies Modem Interface Operation

- • CAPABILITIES
    - • Generator   "Line of Fox" Message Generation
                              Programmable Bit Switches
                              Asynchronous Start/Stop Bit Generation
    - • Analyzer   Character Parity Check
                              Error Count Display
                              On-Line Traffic Monitoring
    - • Speed   Most Teletypewriter and Medium Speed Data
    - • Code Set   Conventional Data Codes

- • LIMITATIONS   Line is Out of Service

Figure 14-11.   CERT Testing at Terminal Location

Tech Control capability because of the quantity and complexity of problems which arise on a network on a continuous basis. Special equipments and facilities can pay for themselves in a year's time, not even counting all the lost time resulting from network degradations. Naturally, all applications and users are different, but the basic capability of knowing how to correct a communications problem, and do it both quickly and efficiently, is in almost every single case the most worthwhile investment a user can make when he gets involved in a communications network.

Knowledge of troubles occurring on a particular line will most probably get to the Tech Control personnel from other personnel observing an apparent trouble and calling it in for isolation and resolution. Also, some of the indications from line monitoring equipment will provide trouble indications. Table 14-5 gives some examples of both of these.

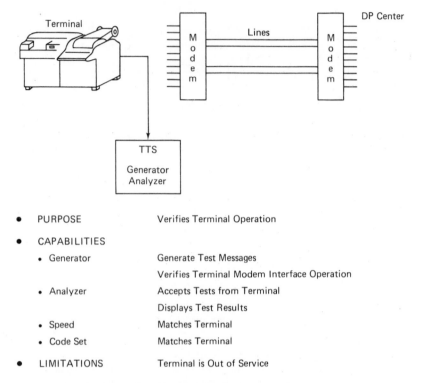

- ● PURPOSE   Verifies Terminal Operation

- ● CAPABILITIES
  - • Generator   Generate Test Messages

                         Verifies Terminal Modem Interface Operation
  - • Analyzer   Accepts Tests from Terminal

                         Displays Test Results
  - • Speed   Matches Terminal
  - • Code Set   Matches Terminal

- ● LIMITATIONS   Terminal is Out of Service

Note: More sophisticated models may be connected to the terminal
         modem to duplicate the functions of the terminal for testing
         from the DP Center over lines and modems.

Figure 14-12.   Terminal Test Set

Test transaction monitoring at the Tech Control location is shown in Fig. 14-14. This can be very important in trouble isolation on terminals which access the DP center over dial lines or half-duplex dedicated lines. These access lines prevent the use of modem and line isolation by loopback testing in that only the single data channel is available over the line or through the modem.

When full-duplex lines are involved (dedicated), both line and modem loopback testing can be performed to isolate trouble to either the line or the terminal location modem by testing from the DP center. An alternate method to perform these tests would be to perform the loopback operations in the opposite direction and do the tests from the terminal location. These tests depend on the line and modems both being full duplex. In the case of the reverse channel modems on a half-duplex line, special test capabilities are usually

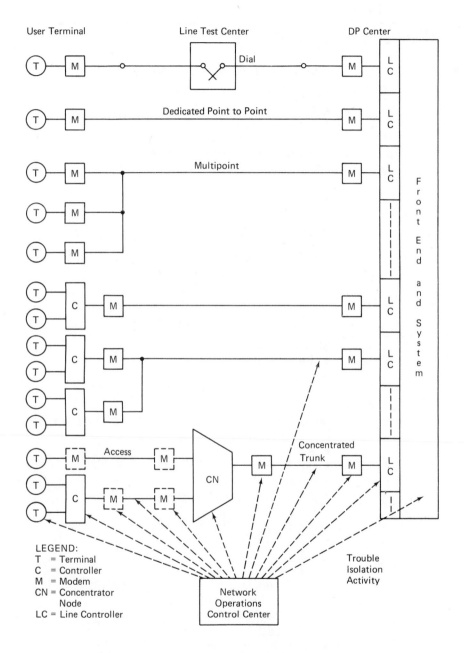

Figure 14-13. Network Trouble Isolation Environment

TABLE 14-5

KNOWLEDGE OF TROUBLE

Due to Tech Control Capability

TECH CONTROL PERSONNEL
- Call from Others
- Line Monitoring Results
- Trouble is Apparently
  Associated with Other Troubles

EXTENT OF TROUBLE
- Network Layout Indications
- Terminal Equipment Indications
- DP Center Equipment Indications
- DP Center Program Indications
- Further Investigation is Required
    User Terminal Operator
    Line Test and Repair Personnel
    DP Center Personnel

Due to Network Layout

SINGLE TERMINAL
- Totally Out
- Impaired
    Device Totally Out
    Controller Impaired

MULTIPLE TERMINAL (SINGLE CONTROLLER)
- Single Terminal Affected
- All Terminals Affected
- Single Device Type Affected
  on Single Terminal
- Single Device Type Affected
  on All Terminals

LINE
- Point to Point
    Dial Line Out
    Dedicated Line Out
- Multipoint
    Single Terminal Affected
    Terminals Beyond a Point Affected

DP CENTER
- Single Port Affected
- All Ports of 1 Front End Affected
- Entire Application Affected

TABLE 14-5 (Cont.)

Due to Observer Capability

USER TERMINAL OPERATOR
- Terminal Totally Out
- Device/s Totally Out
- Controller Impaired
  Single Device
  All Devices

LINE TEST AND REPAIR PERSONNEL
- Single Analog Line Alarms
- Group Analog Line Alarms
- Supergroup Analog Line Alarms
- Mastergroup Analog Line Alarms
- Digital Channel Alarms
- System Alarms
- Preventative Maintenance
  Indications
- Threshold Detection Indicators

DP CENTER PERSONNEL
- Center is Out
- Subsystem is Out
- Application is Out
- Terminal Queue Abnormal
- Line Threshold Detector Indications

built into the modem by the vendor and can be used to isolate the problem to at least the line or the modem. If not available, the user must start with the standard half-duplex line type testing.

Computer Port Testing

Table 14-6 indicates two options in performing computer port testing, as well as listing the arguments for and against each technique. In a practical sense, whether a manual or automated technical control system is employed, the DP center to terminal or "outbound" isolation testing seems more logical from an equipment efficiency and personnel viewpoint, but it should be recognized that if the computerized technical control is employed, it is also an active device that will require maintenance from time to time. In the long run, however,

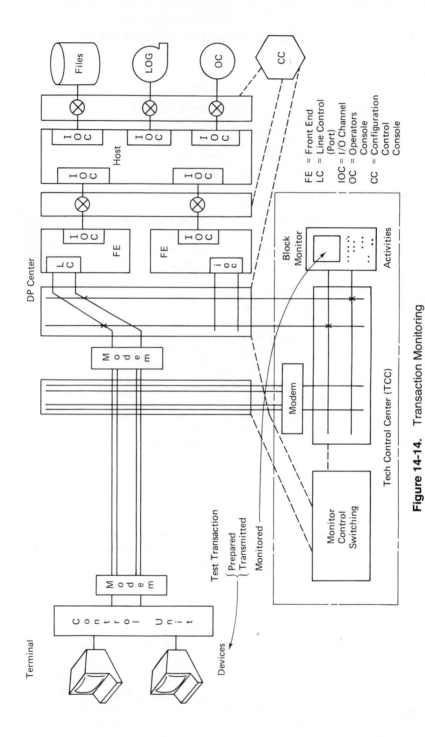

FE = Front End
LC = Line Control (Port)
IOC = I/O Channel
OC = Operators Console
CC = Configuration Control Console

Figure 14-14. Transaction Monitoring

TABLE 14-6

COMPUTER PORT TESTING

Two Options

USER TERMINAL INBOUND
- User is Idle
- DP Center Has Many Ports
- DP Center Personnel Cannot
  Usually See Direct Results

DP CENTER OUTBOUND
- Manual Equipment and Procedures
    Fewer Test Sets
    Faster Trouble Isolation
- Automated Equipment and Procedures
    Continuous Threshold Monitoring
    Personnel See Direct Results
    Statistics Gathering
    Statistics Storing
    Statistics Analysis
    Duplicate System to Maintain
    Active Test Tool

this is a small price to pay for the capability and convenience of having one when a network problem arises.

Loopback testing is pictured for both of the above options in Fig. 14-15. It should be pointed out here that the Tech Control coordination effort is intensified when using the terminal inbound method.

Loopback Testing

Table 14-7 lists types of loopback testing by degree of automation used, activity on the part of test personnel and, equipment and line limitations when using analog lines and conventional modems. It should be noted here that a loopback isolation test which involves sending a test message or transaction using synchronous modems can result in a false assumption that the line and modems are good because the timing phase correction at one or both ends of the line can be faulty and not appear in the test. False assumption has hidden faulty modems where problems appeared as intermittent line troubles to the observer.

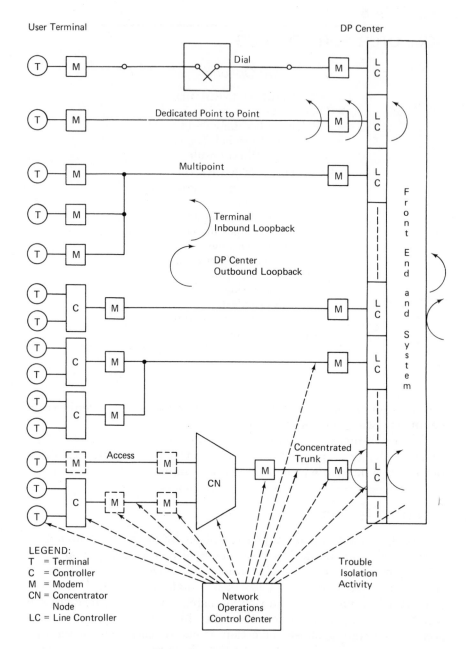

Figure 14-15. Computer Port Testing

TABLE 14-7

LOOPBACK TESTING

MANUAL
- Operated By Someone

AUTOMATIC
- Noted by Someone

DIGITAL
- Limited to Terminal and DP Center
- Several Conductors
- Timing Missed on Lines

ANALOG
- Must be Full Duplex
- Isolates Line Section
- Capability Found in Most Test Boards

USER OPERATES
- User is Idle
- At Location

DP CENTER OPERATES
- At Location

Figure 14-16 indicates the possible locations at the user terminal installation where loopback testing can assist in trouble isolation. The user would be the loopback device operator because of the reasons listed in Table 14-7. On the other hand, the control that must be exercised by Tech Control personnel becomes very important in the light of the effect on other users that loopback testing may cause if they share common equipment.

Figure 14-17 shows loopback test activity which may take place in the Telephone Serving Office nearest a user's location. It is assumed here that the lines are analog and full duplex, equipped with full-duplex (4-wire) modems, and that attempts are being made to isolate either a line fault to the local access loop at the terminal end or the terminals are being operated in a multipoint type arrangement.

Figure 14-18 shows loopback test activity in the DP center for the terminal inbound option of line and modem fault isolation. Loopback testing at the front-end equipment will have to be carefully coordinated with system operations personnel because care will have to be exercised with regard to application work priorities and the host computer system.

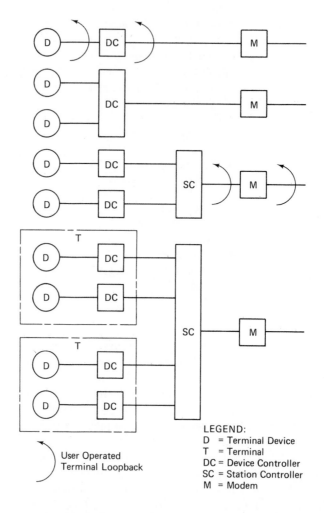

LEGEND:
D = Terminal Device
T = Terminal
DC = Device Controller
SC = Station Controller
M = Modem

User Operated
Terminal Loopback

Figure 14-16. User Terminal Loopback Testing

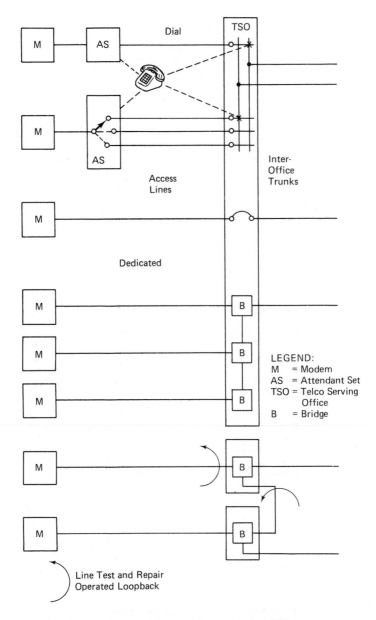

Figure 14-17. Loopback at Telco Service Office

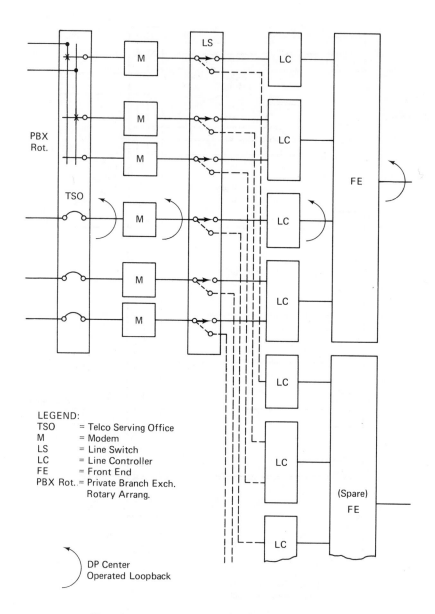

LEGEND:
TSO   = Telco Serving Office
M   = Modem
LS   = Line Switch
LC   = Line Controller
FE   = Front End
PBX Rot. = Private Branch Exch.
             Rotary Arrang.

DP Center
Operated Loopback

Figure 14-18. Loopback Testing in DP Center

TABLE 14-8

TROUBLE ISOLATION PROCEDURES

Rules

TOOLS
- Available—Perform Test
- Unavailable—Go to Next

PERSONNEL
- Available—Perform Test
- Unavailable
  - Temporarily—Wait
  - Permanently—Go to Next

TEST DATA
- Diagnostic Message
- Dummy Transaction
- Live Transaction

OTHERS KNOWLEDGE OF TROUBLE
- Single Terminal, Line, Port
  - Test Personnel Sequential
- Multiple Units
  - Users in Common Path
  - Test Personnel Sequential

Tech Control Center

EQUIPMENT AND LINE FAULTS
1. User Reports Trouble to Tech Control (Out of or Impaired Service)
   a. Single Terminal and Line
   b. First Reported of Multiple Units
   c. Device or Device Controller Trouble
   d. Terminal or Single Terminal Station Controller Trouble
   e. Multi-terminal Station Controller or Modem Trouble
   f. Line Trouble
   g. Data Processing (DP) Center Port Trouble
2. Terminal and Controller Self Test
3. Terminal and Line Test
   a. Remote
4. DP Center Access Line Test (Local lines to TCC and to DP equipment)
5. Modem Test
   a. Local
6. DP Equipment Tests (Front-End T/P)
7. Program Problems

General Trouble Isolation Procedures

Table 14-8 is a list of rules for applying the general network trouble isolation procedures which follow. A unique set of procedures will have to be written to account for the many constraints of a particular system environment, but for the general case a list of the pertinent assumptions and built-in constraints is provided.

H.

Computerized Technical Control Systems

A computerized technical control system, as is typically implemented by several large network operator organizations, is comprised of a small computer system (either a minicomputer or microcomputer) which has features allowing line monitoring, event detection and recording, error (trouble) statistics gathering, storing, reporting, and finally it is set up in a unique area with the access units and manual test equipment. The geographical locations for these Automated Technical Control Systems (ATCS) equipments is logically at or near the DP center location. It may be located in adjacent rooms or different floors of the same building or in a separate system in the computer room of the DP center proper. The uses of ATCS are shown in Table 14-9.

A typical ATCS configuration is pictured in Fig. 14-19. The DP center modems and access jacks, along with the manual test equipment may be in racks alongside the computer system for easy access. The connections for the computer to monitor the modems and channel operation is shown in Fig. 14-20.

I.

Automated Diagnostic and Test Programs

The principal attributes of programs used for diagnostic and test purposes are listed in Table 14-10. The location of the program is optional because of the low-cost microprocessor electronics and the diagnostic programs can be considered to be "hardwired" in terminal units.

TABLE 14-9

COMPUTERIZED TECH CONTROL SYSTEMS

FEATURES
- Line Monitoring
- Event Recording
- Statistics Gathering
- Statistics Storing

LOCATIONS
- NOCC Separate from DP Center
- At DP Center in Separate System
- In DP Center Front End

USES
- Error Detection
- Error Recording
- Transaction Journaling
- Network Data Base Maintenance
- Trouble Isolation
- Trouble Reporting
- Statistical Analysis
- Report Generation

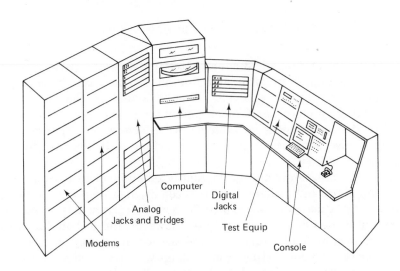

Figure 14-19. Commercial Tech Control Configuration

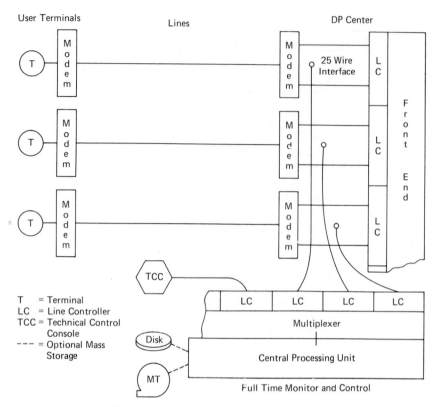

Figure 14-20.   Monitor Connections at TCC

The extent of dynamic diagnostic testing generally performed at this time is digital in form and limited to character, block, and message generation and analysis, using bit matching, character parity checking, protocol and block redundancy checking. On more sophisticated and expensive systems, some degree of response-time testing is also done, especially in conjunction with line monitoring equipment.

The test programs may be manually or automatically activated due to an alarm indication or a sensed condition of suspected trouble, or they may be activated when a traffic activity threshold is exceeded. When automated diagnostics are used, however, there should always be a system of manual override capabilities for emergency purposes.

Network element testing from a diagnostic program stored in a computer is classified into three types based on the level of testing performed. Listed in Table 14-11 are the first two types of diagnostics and the principal features of each type.

TABLE 14-10

DIAGNOSTIC AND TEST PROGRAMS

LOCATION
- Terminal
- DP Center
- NOC Separate Location

EXTENT
- Character Generation
- Test Block
- Transaction or Message

TESTING
- Bit Matching
- Parity Checking
- Protocol Checking
- Response Time Tests

MANUALLY ACTIVATED

AUTOMATICALLY PERFORMED
- Detected Threshold Command
- Low Traffic Periods

TABLE 14-11

COMPUTERIZED DIAGNOSTIC TESTING

TEST CHARACTER PARITY CHECK
- ASCII Code Set
- Idle Character Generation
- Full-Duplex Line
- Character Parity Checking
- Error Event Counting
- Threshold Count Alert

TEST TRANSMISSION BLOCK
- Manual Activation
- Unique ID on Test Block
- Automatic Insertion in
  Line Block Stream
- Receiver Block Checks
- Block Error Counting
- Character Parity Checking
- Time Between Errors
- Error Rate Establishment
- Error Reporting

Parity checking of test characters is performed over full duplex, single terminal, dedicated lines using a code set containing the control or parity bit. Fig. 14-21 shows how the ASCII code set "synchronous idle" character can be generated between transmission blocks on the line and a parity check (VRC) performed at the receiver. If the terminal location has a diagnostic computer, the terminal controller need only store the error counts, then prepare and send an error count message on command of the diagnostic program from the DP center. When a transaction has been prepared by the user at the terminal location and is sent to the line from the terminal controller, the diagnostic computer interrupts the idle character generation and sends the data block, returning to idle character generation at the end of the block transmission. When a response is ready from the DP center, the corresponding diagnostic computer performs a similar interruption of idle character generation and sends the transmission block. Periodically, the DP center diagnostic program causes a diagnostics poll to be sent to the terminal during a lull in traffic and picks

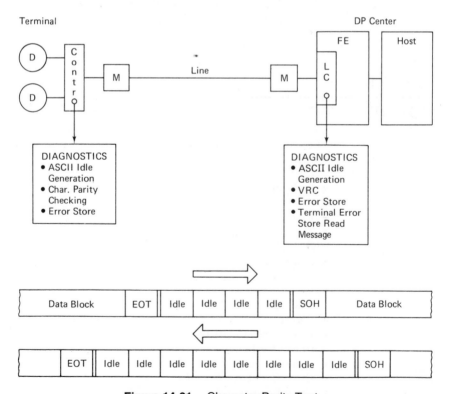

Figure 14-21. Character Parity Test

up the error count for storage and later analysis. This parity checking at either end is interrupted by the presence of the data block delimiter (SOH used in the figure) and restored by receipt of one or two idle character patterns after a block is received. If the terminal location does not have a separate diagnostic computer, it may be possible for the terminal controller to have firmware or software installed to perform the basic storing and transmitting of the diagnostic information.

The second diagnostic test listed in Table 14-11 is the test transmission block. This type of test can be performed on any line type by either manually or automatically inserting a test block on the line when a trouble is suspected. The test block must have a unique identification incorporated so that it is not mistaken for a live transaction. The same block checking can be used for the test block as is used for the traffic.

The blocks containing an error or errors are counted, and these counts stored for delivery to statistical storage in the DP center in the same general manner as for the test character errors. Block error counting is not as accurate as the test character counting because one, or more than one, character error results in only one block error count. In addition, the time between errors may be an important parameter, and the block error tests do not provide this directly; but it should be recognized that effective information throughput is dependent on how many blocks per unit time are received correctly, so even though the total amount of errors may not be available, this block test is important to determine effective information input. Some diagnostic programs incorporate both tests to provide the complete statistics of line performance.

Block generation at the terminal may be performed by the user operator, who can also provide the checking of a known block content and error counting. This would eliminate the need for a set of diagnostic programs at each terminal location within a large network. Finally, the diagnostic program may be executed from a separate Automated Technical Control computer at the DP center. The test block being discussed here is not a formatted transaction, but merely a block of data used to test the data path from the controllers on each end and over the line and modems (see Fig. 14-22).

The features of the third type of diagnostic testing, test transactions, are itemized in Table 14-12. From the standpoint of using the identical data path as live traffic, test transactions are the best of the three test types. As in the case of test transmission blocks, the user at the terminal may manually prepare the transaction using the existing terminal devices and procedures, while the DP center diagnostics

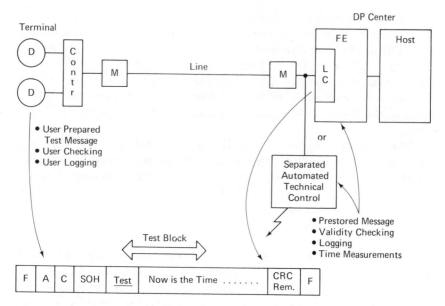

Figure 14-22.   Transaction Test Block

TABLE 14-12

TEST TRANSACTION DIAGNOSTICS

TEST TRANSACTIONS
- User Preparation
- Computer Preparation
- Transaction Log ID
- Normal Transaction Path
- Response Time Testing

NOTE: TESTS MAY ADD TO HEAVY
     TRAFFIC PROBLEM CAUSE!
- Front-End Handling
- Automated Tech Control
  Handling
- Test Response Generation

TRANSACTION ERROR LOGGING
- Audit Trail Tapes
- Statistics Gathering
- Statistics Analysis
- Report Generation

program might use a prestored transaction, prepare a test transaction, or respond to a test transaction. The test transaction must be uniquely identified, again so that it is not mistaken for live traffic. Test transactions may also be used for response-time testing or turn-around testing of a particular application. However, as pointed out in the table, the tests if performed at the same time as normal traffic is sent, can add to heavy traffic problems which may already exist. Diagnostic test transactions can be processed in the communications computer or a separate automated test system.

Figure 14-23 shows the transaction or message interplay on the line. The transaction logging function used for normal traffic accounting and restart purposes may be used for logging the test transactions, or a separate logging function may be implemented at the separate automated test system or the communications computer (front end) and used specifically for this test function.

Regardless of the location of the logging function, its purpose is to gather the statistics of test transaction results to be used in tracking down intermittent network line problems and preparing qualitative network operational reports.

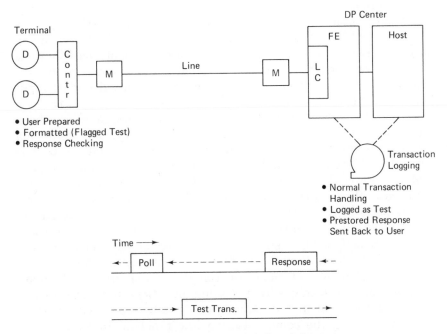

Figure 14-23. Transaction Test Interplay

J.

Test Sequences for Problem Isolation

When trying to isolate problems which occur on a communications line there are two basic types of tests to be performed. First is the digital testing, and second is the analog testing. Digital test refers to the test of information in its digital form, while analog testing refers to those tests which are performed on the communications line itself. Many of these tests utilize the loopback, which has been described previously, and for purposes of this section will mean the return of information back to the source at any one of a number of locations in the network (digital side of modem at transmit end, analog side of modem at transmit end, analog side of modem at receive end, and digital side of modem at receive end).

The most frequent test mode used by far is the digital test mode and is possible with a large range of equipments, all the way from the so-called "free" ones on the communications devices themselves, to the sophisticated and self-contained units. Since most of the tests performed by these devices are in the loopback mode, they will be described first.

When a problem has occurred and the communications line is suspected, the very first test should be a modem self test. Depending on the particular unit, this may consist of one or more push buttons for which the end result is the same. An internal test pattern is generated which is as close as possible to the normal digital input (which has been disconnected), and this test pattern travels through more than 90 percent of the internal circuitry, a simulated telephone line, and then returns to its originating circuitry. The returning pattern is compared with the transmitting pattern, and the user is advised of differences by an indicator type of lamp. It is quite possible that an error could be caused by the self-test circuitry itself, so if this is the case, then a spare modem should be substituted and the same testing performed. If this modem now looks good, the testing should continue with the line if the overall problem still has not been found.

Modem self tests, even when performed at both ends, do not necessarily validate that the modem is operational. First of all, the test patterns do not go through the complete set of circuits which are required for interfacing with the communications line, and second, the bit pattern which is generated may not be the specific pattern which is causing the communication line problem. In addition, an even more common problem which is not found, is an out-of-tolerance timing condition which occurs only when the two modems are communicating with each other.

The next most probable test is what is known as a *remote self test*. In this particular type of operation one modem would be set to generate and compare a test pattern after transmitting the information down the actual line, through the modem at the other end where it is digitally looped back, and then back on the communications line for comparison at the transmit end.

Two alternatives exist with the remote self test. First, without benefit of line test equipment, if both modems have passed the local self test, passing the remote self test would indicate that the user should contact the modem vendor; but if the remote self test fails, it would indicate that the telephone company or the carrier should be contacted.

If there is external test equipment available, the same test should be repeated with externally generated patterns which are more complex. If the results are the same as the self test results, the same conclusions can be drawn with a high probability of being correct.

If however, the local loop fails with the test equipment, a modem failure is extremely probable, but if the remote digital loop results agree with the results of the remote self test, there is no specific place to point the finger.

At this point in time the telephone company should be called with the specifics of the problem being described to them. The telephone company, in all likelihood, will check those line problems which are both most common and easiest to test. If the telephone company testing results in no problem being found (NTF), it's advisable to ask the phone company which checks were made, and then try to use the line again. There have been many instances where the telephone company has been unable to find a problem after testing the line, yet the line has been found to be good after the test sequences have been completed.

If the communications line is still not operational, the telephone company should be called back again and specifically requested to perform a noise check and a frequency run (FREQ), if these tests were not performed before. The FREQ run consists of testing the attenuation at the various frequencies throughout the telephone bandwidth. If this still doesn't work, the modem vendor should be called, and assuming the user does not have any specific internal test capability, the modem vendor and the telephone company must work together to try to isolate the problem. The user must have internal operating procedures to facilitate the modem vendor and the telephone company maintenance personnel working together.

If possible, with the availability of the appropriate equipment, end-to-end testing can also be performed (one way each way). In this case the very same type of test can be performed utilizing the test equipment to an end-to-end basis without a loopback. Because the information is going through the modems at each end and the logic hardware at each end, the probabilitity of detecting errors is better than on a loopback because the total signal path is involved. At the same time, a remote analog loopback should not be performed unless the signal goes through an amplifier at the remote end, because, what the user ends up with is a communication line which is twice as long in distance as it was designed to operate over. (The remote modem outputs a signal level which is the same as the signal level at the transmit end, but if an analog-only loopback is performed, the level being looped back at the receive modem will be at the receive signal level of the remote end instead of at least 16 dB higher, which should be the normal transmit signal level.)

Another test which can be performed in this environment is to test the polling and calling sequences and determine the responses of the individual modems. This is especially critical in a dial-up situation where all the modem/terminal equipment interfaces have a specifically defined relationship with each other.

One other level of digital test capability is available and that is automated test equipment on the digital side at each end. Specific signals as well as data blocks can be sent from one of the test equipments to the other so that the comparisons can be made at each end of a line without a loopback (end-to-end tests), and the entire live system is utilized for the test. It would also be possible for the communications software to be tested here if the test equipment allows for external input of information. (This is very expensive, however, if all remote sites are to have separate test equipments.)

The second significant area of testing is analog testing. This is always the last and the hardest to describe, because the analog world is so much different from the digital world in which people discuss "discrete" elements instead of varying elements which occur in the analog network. As with digital testing, however, analog tests can also be performed in a loopback or end-to-end mode. For these tests though, the loopbacks must be analog, and they must also be remote analog loopbacks so that the analog network can be tested. It is also very important to recognize that with very few exceptions, analog testing which is performed in a loopback mode is nearly 100 percent valid. The reason for the question of validity is the fact that only gross level analog tests can be performed very quickly for most of the parameters to be tested, but detailed tests on an end-to-end basis require personnel at both ends to coordinate the different functions with each other. These are the kinds of tests that take quite a bit of time, and therefore the line could be unavailable for extended periods of time (hours or days).

The first test which is performed on the line in an analog mode is called *continuity*. This shows whether the connection is broken somewhere. Obviously, this is one of the easiest problems to isolate, and assuming that continuity is not the problem, the next test which should be performed is *level testing*. This means the power levels at various points in the circuit must be measured. These measurements can be made in many ways, but with a telephone line it is most convenient to use a decibel (dB) measuring device as was described in Chap. 13.

The testing of an analog line in the telephone company environment is such that a typical communications path has a receive level which is 16 dB less than the transmit level. The 3002 specification identifies the transmit and receive levels with plus or minus 4 dB as the nominal range. If the measurement is anything other than the expected, the circuit is identified as "long" if the difference is more than 16 dB or "hot" if the signal is stronger than expected. This type of testing should give a very good indication across the band as to the loss of signal strength on the line.

A second characteristic that is measured is called *frequency response* and is a measurement of the line response for all frequencies between 300 and 3300 Hz. The amount of deviation from the nominal for each of the frequencies is also identified in the 3002 specification. The user must be aware of the fact that because of the measurement, which is related to a referred frequency, the line may appear to have a satisfactory frequency response on the line, but the level measurement may be out of tolerance.

Another one of the analog measurements is known as *noise measurement*. It is important to recognize that the only noise we are really interested in is that which exists between 300 and 3300 Hz because those are the frequencies where we will be transmitting our data. In order to do this, a filter (C message filter) which was also described in Chap. 13, is used to simulate the line characteristics. Although a C message filter will allow some of the noise from outside the band in and also reduce some of the inband noise, it is good enough to give the user a fairly accurate indication as to whether noise is a problem. This type of noise measurement should be made with the end of the circuit properly terminated, because if it is not properly terminated, additional noise or other kinds of problems can be injected back into the circuit.

A generalized noise measurement using the C message filter is not always adequate to identify the total impact of noise, because some of the noise is only generated in the presence of a signal. Therefore, the signal itself must be generated and transmitted, and then the signal must be eliminated and only the noise measured as a result of that signal. This is the signal which is known as the test tone at 1004 Hz. This test tone is erased or "notched" out by a notch filter which eliminates just the 1004 Hz signal but leaves the rest of the noise which has been generated by that signal. Although the noise at 1004 Hz has also been eliminated, the effect of its elimination is barely noticeable.

Other analog tests which could be performed are those which measure *envelope delay*. This particular test, however, would probably not indicate anything new if the circuit which is being used had been used previously and worked. This is because envelope delay rarely changes significantly without a corresponding change in the other parameters which would have already been measured. Therefore, envelope delay would only be suspected with a new or changed circuit.

Another unique type of noise is called *nonrandom noise* and is a single frequency interference. It is practically impossible for the single frequency noise to be out of tolerance while the total noise is within tolerance and therefore the C-notched filter noise measurement should find this problem also.

A third type of analog measurement is *frequency shift,* where a particular frequency is shifted up or down by the time it gets to the receive end. A 5-Hz change up or down is allowable, and most of the telephone company testing will find frequency shift problems very quickly.

A fourth type of analog problem is *phase jitter* which is really a frequency shift that is occurring frequently and continuously. This is not normally a common problem and is hard to recognize because of the interrelationship between the phase jitter and noise which is measured by the same type of equipment. Noise will always affect a phase jitter meter and usually vice versa. Since these types of measurements are hard to differentiate, it is usually recommended that these be left to the telephone company to perform.

The testing described above is for impairments that are fairly constant and therefore does not apply to the hit type of noise which is a random occurrence and has values which can change instantaneously. The hits, unless they are on a continuous basis, will normally result in random errors which are detected in data transmissions.

Remember, analog tests are not always conclusive, and the only thing a loopback will tell you with certainty is that there is a loss of continuity on the circuit.

K.

Backup/Alternate Procedures

In all of network management and control procedures, the concept of backup and alternate procedures are mandatory. They can cover a myriad of possible occurrences, and the extent of implementation is normally limited by the amount of financial resources which are available to be spent. For purposes of this text, only the basic backup procedures will be described relative to their mode of implementation, as opposed to the specific types of equipments which would be used.

At the first level, the concept of backup should be identified. What does the user really need? Is immediate backup required, or is there some time available during which service can be restored? What is the maximum length of time that the system and/or particular components of the system can be unavailable to users? These are only some of the parameters which must be evaluated prior to determining how much of an alternate capability is required.

If the entire system must be available, then the user is really talking about a completely duplexed set of hardware and software capability at all levels, from the peripheral storage devices at the central sites all the way out to the display devices at the remotes. This is usually impractical, so the majority of cases have single equipments in the remote network, while the central site normally has the duplexed capability. Since we are concentrating on the communications network in this text, those functions which relate to that capability will be described here.

At the central site, the best backup capability to have, from a hardware point of view, is the capability of switching the communications lines from one communications computer to another one in the event one of those computers fails. A second level would be to have alternate termination equipment which could be automatically switched in, and a third level would be to have alternate modulation equipment which could be replaced in a circuit in the event of a failure at the central site. This latter type of switching (the modem) is normally done through a Tech Control and is done manually after a problem has been identified. If an individual circuit fails and is not duplexed it will have to be fixed in order to restore service to the remote location (dial backup will be described later).

Because of the usual lack of duplex capability in a network (due primarily to cost), the user may consider alternate communication paths in the event of a failure. The primary capability here is the use of dial-up facilities when the leased line fails. The recommendation here is for the dial-up capability to originate at the central site, because the availability of central site hardware can be shared across the entire network, and in addition, if there are problems other than the communication line itself, the user would not want the remote sites calling in because the central site may not be capable of communicating anyway. The user would also have the capability of contacting those remote sites in a prioritized sequence which is designed to be the most efficient from a processing or application point of view at the central site.

As a last resort, if it appears that the circuit failure will last for an extended period of time and alternate communication paths are not available, then the user can also consider the transmission of manual information from one remote site to another remote site, or to the central site for entry at a later point in time. Backup procedures can accommodate this type of activity if, in the original design, the situation was planned for (use of courier air freight, priority mail, regular mail, etc). Actual use depends on particular application and time available before information must be included in the system.

It should be recognized in those cases where a dial-up sequence is used after a leased line has broken down, that the dial-up modem operates differently, and is therefore in most cases, a different modem. Because of the potential expense involved in putting two modems at every single one of the remote sites, the user will probably put the dial-up modems only at those sites which, from a priority point of view, will require the quickest reconnection back to the system.

Because maintenance personnel are not available at all sites, and remote site personnel rarely have the necessary technical capability, the planning for backup and alternate procedures for almost all conditions should be made with the idea in mind that the overwhelming majority of all functions must be performed at or from the central site.

QUESTIONS

1. Draw a diagram with typical connections for the telephone company central office hierarchy.
2. Describe six types of equipment provided by the telephone company.
3. What is the most common and effective form of line-access and monitoring equipment? What are two others?
4. Describe the functions of line monitors.
5. Describe two different types of manual test equipment.
6. Draw a diagram of the typical locations for connection of a Network Operations Control Center.
7. When testing computer ports describe two of the areas to be tested and types of information they provide.
8. Describe the various locations for implementing loopback tests.
9. Describe three types of diagnostic testing.
10. Describe a sequence of testing for fault isolation.
11. Describe a sequence for establishing backup procedures.

COMMUNICATIONS SYSTEM TRANSACTIONS AND APPLICATIONS

In any communications system, whether based on a single processing site or multiple processing sites such as a distributed processing application, there is almost always a wide variety of applications which are to be processed by that system. The individual handling of each application may be different for the single central processor mode of operation as opposed to one of the distributed type processing where specific functions may be handled in specific CPUs, so a set of definitions has been developed which is applicable to both methods of implementation. These definitions are not necessarily accepted industry standards as there are no universally accepted standards, so the reader must use these as a baseline for describing, discussing, and analyzing the method whereby each one of the specific transactions is handled.

A.

Inquiry/Response (I/R)

Of the nine different transactions which will be described in this chapter, the one which will be used most often in communications systems is the inquiry/response (I/R). Inquiries from remote locations will be made into the data bases at one or more central processing sites to determine such things as status, and responses will be returned to the inquirers for their use. An I/R is defined as the entry of a request from a terminal for information from a data base, regardless of where that data base resides in the system, and the return of the requested information to the operator in a real-time mode. Real time in this case means that an operator is waiting for the system to respond, the longer the system response time is, the longer the operator has to wait. As will be seen in Chap. 16, this is a critical design criterion.

B.

Record Update (R/U)

A record update is defined as the modification and/or deletion of an already existing record in the system data base. This term should not be confused with the term *file update*, which is taken to mean any change to the data base. R/U has a very specific meaning because of the method whereby different changes to the data base must be handled. This record update can be done by an operator in a real-time situation, or it can be done in a non-real-time situation as a result of inputs which may have been "batched" previously. This batch mode of operation will be described later in this chapter. The significant part of the definition of record update being done in real time is that it is available to users of the system immediately after the update. When the update is not done in real time, it will not be available to users of the system until it finally gets to the file, at a point later in time after initial entry into the system. This initial entry will probably occur at a terminal where it is being collected. Data collection will be described in Section D of this chapter.

C.

Data Entry

Data entry is the creation of a new record in the system data base in real time. Because the process whereby the data base manager creates a new entry in the data base is different from the process it goes through to access an already existing file, the data-entry function has been given a separate transaction definition. This is important because the newer data base management systems are being designed so that they can be physically resident in a single CPU which is a dedicated Data Base CPU. The creation of a new record in the data base will take a longer period of time than a straight access, and even though it is not a significant period of time (because the internal process is different), it is being defined as a separate transaction.

D.

Data Collection

Data collection is the collection of information in a local or remote environment for *subsequent* update into the system data base. The information will be in machine-readable form so that when the appropriate time and/or facilities are available, this collected information can be applied to the data base in either the record update or data entry mode, i.e., modify existing records or create new records in the data base. The function of data collection implies that the information is not available to users of the system at the point in time it is collected. It will only be available to system users after being applied to the data base. For those systems where the information collected can be accessed locally, the local user may perform inquiries against that information; but from an overall system point of view no other user will be able to access it, and therefore this particular transaction must have a unique definition.

The fact that the data collection is implemented in a local environment implies that the local environment must have a storage media to collect the information. It can also be transmitted incrementally or in a batch mode to a central site where two more alternatives exist. If, at the time of transmission the information is applied to the data base and is available to all users, it becomes the combined function of record update and data entry. If however, the information is collected again at the central site for subsequent update, it is still considered data collection. The data collection procedure itself may involve the transmission of the information from a terminal to the central site directly for off-line storage purposes, and in this case we have storage only at the central site instead of at each of the remote sites. This is still data collection because the information is not available to the system users. Until the information becomes available to the system users it cannot be considered a part of the data base accessing system and therefore must be handled separately. Central site collection is sometimes called *spooling*.

E.

Message Switching

Message switching is the transaction which is required when a message must be transmitted between three or more processing sites. These processing sites can be terminals and/or CPUs. Message switching requires three or more locations because there is no routing involved when there are only two locations. Routing is only required when a decision must be made at a particular site as to where the message must be sent. Even in a case where a single central site has multiple terminals connected to it, if a terminal on one line has to communicate with a terminal on another line, the message must go through the central site, where a determination as to the output location must be made. This involves message switching. All of the queuing, buffer management, and routing table functions of the communications software must be included when message switching is required.

F.

Process Control

A process control transaction is one where a physical process is being monitored automatically, and information regarding that physical process is transmitted to another location, where controls are generated *automatically* to control the physical environment. Typical applications of process control are an electrical power grid system, an oil refinery, a chemical plant, etc. Process control is completely automatic without human intervention. Only in the case where limits exceed the capability of the control units will human action be required.

G.

Command and Control

In the command and control environment we have a situation which is very much like the process control environment except that in C/C there is either manual and/or automated monitoring of a physical process; but the control is always initiated by a human. Even though the mechanism whereby the controls are implemented at the physical locations may be implemented by machines, the initiation is still done by the human.

H.

Batch

The batch transaction is defined as the collection and transmission of all of the information to perform a particular stand-alone job to another location for processing. After processing at the second location, it is collected and transmitted all at one time if a return transmission is required. This is pretty much the standard definition of batch operation, except that batch is sometimes described as processing of a particular function at one site and then transmitting to a second site. Either one is acceptable if it is assumed that the information and/or results are transmitted together as one sequence for either processing or use by the other site. Batch can consist of a particular application to be processed as a complete stand-alone job, or it can be considered as a group of data collection functions which will be processed separately and independently once they reach the application site.

I.

Diagnostics

All of the previous transactions involve the day-to-day operation of a typical communication system. They are the functions which must be performed in order for the user to conduct his business. What is usually left out (but is an important part) is validation that the system is operating correctly and in the event of malfunction can be corrected quickly. In order to accommodate this kind of application the user must consider the implementation of a series of diagnostic capabilities (over and above the communication facilities) which will continually test the system operation to determine if malfunctions are occurring or that a failure has occurred. Many times failures occur, but they are not recognized for a period of time because the process does not have to be used all the time. If a diagnostic capability existed, then the failure or malfunction could be recognized almost immediately, and corrective action could be taken long before the process would have to be used again in normal operations. Because the vendors do not normally provide this capability in minicomputers and terminals today (some mainframe vendors do), it is important for the user to consider implementing diagnostics as a separate application when designing the system. The diagnostics should include the communications software and all of the individual hardware elements which make up the system. Because of the already existing capabilities, however, the communications system can be considered a separate item and treated independently.

J.

Distributed Applications

When discussing distributed applications there is a tendency to confuse the application with the method of describing the network. The fact that applications are performed in different locations or under different sets of conditions really has no effect on the physical network itself, which will consist of either dedicated or dial-up circuits operating on either half-duplex or full-duplex facilities (other than quantities and locations). In order to reduce some of the confusion which exists here, three separate definitions will be made relative to distributed processing applications, but it should be kept in mind that they are just specialized system configurations which are implemented with half- and full-duplex circuits and other types of standard communications facilities.

The first definition is *hierarchial distributed processing*. In this mode of processing we have multiple levels of processing capability starting at the terminal level and going to some nodal level, and ultimately anything that cannot be done at either the terminal or one of the nodes is then done at some high-order central site. There may be multiple levels of nodes in a hierarchial network, but those connections are either point-to-point or multipoint circuits configured usually in full duplex. This is shown in Fig. 15-1. It should be noted

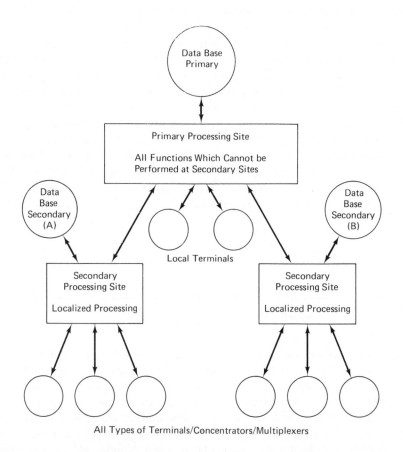

Figure 15-1. Hierarchial Distributed Processing

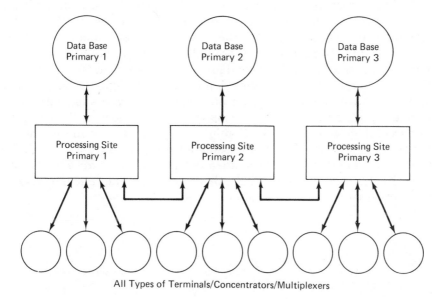

Figure 15-2.   Remote Distributed Processing

that this configuration is representative of IBM's distributed network environment, System Network Architecture (SNA).

The second type of distributed processing is called *remote distributed processing*. This is shown in Fig. 15-2 and consists in this particular case of three independent processing sites, each with the same level of network controls and capability. In the hierarchial process, what cannot be done at one terminal goes upward through the network until it finally reaches a location where the particular processing can be performed. In remote distributed processing, each different site has specific functions to perform, at the same control level, and therefore what cannot be processed at one site is moved to the next site to see if it can be processed there. If not, it goes to the geographic location where it can be processed. In this type of configuration it is also possible for the same applications to be performed at different sites because it is possible that the data bases to be used with the application might be different.

The third type of distributed processing is called *functional distributed processing* and involves the separation of processing functions into separate CPUs. The three functions which are logically separated are Transaction Processing, Application Processing, and Data Base Processing. A more detailed description is provided in Chap. 16 and a block diagram is shown in Fig. 16-4.

In the practical world, where most companies start off with a
single central site and add to it in an incremental mode starting with
terminals and adding CPUs at other remote locations after a period of
time, it is quite probable that there will be a combination of both the
remote and the hierarchial configurations existing at any point in
time. A diagram of this configuration is shown in Fig. 15-3. As can be
seen you have the remote type of distributed processing with the
primary sites, and each of the primary sites has associated with it a
hierarchial type of network. It might be possible in some of these
networks for the secondary processing sites also to have communications paths to other secondary sites, but this may not always be the
case. In the case of IBM's SNA, this particular diagram is a more
complex picture of what they offer.

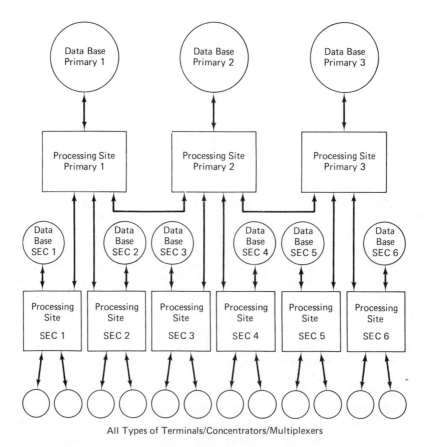

All Types of Terminals/Concentrators/Multiplexers

Figure 15-3.   Combined Remote/Hierarchial Processing

Since the network in many cases may comprise up to 50 percent of the monthly operating costs in a distributed processing application, it is very important to recognize the tradeoffs which can be accommodated and these will be described further in Chap. 16. Still, the mechanism whereby the network is physically constructed will consist of dial and/or dedicated connections operating in either a point-to-point or multipoint environment where it is up to the user to establish what the physical processing capabilities are at each one of the sites being connected. The user designs his own network and then goes to the various common carriers to get the necessary facilities to implement that network.

K.

Packet Switching and Controls

Although it is not truly a transaction or an application in the sense that the previous sections in this chapter are, packet switching is one of the mechanisms that can be used to move information between locations within a distributed network environment. It is therefore included within this chapter for descriptive purposes since no text on data communications today would be complete without a discussion of the packet environment.

In the late 1960s a report by the General Accounting Office (GAO) of the federal government indicated that there were many facilities, supported at least in part by the federal government, which had data processing facilities which were grossly underutilized, while others had facilities which required much more capacity than was available. In order to share the loading more evenly at the different facilities, the concept of a common-user network was initiated, where information from the sites which lacked adequate capacity could be sent to those sites which had excess capacity available, processed at those other sites, and returned to the originating location. For more effective use of the communications facilities, the idea of packet transmission was introduced. Basically, packet transmission means that a message would be divided up into specific length blocks or packets, which would then be sent out individually over the network through multiple locations, and then reassembled at the final location prior to being returned to the user at the receiving end. Because there were multiple paths over which the different packets could be transmitted, they could arrive out of sequence.

Therefore, each packet had appended to it the necessary control information which identified which part of which message the packet belonged to. The validity checking was performed at each location that the packet entered, even if the packet was to be subsequently retransmitted to another point in the network. When delivered to the final packet destination, all of the packets would be reassembled and then transmitted to the end user at the final destination in a format which was compatible with the user's equipment. Because of the multiple routing path capabilities, a packet network can be looked at as an adaptively routed network where individual line failures will not cause the loss of a complete message path.

Once the ARPANET, as it was called, was operational, it was only a matter of time before commercial organizations would follow suit. One of the first companies in the United States to implement a packet network was Telenet and was followed closely by a company called Graphnet, which sent facsimile type information using the packet techniques. It was in Europe, however, that the packet technique was utilized more extensively. In fact, today there are multiple packet networks operating in most of the Western European countries. The United States now has Tymnet, ITT and others as large packet operators, and AT&T is planning on packet services. The primary benefit of these packet services is the capability for transmission of large volumes of data at fixed costs regardless of the distance between end points. This is because the charge is based on the quantity of packets transmitted and not the time or distance involved. The only additional cost to a user is the connection charges at each end. Typically, a user has a leased line to the packet operator in the local environment at each end, which is paid for on a local intrastate monthly rate.

The capability also exists for dialing into the local packet operator location, and the additional charges are the port charges for leased lines and for time of connect charges for the dial ups. These charges are relatively minimal and are in the range of $100 a month for a permanent 9600 bit per second port or 3 to 4 cents per minute on a dial up at 2400 bits per second. Since each of the packet operators has a different tariff, it is necessary to validate current charges with each of them to determine overall network costs. A typical packet switching configuration is shown in Fig. 15-4.

Because packet switching techniques evolved in different locations at about the same time, it was inevitable that it would be implemented differently by different operators. In order to provide a common interface for connection between different packet vendors, a series of standards has been developed for providing common inter-

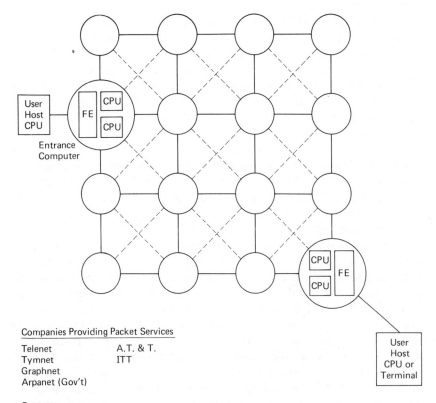

Figure 15-4.   Packet Switching Configuration

faces. These interfaces consist of a series of specifications which defines the interfaces between terminal equipment/host equipment and the common user packet network. The standard which has been adopted by the CCITT is called X.25 and is called "Interface Between Data Terminals Operating in the Packet Mode on Public Networks." The major U.S. carriers, the Canadian Data Network, and all of the major European carriers have agreed to these standards, and this will allow them to connect any user's computers to both domestic networks and eventually connect the networks to each other on an international basis.

What X.25 actually does is to provide a precise set of procedures for "host" type computers to communicate directly with each other in a packet environment by establishing one or more so-called "virtual" circuits between them and then moving the packets of information until the final destination location is reached. A separate interface using other protocols can be implemented to connect to the packet host computer from an external user. This will be described later in this chapter.

In order to understand packet switching a little better, the user must recognize that the services based on packet switching are very much different from those using standard leased lines or dial circuits, which are in effect point to point or end to end. On the end-to-end communications, the user obtains a specific line and is free to choose his own mode of communicating over that link (including speed, format, protocol, and error control) provided that the communicating devices at either end of the link use precisely the same mode of communication. With the packet network, however, the transmitter of data does not establish a physical link with the receiver before starting transmission. Data is sent by the transmitter to his connecting site in the network and is sent to the ultimate destination by whatever combination of routes is fastest at any given instant. The ultimate delivery of information is rapid enough that the user appears to have a dedicated, end-to-end channel, but it is called a virtual circuit. To move the data between the network and the user at either end, the packet carrier provides a set of standard protocols which may be asynchronous, bisync, or other protocol which the vendor may have in his repertoire.

A user's device gains access to the packet network through a communications line that connects it to one of the network's stored-program computers. If the terminal itself can transmit and receive packets, the devices that exchange data over this connection are described by the X.25 protocol as "data terminal equipment operating in the packet mode." Such equipment transmits data synchronously to the packet node computer in a standard format called a packet. Then, at the node computer, the data content of a packet may be reformatted into smaller segments for internal network handling. The segments are transmitted from node to node over the optimum long-haul paths, and at each location which the packet enters it is checked for errors and retransmitted if necessary. At the destination node, the segments are reassembled into the original packet format and passed on to the receiving unit. The fact that the data is reformatted and that complex routing and error recovery techniques are used within the network, is transparent to the user.

Because of the buffering procedures of the packet environment, the physical characteristics of the transmission (bit or byte orientation and speed) sent into the node by the terminal can be different from those transmissions received by the user terminal at the destination node. More important, the network resident software for device support, called a *terminal handler,* can perform the packet mode interfacing function for a device incapable of implementing the packet protocol itself, whether the device is asynchronous or bisynchronous or an emulation of one of these devices. Because of this capability the packet-mode host can communicate with a large variety of both packet-mode and non-packet-mode devices.

With the X.25 network access protocol, the network itself appears to the user's system like a remote concentrator connected to the access link. Therefore the user is mainly interested in the relatively simple procedures and structure for transmitting and receiving to what looks like a concentrator. These are the procedures which are incorporated in the user's system in the form of software routines. Typically, the routines reside in a programmable processor that serve as a front end to the host computer.

For both efficiency and economy, host computer systems are connected to the packet network by single or dual high-speed lines. The physical and electrical signaling characteristics of the access as defined in X.25 use standards like RS232 or V.24/V.28 so that most users already have the appropriate electrical interface.

In actuality the X.25 interface consists of two separate and distinct levels of control procedures. The first is what is known as the *subscriber link-access procedure.* This is the physical movement of data between two physically and geographically separated locations. This level defines a local, rather than end-to-end, protocol. In other words, somewhere else in the network the data which is being received in accordance with X.25 may be itself contained in a higher level protocol for host or application purposes. X.25 only refers to the specific line interface between the host and the system packet mode terminal and the public network. The main purpose of the subscriber link-access control is to connect the user's device to a network. Information is then transferred over the access link in a transmission block called a *frame,* and this is called the packet-level interface. The frame may contain a packet within its information field, and the main function of the frame level control is to ensure that the packets arrive at and leave the network free of error. The frame-level procedure described in X.25 consists of either what is known as the *High Level Data Link Control Procedure* (HDLC) specified by the International Standards Organization or Bisync with transparency. HDLC, when used with either bit- or byte-oriented hardware interfaces, allows for a high level of error free throughput between the user's system and the network.

Using the packet level interface, the user's system looks at the packet network as providing for a number of virtual circuits to which it can link directly for processing in other systems or to other network resident processes which support terminal devices. The concept of virtual circuits can best be visualized by looking at the local interface between the network and the user's devices at each end. These end connections are physical interfaces over which the information is transmitted to and from the packet network. Between the two packet network ends, however, there is no specific circuit established on an end-to-end basis, and therefore the circuit which appears to be established end to end for the user is in effect only local, and the information between the packet network end is sent out on any of the multiple paths that exists in the packet network. This description of the virtual circuit is really an end-to-end concept that describes the "appearance" of the network. The user appears to have a dedicated connection between his devices during a transaction, but in reality it is the capability of the packet network to provide that appearance.

Since the establishment of X.25 there have been additional user-level protocols which provide interface capabilities between different types of terminals and the X.25 interface itself. Of these new protocols, recommendations X.3, X.28, and X.29 were the first and are informally referred to as the international *interactive terminal interface* (ITI). They specifically relate to the support of low-speed, asynchronous terminals by packet-switched networks. They are logical complements to X.25 in that they will allow very specific sets of terminals to interface to packet networks utilizing the already established X.25 interface.

In order to interface different types of terminals into the packet network there is a function which takes place that is called a *Packet Assembly/Disassembly Facility* (PAD). The terminal transmissions are accumulated in a buffer at the PAD and assembled into packets addressed to the host computer at the other end of the virtual circuit. In the meantime the host will be sending information destined for the terminal for which the packets arrive at the PAD where they are reassembled into the appropriate format for sending on to the terminal. As with any remote implementation there are certain functions related to the support of the different types of terminals which the concentrator must provide in addition to buffering the data before forwarding it. These are the functions which are defined in recommendation X.3.

In actuality X.3 identified 12 basic PAD parameter functions which must be provided for start-mode data terminal equipment by packet networks. Recommendation X.28 describes in detail the mechanism by which these functions can be controlled from the terminal, while X.29 specifies the mechanisms for control by the host computer. There are more than twelve functions which can be defined, but they are the basic set which have been agreed on by the international users.

The result of this standardization is that a large number of host computers can all use the same network, which is in fact a distributed nationwide network. On an international basis it means that a terminal in one country will be able to talk to a terminal or a host computer in any other country because all the terminals and the hosts will be compatible.

Because the PAD appears to the packet network functionally like any other X.25 device the network is able to establish X.25 virtual circuits among all the users, hosts, and network PADS with complete symmetry.

With PAD functions still being evolved, it is very probable that additional parameters will be added to the protocols as time passes. In addition it appears that the dynamic changing of PAD parameters will be desirable so that a particular terminal can have its function changed dynamically without changing physical connections to the PAD. What this means is that a terminal could, under network control, be changed from a device which is entering information in a start/stop character mode by operator entry to a mode of floppy disc or tape casette sequential entry. Naturally some operator intervention is necessary, but once the controls are initiated, the terminal, the host processors, and the network will remain compatible.

There are two other functions which must be discussed when describing packet network operation. One of these functions is what is called a *datagram,* which is in reality a single packet message. There are many applications which involve a high volume of single packet size messages which are destined for individual locations or multiple locations. Typical of this could be an inquiry/response type application. Because of the response time requirements back to the initiator, the network throughput must be as fast as possible, and since the interface to the network will only exist for a relatively short period of time for that particular transaction, a different set of parameters is required for optimum network operation. The effort towards datagram standardization is known as the American National Standards Institute (ANSI) X3S3 Committee's Task Group 7 on Public Data Networks. This group is in the process of establishing the parameters which are to be used for a datagram definition. Basically the users of datagrams will have the following characteristics:

1. Send short transaction messages with either a short response or none expected.
2. Potentially send a transaction message to a large number of destinations over a period of hours, without often retransmitting to the same destination.
3. Each transaction will consist of one packet in order to incur the minimum overhead and delay in network handling and destination processing.

The datagram is both a packet-switched service and a subscriber interface to that service. Since the datagram is not yet a completely defined standard there is no formal definition yet, but many of the potential datagram users have agreed to some of the critical components such as the one-packet length, potential out-of-sequence delivery, nondelivery indication being nonmandatory, and the fact that the datagram is self-contained, carrying sufficient information to be routed from a source terminal to a destination terminal without relying on earlier exchanges between the source or destination locations. It should be noted that the datagram interface for character-mode terminals is also compatible with X.28 and X.29.

The final function which must be discussed regarding packet network is the availability of what is known as a *pacuit network*. The pacuit network is neither a national or international type standard, but a specific application of the combination of both circuit- and packet-switching techniques. The California State Universities and Colleges (CUSC) requested in 1973 a system which would have the capabilities of both the packet-switching type of accesses, and at the same time, the capability for establishing end-to-end circuits for direct communication without virtual circuits. To provide the necessary features of both types of switching a system called the Tran M3200 system built by the Computer Transmission Corporation was designed. Pacuit is a highly efficient packet structure containing data traveling between a fixed pair of source and destination locations. The structure itself is a variable-length entity that effectively compacts data in an optimum manner. Because all data in a pacuit system has common source and destination nodes, there is no need for error checking or for storing packets at intermediate nodes along the path. Instead, only source and destination switches perform packet control functions, and all intermediate nodes operate in a pure circuit-switching mode for through-traffic. That means messages are acknowledged only on a network end-to-end basis minimizing the end-to-end delays. In addition, intermediate buffer storage requirements are reduced because the less time packets spend in each node the less queuing goes up, and the logical link established between any source/destination node pair is called a *virtual connection.*

Pacuit and pure circuit-switched data are all time-division multiplexed on trunk lines character by character. Because of a technique known as *dynamic bandwidth allocation* the dynamic reassignment of time slots to different data sources allows the effective utilization of this wide bandwidth and in effect looks like statistical multiplexing which is described in Chap. 10.

Pacuit transmission techniques are not for public network users. Instead they are for those organizations which are large enough to install and implement their own dedicated network. What it does, however, is to provide the best features of both types of techniques while at the same time making best use of dedicated communications facilities.

QUESTIONS

1. Describe an inquiry/response transaction.
2. Describe the relationships between the record update, data entry, and data collection transactions.
3. Describe a message-switching transaction.
4. What are the differences between a process control and a command and control transaction?
5. What is a batch transaction?
6. Describe the operation of a diagnostic transaction.
7. Describe two types of distributed processing transactions.
8. Describe the functional operation of a packet transmission.
9. What is a datagram?

16

SYSTEM CONSIDERATIONS TO EVALUATE

Chapters 1 through 15 of this text have described the basic elements and functions which comprise a data communications network. Also brought out were some of the considerations which are involved when planning a distributed processing type of system. This chapter will bring together many of those individual items and provide the reader with an idea of the overall system trade-offs which must be considered when designing a complete system.

A.

Centralization vs Decentralization

One of the most important considerations in all of system design is to determine the primary mode of processing data. Will it be done at a centralized site, at multiple centralized sites, at remote sites, or will it be done in some mixture of remote and centralized processing?

Even though it is not solely a technical consideration, it appears that in today's environment, the primary decision as to whether to incorporate centralized or decentralized type data processing is really a political decision. Many of today's managers and decision makers grew up in the environment of the "big machine," where IBM had an extensive impact on decision-making processes of the users. The IBM philosophy was that control was mandatory in all system operations, and since it was much easier to control the operation at a single site, a single mainframe processor at one location would be the best choice. Today's environment is somewhat different, however, in that the techniques for control do not have to be maintained at only one site. Functions such as down-line loading, up-line loading, and automated monitoring and logging techniques provide the capability for control to be resident at single or multiple central sites, while at the same time either remote distributed processing or hierarchial distributed processing can still take place somewhere else in the network. Once management recognizes that they do not have to give up control when they go into a distributed form of processing, the decision to go decentralized is much easier.

If the political environment can be eliminated at the time the decision must be made as to whether to go centralized or decentralized, the decision really becomes a standard one of cost versus benefits. The benefits must be looked at from the point of view that they have both advantages and disadvantages, while at the same time they have cost impacts over and above the purchase or lease of computing equipment. Typical of these hidden costs is the requirement to have more capable personnel out at the remote sites. The cost to the company for these additional capabilities adds to the basic cost for operation of the entire system. The second most obvious area of additional cost is the maintenance requirement, in that no single organization can afford to have maintenance personnel for all equipments at all sites. This means calling out the right vendor at the right time to fix any problems which exist. It takes a more qualified person to determine the cause of the existing problem so that the correct vendor can be summoned. To help the personnel perform this function automated and semi-automated test equipment can be employed (described in Chap. 14), but this also adds to the cost of system operation.

When trying to make the decision as to whether a system should be decentralized or not, the user must objectively evaluate the type of business the company is engaged in, and whether that type of business lends itself to a distributed environment. For example, is the company geographically distributed in multiple locations? Are different applications performed at different sites? Do the reporting requirements mandate centralized distribution with short time-turn-arounds, or is time available for coordinating the reports and submitting them less often? How are orders handled? How are the files utilized? Can multiple copies of a data base be utilized within the system with decision-making capability based on the access of only those separate files? These are only some of the decision factors which must be considered on an overall company basis as to how the system will be used. There are other decisions which are more pertinent to the day-to-day operation of the network, and they are the ones that are somewhat more technical in nature.

The technical/operational type decisions usually have response time as the primary requirement at the top of the list. If the system operation is primarily terminal/operator oriented, the operator will most often be waiting for a system to respond to an inquiry. The longer the operator has to wait, the greater the wasted time will be and the greater the overall cost of the system. Response time of the system/network is therefore critical and in most cases is designed to be within six seconds maximum, with two seconds as the desired reponse time. If the system is more batch oriented, where the data is collected remotely and processed at one or more central sites, the response time may not be as critical; but depending on the length of the transmissions between the two locations, first for the generation of information and then for the return of the results, the network response-time design parameters are still critical because of the costs which are involved in the network during transmission times. Right along with the response time, the total volume of traffic must be estimated so that the appropriate network components and facilities can be designed to accommodate those loads. This will be further explored in the next section on design requirements.

Other basic questions must be answered relative to what the system will be required to accomplish with respect to the user's applications. Of the transactions described in Chap. 15 which ones must be incorporated into the system operation for each of the different applications for each location? Have the various dispersed operations of the company done their processing independently in the past with different code sets, equipments, programming languages, procedures, etc? What is the total system cost for doing business in the present environment? If the present system was expanded to accommodate the new requirements, what would the same mode of operation cost for the expanded configuration? These questions must be answered in their total system environment, which includes hardware/software, people, network facilities, and maintenance costs. It is mandatory that this be done because it is no longer feasible to compare just the hardware/software costs due to the fact that the operation and maintenance of a distributed network environment can be substantially greater than for a system which was central-site oriented in the first place. Cost factors of ten to one in cost of operations are not uncommon, so it is necessary to take a look at the total system operation, which includes all the factors which make up the total cost to the company.

Another very important factor to consider at this time is the increase or expansion of services which can be offered to the users or customers of the system. Expanding a given system may cost much less than distributing the capabilities over multiple locations, but, it may very well be the case that the improved response time is such that the user environment will considerably improve, and for the case where external customers are involved, it may mean either obtaining or maintaining a competitive position. The additional costs involved are therefore allocated over improved or additional services as opposed to maintenance of existing services which makes the evaluation more subjective because we end up comparing apples and oranges.

Costs for the decentralized approach must be generated independently for each of the potential modes of implementation. If some applications are to be performed at the central site while others at the remote sites, consideration should be given to altering the mix if a significant cost savings can be brought about (as long as operational requirements are still being met). Along with the location of applications processing, the method of system control must also be considered because the controls can add a significant amount of overhead in both hardware and software to the basic cost of the system. Here is where a substantial amount of human decision is involved, because in order to perform all of the controls at the central sites, the overhead traffic will be greatly increased, and the managers who are going to perform the control at the central sites must assimilate significantly increased amounts of data from multiple sites. This can be partially allayed by generating software to perform those assimilations, but this also adds to the central site overhead and adds to the total system cost. If some mode of control can be delegated to the remote processing sites, and reporting takes place on a weekly, monthly or quarterly basis, then a more reasonable approach can be incorporated which will optimize the use of the system for applications versus the necessity for controls.

As can be seen, the decision as to whether a system should be centralized or decentralized has many subjective areas so all facets should be looked at on an individual objective basis as to its impact on the overall system. A small increase in cost of initial hardware, for example, could result in a significant savings in operating costs which will mean a lower overall cost to the organization. A good example of this trade-off is the use of intelligent or programmable terminals at the remote sites which decreases central site costs as well as potentially reducing the network costs (offset somewhat by additional terminal, operator, and maintenance costs).

B.

Design Requirements

Once the decision has been made to implement a network, whether centralized or decentralized, there are certain basic criteria which must be established so that an optimal network can be implemented which meets the basic system requirements. The design requirements for the network, which must be established as a base, are listed below. Note that the functions are not necessarily in the priority sequence for a particular application. The user must determine which of the design criteria have the higher priority for the system he wants to implement. The functions defined are communications oriented as well as total-system oriented so that the impact of one on the other can be determined at the same time.

1. What are the points to be connected (geographically)?
2. What is the data traffic volume on each individual line (connection between two points)? This includes the traffic which is anticipated to come in from individual terminal locations on a multidrop line.
3. What are the peak traffic volume requirements on each individual line?
4. What is the response time required to the user, average and maximum?
5. What level of data protection is required (parity)?
6. What level of security is required on the individual network segments (encryption)?
7. What is the anticipated growth by the time the system is physically implemented?

8. What is the growth projection for the next five years on a yearly incremental basis?

9. How many new applications must be supported?

10. Of the existing applications, how many will have to be changed and how many eliminated?

11. What are the preliminary budgetary limitations?

Once the above primary design requirements have been established (there are others which will more than likely be application oriented), the various alternatives in designing a network can be investigated. These alternatives involve such things as multidrop lines, multiplexing techniques, data compression, forward error correction, type of protocol, transmission formats, use of microprocessors with firmware, utilization of specialized common carriers, use of alternative to phone company services, and use of third party vendor equipments. In evaluating the different implementation methods, the impact on all areas must be considered, and cost is not the only parameter. Additional people, higher paid personnel, network alternatives, user impacts, and capability for meeting operational objectives must all be evaluated when performing the trade-off analysis.

C.

Response Times

As was described in Chap. 15, the definition of response time is the total time it takes for a transaction to be processed from the moment an operator hits the "enter key" on the terminal, until the response starts to display on either the CRT or the printer at the operator's location. This time is totally independent, although in part consists of the processing times of the different sites which process the transaction was well as the transmission paths over which the transaction must travel.

If it is necessary to include the total preparation time of a request as well as the utilization of the results after the inquiry has been processed, the definition should be considered a *transaction time,* which is the time it takes from the initiation of one transaction until the initiation of the next transaction, regardless of the processes which must be undertaken in between. The definition of response time must include the response time of the system and not just the operator.

Since response times on multidrop lines may also be limited by the amount of terminals on that line, the speed of transmission to all involved locations, the processing at the appropriate application site (includes recognition and data base access), as well as the other functions which can impact the response time, must be identified. They are:

1. TERMINAL BUFFERING If the terminal has a buffer of adequate size to take a complete transmission, it will require only one transmission for an inquiry against a data base and a response to that inquiry. If multiple transmissions must be sent because of limited buffer size or because the operator is transmitting directly on line, the response time is lengthened by the amount of time it takes for each of the individual transmissions to be sent and acknowledged.

2. LINE SPEED The transmission line speed can have a significant effect on response time in two different areas. The first area is terminal-to-node transmission time, while the second is node-to-node transmission time. For example, if the terminal-to-node transmission time is at the rate of 300 bits per second, we have a transmission rate of 75 characters per second, so a 150-character message would take 2 seconds to transmit. If the transmission rate was 2400 bits per second it would only take ½ second for the same transmission. If the system design requirement were such that a maximum second response time was required, it is obvious that at least 2400 bits per second transmission rate would be required between the terminal and the first node.

The other area where line speed is significant is between the nodes and central sites. On these particular segments, it is usual to see a minimum of 2400 bits per second and not uncommon to see 9600 bits per second or up to 50 kilobits per second transmission rates. The higher rates between nodes or between nodes and central sites are required because they are in effect concentrator points, and are required to move much more data and therefore need a greater line capacity which is accomplished by speeding up the transmission rate. Remember from Chap. 13 effective throughput at higher speeds must be considered.

The effect on response time must be measured by taking a look at every individual leg over which a message must move and determining the minimum, average, and peak load time transmission rates to determine the overall impact. It is also necessary to take a look at the possible alternate paths which must be taken by either the initial inquiry or the response to determine what potential impacts they will have. Depending on the application, it might be necessary to specifically limit the paths over which long transmissions must be sent, such as batch entries or long reports to be printed out at the terminal.

3. QUANTITY OF PATHS As can be seen in item 2 above, the quantity of possible paths which may be taken between the terminal and the ultimate destination, as well as the return of the response, is critical to response time. The system designer must make intelligent selections with respect to the routing for each application to determine whether it is operationally feasible to send long transmissions over the same paths as shorter transmissions. Remember that the longer the transmission takes on individual legs, the longer the overall response time will be. This will cause an additional load on the routing software because of instead of just looking at an address it must also determine a type of application, and possibly even the length of the message, so that the least amount of time is required to move the transmission from the terminal to the location where it has to be processed and back.

4. QUEUING AT TRANSMISSION NODES Almost all transmission nodes are store-and-forward types of devices. This means an entire message must be brought in and validated before it can be transmitted to the next destination. Because there are many lines and sometimes multiple terminals on the same lines, the possibility of malfunctioning or inoperative equipments or of queues building up at a particular node must be analyzed. The longer these queues build up, the longer time it will take for a particular transmission to leave that node and go to another node. This may have a very significant impact on the response time.

5. QUEUING AT ACCESS SITES Along with the queuing at a transmission node, we also have a situation where queuing at an access site can be encountered. When it comes to the determination of the capacity of a particular central site, one of the biggest areas of uncertainty today is the quantity of data base accesses which can be accommodated per unit time. Many users will put multiple disc drives on the same controller because it is less expensive to do so. This configuration forces a queuing situation to develop for those files which are connected to a particular controller, because only one disc can be accessed at a time (some controllers can read to one and write to another). Instead of a new or different CPU to perform data base accesses, all that may be needed to improve throughput at the data base accessing site is to add some more peripheral controllers in parallel and reconfigure the data base so that more accesses are available per unit time. If the situation is such that data base

accesses must be queued because of the volume of accessing required, the response-time values increase, and the recovery problems which would occur as the result of a failure at the central site are also increased significantly.

6. POINT-TO-POINT VS. MULTIPOINT LINES   We saw in Chaps. 4 and 5 that only one terminal on a line can be transmitting or receiving at a time. Therefore, in the case of a multidrop line, if one terminal is busy, another one cannot be transmitting at the same time. Even with the use of full/full duplex protocols only one terminal can transmit while a different terminal receives. This means that if two terminals have to transmit at the same time, one must wait its turn while the other finishes its transmission or reception. This creates a situation where terminal queuing is an important factor to consider. It is possible that the multiplexing techniques described in Chap. 5 can be used to give each of the locations the capability of point-to-point connections even though single high-speed long distance lines are still used; so the response time analysis must also consider the individual response time requirements at each location, the length of messages to be transmitted, and the possible queuing which would occur during low traffic times, average traffic times, and peak traffic periods.

7. LENGTH OF TRANSMISSION   It is obvious that the length of transmission must be considered in the response time, because even with different transmission rates, the total amount of data must be moved. As the messages get longer over a fixed capacity transmission line (regardless of the speed) the response time must increase. This does not mean that the transmissions should be shortened, since that may be operationally unfeasible to do, but the applications should be investigated to make sure that the transmissions which do occur are the most efficient for that application. Excess data transmission should be avoided at all locations because that excess data will have to be transmitted not only from the terminal to the first node but also on every individual path which it must take to get to the final destination.

8. DIAL-UP CIRCUITS VS. POINT TO POINT   If a system utilizes dial-up circuits, the dial-up time, connection time, and answer of the circuit time (handshaking) must all be included in the response time. These cases are point to point, where the terminal dials the site to be accessed directly (no multiple paths). In this sequence, however, the time it takes to establish the dial-up connection must be included in the response time for at least the response to the first transmission. Once a circuit has been established, subsequent transactions (during

the time the circuit is there) will only require consideration of the other factors described for leased-line circuits.

9. PROPAGATION DELAYS   Propagation in this sense means the propagation of electrical signal, not the data transmission rate. This is only significant when you have very long transmission distances to cover. Most common of these is the satellite situation where absolute minimum round trip times for a single satellite transmission are in the order of 600 milliseconds. In practical situations, for those users who are using satellites today a satellite response time utilizing only a single satellite hop is in the order of 1 to 2 seconds. This is over and above the data transmission rate because regardless of what the data transmission rate is, it still takes the same amount of time for the signal to reach a satellite, be retransmitted to the receiving station where an access is made, and then return via the same path. For those applications where two or three satellite hops are to be accommodated, the system designer must not only look at the propagation delay with its impact on response time, but also the impact on the error-handling procedures which may occur on any leg of the total transmission path. This particular problem is not an easy one to solve and will be discussed further in section F of this chapter.

10. PRIORITY HANDLING   For those systems where there are two or more priority levels, the sequence and time frames for the different priorities must be established so that a projected queuing sequence can be established and the user can be made aware of the probability of queues being delayed due to higher priority messages which must be moved. This priority analysis must be made for transmissions *from* terminals as well as *to* terminals and, in addition, must be reviewed for node-to-node transmission and node-to-central-site transmission.

11. AVERAGE VS. PEAK LOADS   Although we have discussed some of its related impacts on the above items, the case of average and peak loading must also be considered as a separate entity. The reason for this separate consideration is the impact on the design of the system relative to the implementation of point-to-point circuits, multidrop circuits, and multiplexing requirements, because many operational situations have maximum response time requirements even during the peak load situations. The user should be aware, however, that to design a system for peak load handling may be an extremely expensive design because of the excess and unused capacity which will be available during the time that the peak load handling is not required. To alleviate this situation, if possible, it might be more advisable to operationally schedule the workload so that the peaks of the peak load times are not as high in relation to the average load as they

might otherwise be, if other functions which don't really have to be done at the same time could be moved to a different time from when peak loads would otherwise occur.

12. QUALITY OF TRANSMISSION MEDIA   This particular factor is very often ignored. Most users assume that transmission facilities are the same regardless of the locations connected because the telephone company must meet the same basic set of requirements at all locations. This is definitely not true. The basic criteria can be met with different kinds of facilities that have their own inherent error rates as well as different facilities (usually newer vs. older). Even at the same location, the quality of the lines can vary significantly, which in turn means that one of them may exhibit a much higher volume of errors than another. Each individual location and its connection to the local telephone company serving office must be evaluated separately because it is these local loops which usually have the most problems. For those locations where the error rate occurrence is higher, the system designer must include those factors into the response time calculation, because each time a message is transmitted, if there is an error, it must be retransmitted unless there is a forward error correcting code. Here too, the length of the message will have a substantial impact on the response time if it must be retransmitted due to an error.

13. TYPE OF APPLICATION   Some response time calculations will be affected by the particular application which must be processed. In some cases information will have to be obtained from different locations and assembled prior to a response. Other applications will require a certain amount of physical data processing on the information being obtained. For those types of functions, the time for calculation, assembly, etc., must be included in the anticipated response time.

14. SPEED OF OUTPUT DEVICE   This particular factor is only pertinent where a printing type of output device with a limited printing speed is used. If the information to be used starts at the beginning of the print cycle, in most cases, except for teletypes, the response time will not change. But there are other applications where the information to be used is in the middle or at the end of the response message. If the response is printed out on a printer which has a limited print speed (characters per second vs. lines per minute), the total response time consideration may have to include the total time for initial input as well as the print time it takes to get to the area of the response that the operator has requested.

The above factors have the most significant impact on response time, but the user and designer must always be aware of the fact that individual applications and operations may have additional factors which may affect the response time. Any additional time required by the operator, transmission facilities, data processing facilities, etc., between the time the enter key is depressed and the usable information begins to display at the operator's location will increase the response time and must therefore be factored into the response time considerations.

D.

Capacity/Throughput

There are many factors which affect the capacity/throughput of a data communications system. The most obvious one of these is the transmission rate of information on the communication lines between the central and remote sites. This has a further limitation in those configurations where terminals are multidropped on the line because only one remote location on the multidrop line can be transmitting at one time. Therefore, it is not really just the capability/capacity of the terminal controller itself but the quantity of terminal controllers on any one line and the volume of traffic which they will generate.

The second area, which is not as obvious as the first, is the capability of the central site hardware to handle multiple incoming/outgoing communication lines. Regardless of the speed of the lines and the capabilities of the terminals on those lines, if the central site hardware cannot handle the lines simultaneously, the capacity of that particular system is seriously degraded. Most 16-bit word size minicomputers with 64K bytes of memory can handle up to approximately 16 communication lines at 2400 bits per second; but other factors such as communications software design, availability of peripheral storage, availability of buffer areas in main memory, and types of protocol will all have differing effects on the potential capacity of the system. Since there is an extremely wide variety of hardware/software capabilities for different minicomputers, combined with the fact that good quantitative methods are not available to make those projections, this particular section will deal with the capacity and throughput of the primary limitation of transmission capability, that being the potential capacity of a communication line itself.

Describing a communications line in terms of its transmission speed is actually a method of specifying the absolute maximum instantaneous data rate. This speed, however, is not attainable on a continuous basis because of overhead transmission requirements (polls and calls) and errors which cause retransmission of the same information. The real parameter of importance is how many usable characters of information can be transmitted per second.

The term which is usually used to describe the effective rate of information transfer is the TRIB. This stands for *transmission rate of information bits* and is a measure of the effective quantity of true information which is transmitted over a communication line per unit time. The TRIB depends on the various components that make up the communication line. The efficiency of use of those components is also important because there are different modes of utilization which have a different impact on the TRIB in each case. These are such things as the type of protocol and the error detection and correction technique.

In order to calculate the throughput of a particular communication line, we will consider a point-to-point case where a transmission line is terminated with a modem at either end and a data processing type device on the digital side of the modem. A specific formula has been derived by various network designers which will take into account the significant parameters affecting the information-carrying capacity of a communication line. The formula is given below.

$$\text{TRIB} = \frac{B(L - C)(1 - P)}{L/R + T}$$

TRIB is the net quantity of information bits which are effectively transmitted per unit time (in this case, seconds).
B is the number of information bits per character.
L is the total block length in characters.
C is the average number of noninformation characters per block (overhead characters like the SDLC frame characters).
P is the probability of an error occurring in a particular block.
R is the modem transmission speed in characters per second.
T is the time interval between blocks of the transmission in seconds.

This equation has been derived by a number of sources and is applicable to both full-duplex and half-duplex operations for one-way transmissions. For a system which has yet to be designed, this particular equation can be used to calculate an optimum size block length, because on a mathematical basis this equation provides an increasing TRIB as the block length increases until a specific point is reached, at which time the TRIB will begin to decrease as the block length increases. The point at which the TRIB is the maximum is obviously the optimum block size. For purposes of determining the effective throughput on an already existing system, all one has to do is to plug in the different parameters in the equation to determine the effective data throughput on that particular communication line.

For a half-duplex protocol, where each block transmitted is separated by the time it takes for an acknowledge to be received, the T parameter will obviously decrease the effective data throughput significantly. The bisync protocol is a half-duplex protocol and can be measured in this mode. For a full-duplex protocol such as SDLC, the parameter T disappears as long as continuous transmission is taking place. If, over a period of time, occasions arise where the 7-block maximum transmission takes place from one end to the other before an acknowledgment has been received, then some factor for T must be included in the equation (on some form of average basis depending on observed characteristics). The only function which is of a random nature in this equation is P, which is the probability of error. Also, since errors on a communications line occur in bursts, the fact that there are multiple bit errors does not mean that multiple blocks will have to be transmitted. Typically however, using a block length of approximately 400 characters, P for a typical communication line can be assumed to be, for calculation purposes, 0.01. For a full-duplex case we have the calculation here with the following assumptions:

B = 7 information bits per character
L = 400 characters
C = 10 overhead characters per block
P = 0.01
R = 2400 bits per second
T = 0 (this is a full-duplex link where continuous transmissions are occurring in one direction)

Performing this calculation we get the following equation:

$$\text{TRIB} = \frac{7(400 - 10)\,(1 - .01)}{400/300 + 0} = 2027 \text{ bits/sec}$$

As can be seen, the effective throughput at 2400 bits per second, even with continuous transmission, ends up being 2027 bits per second.

One additional factor must be considered here, and that is the case specifically for SDLC. Because SDLC does not retransmit only the error block, but the error block and all subsequent blocks that have been retransmitted, we have a slightly different formula which must be used for SDLC. This formula will take into account the fact that multiple blocks may be retransmitted when an error occurs because of the "Go Back N Technique." The formula to be used is as follows:

$$\text{TRIB}_{\text{SDLC}} = \frac{B(L - C)(1 - NP)}{L/R + T}$$

As can be seen, the formula changes only with the addition of N, which stands for the average number of blocks that must be retransmitted. For typical point-to-point circuits where continuous communication is involved, N has been observed to be in the order of magnitude of 2. Using this factor we can now calculate the effective SDLC throughput using the same parameters as the previous example. This is shown in the following equation.

$$\text{TRIB}_{\text{SDLC}} = \frac{7(400 - 10)(1 - 2 \times .01)}{400/300 + 0} = 2007 \text{ bits/sec}$$

In this case we have an effective throughput of 2007 bits per second. Also for these particular parameters, as N increases, the effective throughput will go down by approximately 20 bits per second for each additional block of information which must be retransmitted. Since N can be a maximum of 7, the effective throughput can be reduced up to 100 bits per second more as long as continuous transmission is maintained (original calculation was for 2 blocks). If such a case arises where 7 blocks are transmitted and there is an additional wait time required before the acknowledgment is received, then the entire equation must be recalculated to further include the T factor.

It should be noted that the calculations shown here are for point-to-point continuous transmissions. In the case of the multidrop lines the probability is substantially increased for more blocks to be retransmitted when an error occurs, because the central site may be transmitting to one remote terminal while receiving from another remote terminal, meaning continuous two-way transmission between the same two points is not taking place. This obviously complicates the calculation and, in fact, must really be analyzed as to observed characteristics as opposed to a quantitative calculation where the parameters can be more easily identified and specified. The other factors which must be considered are the polling and calling, which are required to determine whether individual remote sites have messages to transmit or whether they are in a condition to receive messages. This particular timing sequence, as well as the time frame to answer the polls and calls when there is no information to be transmitted, is a function of software and adds to the time between message blocks. It would have to be determined from measured characteristics as to what the poll/call cycle times are to determine the impact on line capacity.

When the anticipated loading on a line is relatively light and then begins to increase, the calculated capacity can be used to determine when a new line will be needed. It should be noted, however, that the parameter P increases as the transmission rate increases, and if observed characteristics so indicate, it might be advisable to reduce the transmission rate to something like 4800 bits per second, because a lower error rate may actually increase the TRIB. This is quite possible, depending on the quality of the communication lines. In many installations the effective throughput has been demonstrated to be better at 4800 bits per second than at 9600 bits per second because of the difference in error rates encountered.

Another factor, which may possibly override completely the line capacity calculation, is the fact that the traffic load itself may be so low that transmission rate capacity is a negligible parameter. For these cases, there are usually multiple remote terminals connected to the same line, and when this is implemented the response time again increases because of the additional polls which must take place to the other locations on the same line. Also, it is the capability of the minicomputer at the central site, along with its communications software, which contributes to the actually encountered limitation. Because of the overhead functions which must occur on each line for line control and error detection/correction, it is really the capacity of the processing at the minicomputer which contributes to the reduced transmission capability on an overall line basis instead of just an individual bit per second basis on an individual group of lines. What this means to the user is that the transmission speed for the existing lines can actually increase and yet have relatively minor impact on the minicomputer capacity, but if a new line is added, even at a lower transmission rate, its impact may be very significant. Experience has shown that a typical 16-bit word minicomputer with 64K of main memory can in reality only efficiently handle somewhere between 8 and 16 lines, which are operating at 2400 bits per second.

As a general rule, therefore, a user can consider that just about any speed line up to 9600 bits per second can be interfaced to a 16-bit minicomputer with a 64K main memory and have a capability of interfacing somewhere between 8 and 16 of those lines before the throughput will begin to slow down because of the overhead handling and, in turn, reduce the instantaneous capacity where all lines will try to be busy at one time. Why consider only 64K memory? This is the optimum size for memory addressing with a 16-bit word and is the most prevalent design for dedicated communications processes using 16-bit word computers.

E.

Security/Privacy/Encryption

Over the years, the data processing user has been primarily concerned with the integrity of his data. Integrity in this case means the representation of true information and the transmission of information without errors. Many error detection and correction techniques (described in Chap. 10) have been developed and are primarily implemented today to validate the transmission of information over communications lines, as well as to validate the transmission of information between co-located computers and the various component parts of a data processing device (such as in and out of main memory).

Various government and military organizations, however, have also been vitally interested in protecting information from sources who would use the information to the detriment of national interests. More recently though, the same techniques that have been used by government organizations to protect their information from unauthorized users are finding their way into the commercial environment. The subject of data protection from overt access by unauthorized entities is called *security*. There is another related situation where authorized users of a system are not necessarily authorized to access all portions of the information residing within a system. Protection of the individual portions of a file from system users who would otherwise be authorized to access different parts of the information is known as *privacy*. In the real world environment security is sometimes interpreted to mean the prevention of access and privacy to mean the authorization to release information. The techniques which are available to a user can be employed to implement either/or security and privacy. Both can be based on either physical or logical parameters, and the intent of the user determines whether the technique is being used for security or privacy purposes. In order to maintain a correlation between the technique and its effects, each one will be discussed relative to its most often used implementation.

The first set of techniques relate to the physical protection of information and are normally associated with security. Primary among these is the technique of *encryption*. Encryption is a method of modifying information which is being transmitted on a communication line so that an unauthorized entity can physically collect bits being transmitted but will have no way of determining the real meaning of those bits. What is physically accomplished is the modification of a known bit stream by what is in reality a pseudo-random bit stream so that anyone looking at it externally would only see what appears to be a random bit stream. If the authorized receiver knows what the pseudo-random bit stream was to start and at the same time knows where the information bit stream has started, the receiver can apply the inverse of the pseudo-random bit stream to the actual received bit stream, which will then yield the original data back to the user.

A typical diagram of where an encryption type device, called a *crypto,* would go in a circuit is shown in Fig. 16-1. As can be seen in this particular diagram, the transmitter and the receiver are in their normal line configurations, but instead of the RS232 interface being tied directly to the digital side of the modems, the crypto is inserted which then interfaces to the modem. Both sides of the crypto are configured to meet the RS232 interface standard. It is therefore transparent to the user except for the time it takes to synchronize the receive crypto with the transmit crypto.

As far as the information appearing on the communication line, it appears to be a continuous stream of bits with no discernible start and stop of information. Because of this continuous mode of operation (usually synchronous), cryptos are almost entirely used in point-to-point circuits which are leased. Although there are cryptos which can be used on a dial-up circuit, the crypto synchronization which must take place every single time a call is made may allow an unauthorized observer to eventually break the code. For what is considered a casual protection (sometimes used for privacy purposes only), the dial-up type of encryption can be used because it has been determined that the time and expense of breaking the code is usually significant enough to maintain the desired level of protection.

Since all codes can eventually be broken, it is really only a matter of what level of protection the user desires. As a standard, however, there is a mathematical algorithm available in semiconductor chips which is based on a National Bureau of Standards (NBS) specification which uses what is known as the "56-bit algorithm." In simple terms, what this means to the user is that there are 2^{56} possible combinations of codes which are available that can be reset (on a manual basis) any time the user desires. The level of protection is considered more than adequate to protect most commercial grades of data transmissions. The cost for these chips is approximately $300 for a pair (need one at each end), but it is expected that cost will go down as the volume of production increases.

It must be recognized by the user that if it is determined that a form of encryption is needed to protect data transmissions, the effective throughput, even on point-to-point circuits, will be decreased; in

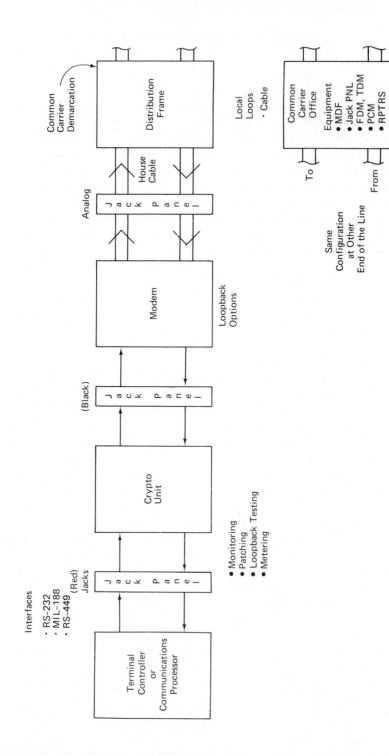

Figure 16-1. CRYPTO Configuration

addition to errors, the cryptos may go "out of sync," which will require retransmission of the data being transmitted as well as resynchronization of the cryptos. For this reason the user must also recognize that the multidrop circuits will suffer from these same disadvantages. Even though all of the receive cryptos at the remote sites can be synchronized to one transmitting crypto, each time a response is required from one of the remotes, the transmitting crypto at the remote site must go through a synchronization sequence to the receiving crypto at the central site prior to any data transmission. This sequence is necessary because all of the transmitting sites will be at a different point in the encryption algorithm sequence so that the central site, after completing the reception of a message from one remote site, must go through a complete synchronization sequence before receiving from another remote site on the same line. If this precludes the utilization of multidrop lines, the user must review the required additional costs for installing multiple lines. This is usually where the requirement differences between security and privacy are significant, because for most user applications, the requirements for privacy are not as severe as those for physical security.

There are other methods of incorporating security type protection techniques for a user and one of these is the scrambling of information when stored on a disc. This scrambling, provided by software or firmware, generates information modifications so that it is in fact encrypted. Only an authorized user who goes through the appropriate access screens, meeting all the intended requirements, will be able to retrieve the data correctly after being decoded by the decryption algorithm. Any other user, even if he obtained the physical bits of information, would still not be able to determine the true information stored on the disc. This particular technique is used primarily in those applications where there are multiple users of the same system and only specified users authorized to access specific levels of information. If one of the other users should inadvertently access the physical storage locations on the discs, then he would not be able to determine what the information really meant.

Another method of maintaining physical security is the implementation of a private communication facility. By doing so, a user will be able to protect more adequately the physical components over which information is being transmitted, whereas over a public communication network the same level of physical security cannot be maintained. In conjunction with the private communications facilities, the user can also limit access to his entire physical facility, which will protect data, and as a second level of protection, limit access to the computer room or library where the sensitive information is being stored. These types of protection are used when data is considered to be in physical jeopardy (intruders, saboteurs, terrorists, etc.) or when otherwise authorized users have to be segregated physically from nonauthorized users who share the same physical facilities.

One other method of maintaining security, which may or may not be implemented on a data processing system, is the establishment and maintenance of a classification system, where physical access to the information is not permitted unless the potential accessor has appropriate physical authorization. In the case of documentation this may be a specific clearance level identified by such items as a badge or special document, while on a data processing system this may be via the use of specific code words or use of specially pre-identified terminals.

When the subject of privacy is discussed in today's environment, a situation exists which transcends the implications relative to just a data processing system. The federal government, as well as each individual state and most foreign countries, has passed laws which very significantly curtail the potential users to which information regarding personal facts can be disseminated. These laws vary from location to location and therefore make it extremely hard for a potential user to determine when he is in violation of the laws. There is even a significant level of concern today that if information just passes through a particular geographic location, it will be subject to the laws of that location even if it is not generated or used at that location. The situation gets even more hazy as a result of the continuing changes of those laws and regulations.

The long-term potential impact of this situation is one which will apparently involve all those who are using and transmitting personal information. The right-of-privacy laws were designed to protect individuals in the dissemination of information to people or organizations which have been determined not to have a legitimate right to look at that data, and it is the question of these legitimate rights which are in the state of most turmoil. It would appear in the present environment that the tendency would be toward more strict regulation with more limited access, as opposed to a loosening of the restrictions. For this reason the use of protective techniques such as encryption are used to inhibit external access to information, while internal logical methods are used to inhibit access to users with a predetermined level of authorization.

The logical methods of maintaining privacy in a particular system are predominantly based on the access limitations of a data processing system. These access limitations are items such as passwords, access keys, organization and user ID, terminal ID, and operator-entered authorization codes. The key item to consider here is that almost all of the necessary authorization coding must be contained in the format of the inquiry being made into the data base. As was discussed in Chap. 8, the format can be used extensively to identify who is trying to access a particular item of data as well as identify where the access is being made from. Even if unauthorized users can obtain the appropriate authorization codes for operator entry illegally or inadvertently, they can be forced to make to accesses from physical terminals which can be kept under total visual surveillance. This can also be considered a level of physical security, but as was stated earlier in this section, it is the combination of physical and logical techniques which implement the techniques of both security ad privacy.

F.

Satellite Considerations

One of the most significant technology advances which is now available to most network users is the capability for transmitting information via satellites. The satellites which are being used are known as *Geosynchronous Satellites*. The name implies that the satellite always maintains the same relative position over the face of the earth; in other words, it appears to the user to be always in exactly the same position when the user is looking at it. The orbits for these satellites are approximately 22,300 miles above the earth's surface, which is the optimum distance for orbiting dynamics. Many different organizations have put communications satellites in orbit including AT&T, Western Union, Comsat, RCA, and shortly SBS (Satellite Business Systems), which is jointly owned by IBM, Aetna Insurance, and Comsat.

The advantages of satellite communications are primarily the reduced probability of errors in transmission because of the characteristics of the communication path and the very high volume of communications activity that can take place in a relatively narrow frequency band. The disadvantages in the meantime are the propagation delay time, the fact that in the event of a failure it is not very easy to fix, and the substantial initial cost of placing a satellite in orbit. For these reasons only the larger communications-oriented organizations can afford to launch a satellite because they can sell the services provided by that satellite to many other users.

A schematic representation of the satellite system configuration is shown in Fig. 16-2 where we see two ground station antennas which are communicating from different geographic locations to the satellite. The satellite acts as a relay on a direct path to move information from one ground location to another. Typically the mode of communication to and from the satellite is in the microwave range and at a speed of 50,000 bits per second or more. Users may be capable of using satellites at a lower rate, because the satellite

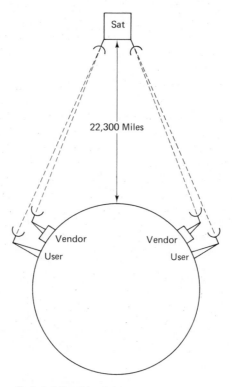

Technical Considerations

Total volume of data to be transmitted
Peak system loading
Block size for optimum throughput
Propagation delays
Type of protocol to be used
Speed of transmission link
Costs of dedicated link vs. costs of vendor service
Compatibility of user system to vendor offerings
Ease of expansion to multiple locations

Figure 16-2.   Satellite Considerations

manager can take multiple low-speed users and multiplex them into the higher range for efficient satellite transmission.

As the satellite capability expands and more and more satellite channels become available, the capability will exist for individual users to have dedicated channels for their own private use. This appears to be one of the primary objectives of the SBS satellite which is presently scheduled for launching in the latter part of 1980. A user will be able to install his own ground station antenna on the roof of his buildings at different ground locations and lease a dedicated link to the SBS satellite from each of the ground stations on a monthly basis. In that kind of environment the user can transmit any type of information he wants between his connected locations up to the full capacity of the channel.

For those applications which are becoming more and more data communications oriented such as the "office of the future," facsimile, closed circuit TV, electronic mail, etc., the feasibility for implementing a dedicated link becomes more and more attractive, especially to the larger users.

Once a user is large enough to afford a dedicated satellite link there is really only one disadvantage to the utilization of that link (assuming the cost can be justified). The disadvantage is the propagation delay which is inherent in the movement of information from the ground to the satellite and back to the ground. With a height of 22,300 miles it takes approximately ⅛ of a second for an electromagnetic transmission to reach the satellite and another ⅛ of a second to come back to earth. The processing time between the ground stations and the satellite adds approximately another 50 milliseconds to a one-way link, giving approximately a 300 ms time delay from transmission to reception. For those applications where a response is required there is at least another 300 ms required for the response to come back from the receiver to the transmitter. This means an absolute minimum time of 600 ms round trip. In actuality satellite users are experiencing somewhere between one and two second response times for acknowledgments to individual transmissions.

This type of delay means that for typical 50,000 bit per second transmissions, there must be adequate buffering at both the transmit and the receive end to accommodate not only a single round trip delay time but adequate buffering for the total amount of retransmissions allowed before transmission of new information will cease. If the allowable amount of retransmissions of an error block is 3 for example, and there is just a single satellite link, the user is talking about storage for a minimum of 150,000 bits for each link. The problem is compounded even further when you get into multiple satellite hops such as would occur on international communications. If end-to-end communications are required, the propagation delay must be factored in and a decision made as to whether to transmit end to end or use store-and-forward techniques will be employed every time the message comes back to the ground to reduce the total amount of buffering required at each end. One possible alternative to the end-to-end link, however, is the connection to a packet-switching network, where the virtual circuit will take over and handle all of the error detection and correction for the user. (The packet network may use satellites too so response times must be considered.) What we are talking about primarily here is the satellite link for a dedicated in-house system where a single user must accommodate the propagation delays inherent in that satellite transmission.

One of the interesting factors in the satellite situation is the inherent limitation of SDLC which was described in Chap. 7. SDLC, as was shown, is limited to transmitting 7 blocks of information before the transmitter must stop and wait for the acknowledgment of at least 1 block of information. On a satellite link where there is a 1-second response, we have the possibility for 50,000 bits to be in transit before an acknowledgment can be received. If the average length of the SDLC block is less than approximately 7,000 bits (a little over 750 characters), then the user is faced with actually operating in a half-duplex mode on what is really a full-duplex communications link. This is because the propagation delay exceeds the capacity of the bits contained in the blocks being transmitted (7000 bits $\times$ 7 blocks = 49,000 bits). Due to this potential limitation IBM will probably either come out with a modification to SDLC or a brand new protocol when SBS is finally launched. This does not mean, however, that SDLC is not a good protocol for satellite communications. For many users, transmission at lower rates is still required, and the propagation delay will have much less of an impact. SBS in the meantime can take the lower transmission rates coming in from different users and multiplex them up to the minimum 50,000 bit per second transmission rates. It is also interesting to note here that starting in 1978 the consent decree which IBM signed back in 1968 to exit from the service bureau environment expires, and IBM can start to establish some kind of service bureau operation. If actually established, these service bureaus can be used as concentration points for low-speed users, as IBM will probably have their own dedicated antennas and channels which IBM can then use in a common carrier mode. This creates the situation where IBM and AT&T will be competitors for large segments of the communications traffic of the future.

From the user's point, this means that serious consideration must be given to the alternatives of data transmission in the future, especially where there are very heavy volumes of data to be transmitted. In all likelihood the capacity on land facilities will not be able to handle the higher volumes except at a significant cost increase. The alternatives will be between dedicated satellite transmissions and packet networks where the charges are based on volumes. If the user establishes standards today which can be adapted to the packet mode of operations, it appears that the interfaces to the satellites will also be compatible with those protocols, and the potential user can either go on a public network or his own private network utilizing the satellite capabilities.

To give just a rough idea of the costs which may be involved the present estimates are for approximately $100,000 each one time cost for ground stations and approximately $20,000 per month for a 50,000 bit per second dedicated path.

Another potential alternative will be the XTEN service from Xerox which will provide for dedicated user facilities on the ground (antennas), but Xerox will provide ground concentration points in at least 100 cities from which they will lease one of the carrier's satellite links (or multiples). This appears to be the same mode of operation as using service bureaus from IBM, but the difference is that XTEN will use microwave from the user to Xerox, while IBM seems to be relying on local-loop telephone company connections to get to and from the user.

G.

Central Site Hardware Configurations

When considering the various alternatives of system configurations, it is necessary to evaluate the alternatives for the hardware at the central sites. The most common user configuration implemented today is shown in Fig. 16-3, where we have a large mainframe and a communications front-end computer which is responsible for handling all of the external communication line interfaces. This particular configuration is continually evolving, especially with respect to the front-end processing capability. The communications front end is no

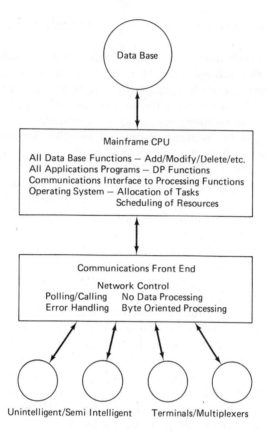

Figure 16-3. Mainframe and Communications Front End

longer just a communications line interface, but also performs processing, searching, and even transaction handling so that those functions no longer have to be performed in the large mainframe. This is
typical of what is known as the *two-machine configuration,* or
Transaction Processor and Applications/Data Base Processor.

With the growth of the stand-alone and independent software
packages for communications handling which are resident in the
transaction processor, there has also been a growth of stand-alone,
independent data base management system packages (DBMS), where
such third party data base software packages such as Total and IDMS
are also being incorporated into machines in a stand-alone environment. This means the communications function resides in one
machine, the data base management system resides in a second
machine, and the specific applications to be performed at that site are

resident in a third machine. This configuration is shown in Fig. 16-4 and is known as the *three-machine configuration,* the *front end/back end configuration,* or the *front door/back door configuration.*

As both the two-machine and the three-machine configurations proliferated in the user environment, especially with minicomputers, it was necessary to develop a new method of tying the CPUs together in a local environment, because the minicomputer is not able to perform the same magnitude of jobs as a big mainframe and also cannot do those jobs at the same speed either. What the minicomputers can do, however, is to take the different jobs that exist on a large mainframe, have them split into smaller or separate jobs, and perform those functions on separate machines. It is then necessary to tie all of the machines together so that specific applications can transfer

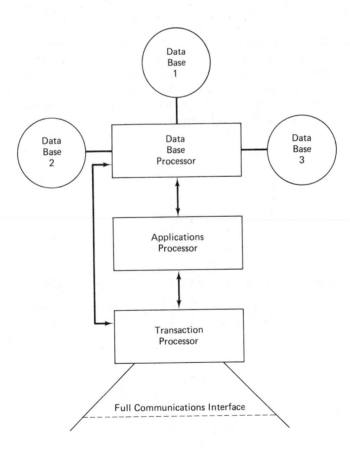

Figure 16-4.   Three-Machine Configuration

information to each other as well as access different data bases which reside on different CPUs.

After going through quite a few different methods of interconnection, it appears that the most common form of minicomputers communicating with each other in a local environment is via a *buss*. The buss is designed so that the CPUs can communicate with each other through a specific buss interface at rates which exceed 1 million bits per second. The buss can be a serial interface which would be handled as if it were a standard communications type interface, in other words with a specific protocol.

A standard communications protocol such as SDLC can be utilized on this link just as if it was a standard communication line, with the rate of transmission the only thing being different. One possible configuration is given in Fig. 16-5, which shows multiple two-machine sets tied together via a buss which connects all of the transaction processors together. Transaction processors each communicate with the terminals in the remote environment and also communicate with other transaction processors which are connected to other applications and data bases. The very same type of buss configuration can be implemented for the three-machine configuration where only the transaction processors will be connected to each other. The reason for tying only the transaction processors together is

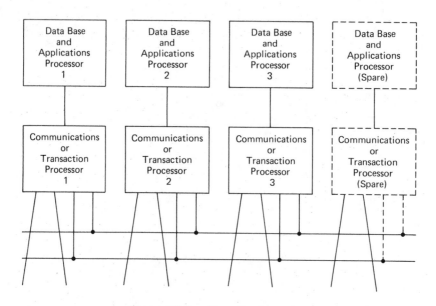

Figure 16-5.   Buss Configuration

that they must perform all of the standard communications and routing functions anyway. To put the same kinds of functions in an applications or data-base-oriented machine would mean a memory and software overhead which would result in less efficient utilization of that minicomputer. Because most 16-bit word minis can handle up to 16 external communication lines, in most networks there will be more than one transaction processor in addition to multiple computers for the other dedicated functions, and it is not necessary to have a symmetric machine configuration as shown. There can be any amount of each of the types of machines as long as the interfaces between the machines are exactly the same and the system is *message oriented*. Message oriented means that each message transmitted throughout the system has enough information to identify it as to where it's going, where it came from, what is being done with it, its priority, and all other functions which allow the CPU in which it resides to determine the full process which must be performed on it.

As was described in Chap. 15 under Distributed Applications, what we really see here is a form of functional distribution. It is quite possible for this type of configuration to exist at multiple central sites where different applications can be performed. It would also appear that this mode of configuration, multiple minicomputers tied together via a buss arrangement through their transaction processors, is the way most vendors are configuring their central sites today.

QUESTIONS

1. What is the primary trade-off when evaluating centralized vs. decentralized processing? What are some of the secondary parameters?

2. Describe five significant criteria which must be included when establishing a set of communication system design requirements.

3. Define response time. Describe some of the factors which affect response time.

4. What are some of the factors which affect the capacity and throughput of a communication system?

5. Describe the process of encryption. Draw a diagram showing where a crypto is configured in a circuit.

6. What are the advantages and disadvantages involved in satellite communications?

7. Draw a diagram of a functionally separated CPU processing configuration and describe the functions of each of the CPUs.

chapter

17

SYSTEM IMPLEMENTATION AND SUPPORT

When implementing a data communications system there are certain functions which, although they may appear to be peripheral in nature, have a very strong bearing on the successful operation of the system. They involve such functions as documentation, standards, procedures, personnel, and vendor interfacing. Without the appropriate documentation for personnel to refer to, a communications system is destined to be down for much longer periods of time than is necessary. The establishment of standards both for procurement and operational interfaces is mandatory for an orderly growth and/or expansion of the system. At the same time, a definitive and detailed set of procedures is necessary for maintaining and operating the equipment. In order to do this, the appropriate personnel must be hired and trained so that they are aware of the operational considerations, not only for the communications system but also for the user's applications. Last but not least of these is the vendor-support interface requirements, which must be established and maintained early in the implementation sequence. Many problems can only be resolved with the vendor's help, and if an appropriate path is not established early, the system will again be down for longer periods than necessary.

A.

Documentation

The one primary area where most system implementors fail in their responsibility is the generation and maintenance of appropriate documentation. No design can take place unless the requirements are specified and all of the design personnel know what they are. This can only be done by documenting the requirements and making the documentation available to designers. During the design phase all changes, additions, and deletions must be integrated into the documentation as they occur, or else different designers will be designing to different requirements. As new requirements and specifications are established, they too must be documented so that there is a continuous record of what is happening in the development of the system, and all designers must be made aware of those changes. It is an outright fallacy, as is proven by the experience of almost all designers, to believe that changes to existing documentation can be assembled externally to the document and upgraded at a later time. As a practical fact this almost always never gets done, and during the interim different people will have different versions of what is supposed to be the same document.

In many cases it is advisable to establish a separate internal organization which has the sole responsibility for maintenance and upkeep of the system documentation. No document can be considered correct unless that document matches what is in the central source or library. Individuals assigned the responsibility to make sure that the documentation is updated must make sure that the changes are continually fed into the central library, because the central library will provide copies of that documentation to other users continuously. The central library can be just a bookcase, but some centralized location must be established as the master document location.

A very significant problem which usually arises with documentation is the actual implementation of changes. There can only be one person or one specific group authorized to change the documentation. Whatever review cycles are used, there must be a signoff of changes to the basic documentation. Even though there may be what appear to be desirable changes, they must be incorporated through the appropriate change control organization so that an accurate record of how many changes and what they are can be maintained. As a general rule along these lines, it is usually grossly inefficient to add or change requirements during the design phase unless there is an outright error in the original design. The reason for this is that the implementation and integration of the changes means that the original design will be delayed and, in most cases, means that the acceptance criteria will be changing at the same time. The best procedure to use in this case is to keep the potential changes in a separate "to be implemented" list, and only after the basic system is operational, should the changes be implemented. A side advantage of this mode is that in most cases the changes themselves can be combined so that the total amount of effort involved in installing them is actually less than it would have been if they were done one at a time. This results from the fact that many of them may affect the same areas of both hardware and software design.

At the top of the list of some of the basic documentation which is required must be the *Functional Specifications*. The functional specifications defined from a user level point of view is what the system is supposed to be doing when it is operational. A separate subset of specifications is needed for the communications network, applications processing, data base, and software for both on-line and off-line functions.

The next level of specification is the hardware design specification which defines the design criteria for each of the individual pieces of hardware which will go into the system—devices such as the CPU, controllers, modems, tech control, test equipment, communications media, power sources, peripherals, recovery hardware, cabling, etc. Each one of these specifications must be defined so that it meets the overall functional specifications. Also each must be validated so that it is compatible with the other hardware items being specified.

The third level of system documentation is the system design specification for both hardware and software. These specifications establish the detail design specifications for implementing the functions defined under functional specifications, and include such items as the I/O system, restart/recovery, formats, forms control, protocols, statistics gathering, editing requirements, routing, file management, system start/load, the transaction processing subsystem, the data base management subsystem, the file management organization, the details of the applications, and the support software. Also included within the system design specifications are the hardware/software interfaces such as the controllers, communication line interfaces, peripheral interfaces, and the network connectivity requirements.

The next level of documentation involves the facilities specifications which includes such functions as power distribution, cable ducting, environmental controls, floor loading, fire/smoke detection, security access, storage, libraries, and the repair/maintenance criteria. These specific layouts must also include appropriate locations for personnel to provide the necessary operation and maintenance function for the system.

Included also within the documentation requirements are the system operational and maintenance specifications. These documents describe the requirements for operating the system and the levels of operational capability which must be maintained. Such functions as MTBF (Mean Time Between Failure), MTTR (Mean Time to Repair), and UTR (Up Time Ratio) are just some of the parameters which can be specified in these documents.

Any other document which specifies the requirements for a particular application or activity must be defined in a specification for that function. Without a clear, concise, and comprehensive set of specifications the actual system design activity may be completed with either errors or absence of required functions. It is up to the system designer to determine that all of the basic requirements called out in the functional specifications are truly included in both the hardware and system design specification.

B.

Procedures

Along with the specification documentation there is another set of documents which is every bit as important. These are the procedures which are required to physically implement the applications once the system has been designed and is operational. Primary among these are the *operating procedures* which describe in extreme detail the step-by-step sequences of operations which must be performed by the operators to accomplish each one of the specific individual applications which are inherent in the system. Operational procedures are designed for describing the way the system should run if it was running correctly. If there are errors or malfunctions in the system a different set of procedures must be implemented, and they are the *error procedures*.

The error procedures are those steps which must be taken in the event the system does not operate in accordance with the operational procedures. They must be exercised first so that alternative operations can be implemented to accomplish the application in the event the backup facilities are available. These error-handling procedures are different from the error detection and diagnostic procedures which are used to isolate and correct problems.

A complete set of diagnostic procedures is necessary for each individual area of the system as well as for the entire system as a whole. Once the overall system procedures for diagnosing a problem have isolated the problem to a specific subsystem, then the individual subsystem procedure can be used to further isolate the specific problem. In the case of a communications network, where the actual facilities being tested may not be in a local environment, it is necessary to have over and above the specific procedures a comprehensive set of test equipment and substitution facilities which will allow for the replacement of potentially defective components (such as modems) with spare units so that quicker isolation of the specific problem can be made.

Another set of procedures which is every bit as important as the operational and maintenance procedures are the change control procedures. Without a specific sequence for the change control process, it will be impossible to have different versions of the same document existing at the same time, and, in addition, there will be cases of personnel being unaware of the changes because they didn't know that somebody else was making them. Part of the requirement for all of the procedures, therefore, is to make sure that when changes are actually issued they be incorporated immediately and identified as to the level and date of the change incorporation.

Although it involves a procedure and a specification, the preventive maintenance (PM) requirements and procedures must be adhered to, not only to ensure that the system components remain within the appropriate warranties, but also to prevent failures which result during normal system operations. Typical PM procedures are applicable to peripherals with mechanical components, but the same thing applies to data processing equipments, especially in the communications area where there can be degradation of components or facilities over a period of time.

C.

Standards

In order to design a system with minimal interfacing problems between the various subsystems such as communications, applications, data base, etc., there must be a set of standards established which provide for a definition of what is supposed to take place when those functions interface with each other. These interface standards include not only the physical interfacing, but also the electrical signal interfacing and the functional interfaces.

There must typically be common hardware standards such as the processors, discs, magnetic tapes, modems, and terminal interfaces, all of which allow the necessary traffic to move from one device to another as well as from one physical location to another. In the software area another set of standards must be established for such functions as file structures, I/O access methods, directory structures, audit control software, security, privacy, recovery, diagnostics, program languages, forms, edits, and software module interfaces.

With respect to the network standards there must be standard code sets, formats, protocols, queuing, and physical electrical level interfaces such as RS232C which allows for the user to interface with external communications equipments. With regard to specific network standards, many of them have been defined all throughout this text for interfaces dealing with such functions as modems/terminals, user interface/packet network, and specific message protocols.

D.

Personnel

Still another area of critical implementation sensitivity is the requirement to have sufficient quantities of trained personnel to operate and maintain the system. Independent of the system users, there are two functions which the operational personnel must perform. These two functions are operations and maintenance. During the times of normal system operation there may be relatively little activity for the personnel to perform, other than to make sure the appropriate operational capabilities exist when a particular application must be accomplished.

It is when the system begins to degrade and/or actually malfunction, that the capability of the operational personnel is most critical. They must be able to isolate, define, and then correct any problems which are degrading the performance of the system. In most organizations, very few people pay much attention to the system operation when all is going well, but when the system is malfunctioning all eyes and pressure are on the applicable maintenance personnel to correct the problem as soon as possible. This is especially evident in those systems where on-line/real-time applications are taking place, because all the time the system is either degraded or nonoperational, operators are nonproductive, and business is most probably being lost.

The best way to ensure that the system is maintained in an operational state is to hire and train experienced personnel. The basic backgrounds must include a familiarity with the function to be performed, and then the using organization can add the necessary local or in-house training which will adapt the capabilities of the individual and his background to the specific requirements of the organization. The key to this function, however, is the availability of both adequate and comprehensive material, as well as competent instructors. It is extremely hard for new personnel, even though they may be experienced in the appropriate basic discipline, to adapt to a new system without training, not only in the specific system components for which they will be responsible, but also in how those components relate to the overall organizational use and application.

The actual education can start either on an in-house basis or externally via classes. Many vendors offer classes to using organizations on either a low cost or minimum cost basis which will train operations personnel in the use of individual pieces of hardware. It is up to the using organization, however, to provide the training as to how those individual hardware and software elements are used to accomplish the actual system applications.

For those personnel where the basic disciplines are known and adequate, the best training is OJT (On the Job Training). The OJT can be augmented by classroom exercises which incorporate use of the individual equipments in the environment in which they are being used.

In addition, overview type course material can be presented either on an in-house or external basis, even for experienced personnel, so that their own particular job functions can be placed in the context of the overall system operation. This type of education can be taken either as a group or on a self-study basis as long as there is adequate material and instructional personnel to answer any questions which may arise. It should be noted, however, that many of the procedures and techniques which are used by experienced personnel have only arisen due to the fact that they have performed the same job at other locations or for a period of time at the present location. It would be extremely desirable to take these specific procedures as they evolve and document them so that future personnel who are hired will have the benefit of the experience of those people who have already developed a system expertise.

As it pertains specifically to the communications environment, the real world situation is such that very few people are available who have the appropriate background and knowledge to maintain a large network. As such, it is very hard to find them and then keep them after they have obtained even more experience. It is therefore necessary to provide the appropriate incentives, both monetary and professional, to keep these personnel in whom a significant investment in time and effort has been made.

One other major function must be discussed when describing the personnel requirements. That is organization. The organization as it refers to a communications network must be set up to function twenty-four hours a day, seven days a week. This is because most environments that use a network are operational twenty-four hours a day, and even though the utilization may not be high during specific time frames, the potential for failure is the same at all times. There must be appropriate shift coverage not only for the standard five-day week but also for the weekends, even if it is on a limited basis, because dedicated communication facilities can degrade or fail at any time. What may alleviate this situation somewhat is the use of automated monitoring and test equipment which will reduce the amount of personnel required for maintenance. In most cases where systems have 16 lines or more, this automated test equipment, even though there may be a high initial cost, will probably pay for itself within a year or two due to the reduced personnel required and the reduced cost involved in isolating and correcting problems over a period of time.

The organization which is responsible for system operation and maintenance must have a clear-cut path of authority for correcting problems within its own environment and also a very specific and clear-cut path for correcting problems in which other organizations are involved. At the same time there must also be a good working relationship with the system users as well as the designers, because many problems can arise which are operational in nature and not due to the failure or malfunction of any specific piece of hardware or software. Appropriate chains of commands must be established so that they are clear and known to all operating personnel and it is also necessary to identify the contact personnel in other using organizations, so that if specific line managers are not available, for whatever reason, then the necessary coordination for correction of interdisciplinary problems can continue. Naturally, specific procedures must be written and adhered to for correction of those problems which affect other organizations, especially where there is the possibility for either degradation or absence of service for a period of time.

E.

Vendor Interfacing

Last but not least in the system implementation and support area is the interface requirement for dealing with vendors. These vendors include both hardware, software, network, and system types who are providing either a product or a service to the using organization. It is mandatory to establish the appropriate communication links between the various vendors and using organizations, and depending on the specific implementation, it may also be necessary to establish communication links between some of the vendors directly. It is a very common occurrence to have a situation where the user is experiencing some problems for which a vendor does not want to take responsibility, whether for technical or financial reasons. It is therefore necessary to have a very good in-house understanding of the vendor's product or service so that a strong case can be made for identifying that particular vendor as the cause of the problem. It is also very common to have situations arise where a particular problem is the fault of more than one vendor, and in some instances the user may be a part of the problem. Here too it is mandatory to have a good understanding of the overall system utilization so that the appropriate vendors can be identified to fix problems which arise.

If there are problems in which there are multiple vendors potentially involved, a procedure must be established whereby all of the involved vendors can be brought together at the same time to try and solve the problem. It does no good to have one vendor at a time try and solve the problem, because he will take no responsibility for the other vendor's product or service, and therefore the problem may still exist even though the one vendor has done all he can do for his own product. At these sessions the user must also have a qualified representative in order to make any necessary interface type decisions, because all during the time the vendors are discussing the problem, the user is the one who has the degraded or nonexistent operational capability.

As an additional level of management control, the necessary communication paths to the various levels of vendor management organizations must also be established, because it is another common occurrence to have maintenance personnel who do not have the authority to make changes involving either time or money. Many times problems must be solved by the addition of new facilities, extra modification to existing facilities, new software, additional time utilization, etc., where the vendor site personnel do not have the authority to permit such action. If critical problems arise where significant user impact could be involved, then it is necessary to have immediate access to the appropriate vendor management levels so that at least interim authorization can be obtained to permit resumption of user system operation. It should also be recognized that all applicable documentation generated by the vendor due to changes which arise as a result of the maintenance activity must be made available to both the vendor's site personnel and/or the user personnel, so in the future the same problem can be corrected more quickly.

QUESTIONS

1. Describe at least four levels of documentation required to support a communication system and identify the biggest problem facing the maintenance of those documents.
2. Describe four types of procedures required to effectively implement a communications system.
3. Describe four types of standards involved in communication networks.
4. Describe three methods for providing training to communications personnel.
5. Describe a method which can be implemented which will reduce vendor interfacing problems to a minimum.

GLOSSARY OF TERMS

ACD   Automatic Call Distributor   A switching system which automatically distributes incoming calls in the sequences they are received to a centralized group of receivers without human interface. If no receivers are available the calls will be held until one becomes free.

Acoustic coupler   A type of modem that permits use of a telephone handset as a connection to the public telephone network for data transmission, by means of sound transducers.

AC Signaling   The use of alternating current signals or tones to accomplish transmission of information and/or control signals.

ACU   Automatic Calling Unit   A device which places a telephone call automatically upon receipt of information from a data processing type machine.

Adapter   (Data Set Adapter, DSA) The hardware unit which performs line control functions to a modem.

ADCCP   Advanced Data Communications Control Protocol   A communications protocol endorsed by the American National Standards Institute.

Algorithm   A prescribed set of well-defined rules or processes for arriving at a solution to a problem. A mathematical process.

Alphanumeric   Made up of letters (alphabetic) and numbers (numeric).

Alternate route   A secondary communications path used to reach a destination if the primary path is unavailable.

AM Amplitude Modulation   Transmission of information on a communictions line by varying the voltage level or amplitude.

Ambient noise   Communications interference which is present in a communications line at all times.

Amplifier   A unidirectional device which increases the power or amplitude of an electrical signal.

Amplitude variation   (Ripple) Unwanted variation of signal voltage at different frequencies on a communications line.

Analog signal   A signal which changes in a nondiscrete manner (smooth transitioning to different levels).

Answer back   A transmission from a receiving data processing device in response to a request from a transmitting data processing device that it is ready to accept or has received data.

Application program   The computer program that performs a data processing rather than a control function.

ARQ   Automatic Retransmission Request   An error detection and correction technique which attempts a retry when an error is detected.

ASCII   American Standard Code for Information Interchange   A data communications code set.

ASR   Automatic send-receive.

Asynchronous   Not synchronized by a clocking signal. In code sets, character codes containing start and stop bits.

ATC   Automated Technical Control   A computer system used to maintain operational control of a data communications network.

Attenuation   Loss of communication signal energy.

Automatic dialer   A device which will automatically dial telephone numbers on the network. Operation of the dialer may be manual or automatic.

AWG   American Wire Gauge   Wire-size standard used in communications line media descriptions.

Backup   The hardware and software resources available to recover after a degradation or failure of one or more system components.

Balanced circuit   A circuit terminated by a network whose impedance balances the impedance of the line so that the return losses
are negligible.

Balancing network   Electronic circuitry used to match two-wire
facilities to four-wire toll facilities. This balancing is necessary to
maximize power transfer and minimize echo. Sometimes called a
hybrid.

Bandwidth   The information-carrying capability of a communications channel or line.

Baseband   The frequency band occupied by information-bearing signals before they are combined with a carrier in the modulation
process.

Base group   Twelve communications paths capable of carrying the
human voice on a telephone set. A unit of frequency division
multiplexing systems bandwidth allocation.

Baudot   A five-level code set named for the early French telegrapher
who invented it. International Telegraph Alphabet (ITA) # 2 is
the formal name.

Baud   Data communication rate unit taken from the name Baudot
and used similarly to bits per second (bps) for low-speed data.
Defined as the number of signal level changes per second regardless of information content of those signals.

BCH   An error detecting and correcting technique used at the communications receiver to correct errors as opposed to retry attempts as in ARQ. Named for Messrs. Bose, Chaudhuri, and
Hocquengham who developed it.

Beam   Another name for microwave radio systems which use ultra/
super high frequencies (UHF, SHF) to carry communications,
where the signal is a narrow beam rather than a broadcast signal.

BERT   *Bit Error Rate Testing*   Testing a data line with a pattern of
bits which are compared before and after the transmission to
detect errors.

Bias   Communications signal distortion with respect to bit timing.

Bit   Binary digit contraction. The smallest unit of data communications information, used to develop code representations of
characters.

Bit rate   (See bps) The rate at which bits (binary digits) are transmitted over a communications path. Normally expressed in bits per
second (bps). The bit rate is not to be confused with the data
signaling rate (Baud) which measures the rate of signal changes
being transmitted.

Bit stream   Refers to a continuous series of bits being transmitted on a transmission line.

BLERT   Block Error Rate Testing   Testing a data line with groups of information arranged into transmission blocks for error checking.

Blank   A condition of "no information" in a data recording medium or storage location. This can be represented by all spaces or all zeroes depending on the medium.

Block   Some set of contiguous bits and/or bytes which make up a definable quantity of information.

Blocking   A condition in a switching system in which no paths or circuits are available to complete a call and a busy tone is returned to the calling party. In this situation there is no alternative but to hang up and try the call again. Also referred to as denial or busy condition.

Block multiplexer channel   A computer peripheral multiplexer channel that interleaves blocks of data. See also byte multiplexer channel. Contrast with selector channel.

bps   Bits per second   The basic unit of data communications rate measurement. Usually refers to rate of information bits transmitted.

Break   A signal used to "break in" when the opposite party/unit is sending. A feature of dial, point-to-point teletypewriter systems operating in half duplex.

Bridge   Equipment and techniques used to match circuits to each other ensuring minimum transmission impairment. Bridging is normally required on multipoint data channels where several local loops or channels are interconnected.

Broadband   Refers to transmission facilities whose bandwidth (range of frequencies they will handle) is greater than that available on voice grade facilities. Also called wideband.

Broadcast   The ability to send messages or communicate with many or all points on a circuit simultaneously.

BSC   Bisynchronous   An IBM developed data link control procedure using character synchronization.

Buffer   A storage area for a block of data.

Burst   A group of events occurring together in time.

Burst error   A series of consecutive errors in data transmission. Refers to the phenomenon on communication lines that errors are highly prone to occurring in groups or clusters.

Buss A single connective link between multiple processing sites (co-located only) where any of the processing sites can transmit to any other, but only one way at a time.

Byte Some set of contiguous bits which make up a discrete item of information. Most common bytes are 6 or 8 bits long.

Byte multiplexer channel Multiplexer channel which interleaves bytes of data from different sources. Contrast with selector channel.

Cache memory A high-speed computer memory which contains the next most likely instruction or sequence of instructions to be executed upon completion of the present instruction.

Call setup time The overall length of time required to establish a switched call between pieces of data terminal equipment.

Carrier An analog signal at some fixed amplitude and frequency which is then combined with an information-bearing signal in the modulation process to produce an output signal suitable for transmission.

Carrier system A method of obtaining or deriving several channels from one communication path by combining them at the originating end, transmitting a wideband or high-speed signal, and then recovering the original information at the receiving end.

CCITT Consultive Committee for International Telephone and Telegraph An international standards group.

Centrex A type of private branch exchange service where incoming calls may be dialed direct to extensions without operator assistance. Out-going and intercom calls are dialed by extension users.

CERT Character Error Rate Testing Testing a data line with test characters to determine error performance.

Chain A series of processing locations where information must pass through each location on a store-and-forward basis in order to get to a subsequent location.

Channel A data communications path.

Channel bank Communication equipment performing the operation of multiplexing. Typically used for multiplexing voice grade channels.

Character A language unit composed of a group of bits.

Character parity A technique of adding an overhead bit to a character code to provide error-checking capability.

Circuit switching A method of communications where an electrical connection between calling and called stations is established on demand for exclusive use of the circuit until the connection is released.

Clocking Time synchronizing of communications information.

Cluster A group of user terminals co-located and connected to a single controller through which each terminal is afforded the opportunity to access a single communication line.

Coaxial cable Two-conductor wire whose longitudinal axes are co-incident. Cable with a shield against noise around a signal-carrying conductor.

Common communications carrier A company whose facilities are available to the public and which are subject to public utility regulations.

Common mode The high-speed modem interface name.

Communications line controller A hardware unit that performs line control functions with the modem.

Compandor A device used on some telephone channels to improve transmission performance. The equipment compresses the outgoing speech volume range and expands the incoming speech volume range on a long distance telephone circuit.

Concentrator An electronic device which interfaces in a store-and-forward mode with multiple low-speed communication lines at a message level and then retransmits those messages via one or more high-speed communications lines to a processing site.

Conditioning A technique of applying electronic filtering elements to a communications line to improve the capability of that line to support higher transmission rates of data on that line. (See equalization.)

Connecting block A cable termination block where access to circuit connections is available.

Contention Competition by users for the use of the same communications facilities; a method of line control in which terminals request or bid to transmit. If the channel is not free, the terminals must wait until the channel is free.

Control console A computer device used for human control of system operation.

Control line timing Clock signals between a modem and communications line controller unit.

cps Characters per second A data rate unit used where circuits carry bits forming a data character.

CPU Central Processing Unit The computer control logic used to execute the programs.

CRC Cyclic Redundancy Check An error-checking control technique utilizing a specifically binary prime devisor which results in a unique remainder.

Crossbar A type of common control switching system using the crossbar or coordinate switch. Crossbar-switching systems are ideally suited to data switching due to their low-noise characteristics and can be equipped for Touch-Tone dialing.

CTS Clear to Send A control line between a modem and a controller used to operate over a communications line.

Cursor A lit area on an electronic display screen used to indicate the next character location to be accessed.

CXR Carrier A communications signal used to indicate the intention to transmit data on a line.

DAA Data Access Arrangement A telephone-switching system protective device used to attach non-telephone-company-manufactured equipment to the carrier network.

Data base A collection of electronically stored data records.

Data compression The technique which provides for the transmission of fewer data bits without the loss of information. The receiving location expands the received data bits into the original bit sequence.

Datagram A user capability in a packet network in which a complete message can be contained in the data field of a single packet and is delivered to the destination identified in its address field.

Data switcher A system used to connect network lines to a specific data processing computer port.

Data set (Modem) An electronic terminating unit for analog lines which is used for data signal modulation and demodulation.

dB Decibel Power level measurement unit.

dBm Power level measurement unit in the telephone industry based on 600 ohms impedence and 1000 hertz frequency. 0 dBm is 1 milliwatt at 1000 Hz terminated by 600 ohms impedence.

DCE Data Communication Equipment The equipment installed at the user's premises which provides all the functions required to establish, maintain and terminate a connection, the signal conversion and coding between the data terminal equipment and the common carrier's line, e.g., data set, modem.

DDCMP Digital Data Communications Message Protocol A DEC data communications line protocol.

DDD Direct Distance Dial The North American Telephone dial system.

Dedicated line A communications line which is not dialed. Also called a leased line or private line.

Delay distortion A distortion which occurs on communication lines due to the different propagation speeds of signals at different frequencies. Some frequencies travel slower than others in a given transmission medium and therefore arrive at the destination at slightly different times. Delay distortion is measured in microseconds of delay relative to the delay at 1700 Hz. This type of distortion does not affect voice but can have a serious effect on data transmissions.

Demodulator A functional section of a modem which converts the received analog line signals back to digital form.

Dial line A communications line which is dialed.

Dial up The use of a rotary dial or Touch-Tone telephone to initiate a station-to-station telephone call.

Digital A two discrete state signal.

Distortion The unwanted modification or change of signals from their true form by some characteristic of the communication line or equipment being used for transmission, e.g., delay distortion, amplitude distortion.

DMA Direct memory access from I/O and peripheral controllers without going through the arithmetic processing unit.

DQM Data Quality Monitor A device used to measure data bias distortion above or below a threshold.

DTE Data Termination Equipment Equipment comprising the data source, the data sink, or both that provides for the communication control function (protocol). Data termination equipment is actually any piece of equipment at which a communications path begins or ends.

EBCD Extended Binary Coded Decimal A code set with the numeric characters arranged in order with the code representation equal to the number value.

EBCDIC EBCD Interchange Code An eight level code set used frequently on communications lines with IBM terminals and computer systems.

Echo distortion A telephone line impairment caused by electrical reflections at distant points where line impedances are dissimilar.

EIA RS-232 Electronic Industries Association The standard interface between a modem and line controller for voice grade communications lines.

Electronic Switching System   ESS   A type of telephone switching system which uses a special-purpose stored program digital computer to direct and control the switching operation. ESS permits the provision of custom calling services such as speed dialing, call transfer, three-way calling, etc.

Emulation   The act of imitating or performing as if a device or program were something else.

Encryption   The technique of modifying a known bit stream on a transmission line so that it appears to be a random sequence of bits to an unauthorized observer.

End office   The first telephone office that a data line is connected to over the local loop or access line. The end switching office for a dialed connection.

Envelope delay   An analog line impairment where a variation of signal delay with frequency occurs across the data channel bandwidth. (See delay distortion.)

Equalization   A technique used to compensate for distortions present on a communications channel. Equalizers add additional loss or delay to the signals in inverse proportions to the channel characteristics. The signal response curve is then relatively "flat" and can be amplified to regain its original form. Also see distortion.

ER   Error Rate   The number of errors per unit of information in the test to establish the error rate.

ESS   (See Electronic Switching System)

F1F2   A type of modem which operates over a half-duplex line (2 wire) to produce two subchannels at two different frequencies for low-speed full-duplex operation. (See reverse channel.)

Facility   A transmission path between two or more locations without terminating or signaling equipment. The addition of terminating equipment would produce either a channel, a central office line, or a trunk. Various types of signaling would also be used depending on the application.

FDM   Frequency Division Multiplexing   A multiplexing technique where a data line bandwidth is divided into different frequency subchannels used to share a data line between several user terminals.

FDX   Full Duplex   The capability of transmission in both directions at one time. Also, a four-wire circuit.

Fe   Format effectuation   Characters of a code set used to format information to be sent for processing.

FEC   Forward Error Correcting   A coding technique used to correct errors in transmission at the receiver by use of redundancy included in the transmission block.

FEX   (See Foreign Exchange Service)

Fiber optics   Plastic or glass fibers which carry visible light containing information in cables.

Filter   Electronic circuitry which blocks some components of a signal while allowing other components to pass through uniformly. For example, a high-pass filter blocks all frequencies in a signal which are below a specified frequency called the "cut off."

Firmware   A set of software instructions set permanently or semi-permanently into a read-only memory.

Flag   A bit field or character of data used to set apart the data on either side of the flag. A delimiter.

Flexible disc   (Floppy disc) A magnetic storage unit constructed of thin plastic and intended to be expendable due to the recording heads riding on the recording surface.

FM   Frequency Modulation   A method of transmitting digital information on an analog line by changing the carrier frequency to different values.

Foreign Exchange Service   FEX   A service that connects a customer's telephone to a remote exchange. This service provides the equivalent of local telephone service to and from the distant exchange.

Format   A structure of a message or data such that specific controls or data can be identified by its position during processing.

Forward error correction   The technique which provides for the transmital of additional information with the original bit stream such that if an error is detected the correct information can be recreated at the receive end without a retransmission.

Frequency offset   Analog line frequency changes which is one of the impairments encountered on a communications line.

Frequency Shift Keying   FSK   A form of frequency modulation in which the carrier frequency is made to vary or change in frequency at the instant when there is a change in the state of the signal being transmitted, i.e., the carrier frequency on the line during a "one" or marking condition would be shifted to another predetermined frequency during a "zero" or spacing condition.

Frequency stacking   Another name for FDM which implies how the multiplexing is performed.

Front end   An auxilliary computer system which performs network control operations, relieving the host computer system to do data processing.

FSK   (See Frequency Shift Keying)

Full duplex   A four-wire circuit or a protocol which provides for transmission in both directions at the same time between the same two points.

Full/full duplex   A protocol which, when operating on a multidrop line, is capable of transmitting from the master location to one of the slave sites and, at the same time, the master location can receive a transmission from a different slave site on the same line.

Gain   The degree to which the amplitude of a signal is increased. The amount of amplification realized when a signal passes through an amplifier, repeater, or antenna. Normally measured in decibels.

GHz Gigahertz   An analog frequency unit equal to 10^{+9} hertz.

Gaussian noise   A noise whose amplitude is characterized by the Gaussian distribution, a well-known statistical distribution (white noise, ambient noise, hiss).

Geosynchronous   A communications satellite orbit at the correct distance from earth and at the correct speed to appear fixed in space as the earth rotates.

Group channel   A unit or organization on telephone carrier (multiplex) systems. A full-group is a channel equivalent to 12 voice grade channels (48 kHz). A half-group has the equivalent bandwidth of six voice grade channel (24 kHz). When not subdivided into voice facilities, group channels can be used for high-speed data communication.

Guard frequency   A single frequency carrier tone used to indicate the analog line is prepared to send data. Also the frequencies between subchannels in FDM systems used to guard against subchannel interference.

Half duplex   A communications line consisting of two wires or a protocol capable of transmitting only one direction at a time.

Hamming code   A FEC technique named for its inventor. Corrects for a single bit received in error.

Handshaking   Line termination interplay to establish a data communications path.

Harmonic   Frequencies which are multiples of some fundamental frequency.

Harmonic distortion   A data communications line impairment caused by erroneous frequency generations along the line.

HDLC   High Level Data Link Control   An ISO standard data communications line protocol.

Hertz   Internationally recognized unit of measure for electrical frequency. The number of cycles per second. Abbreviated Hz.

Hit on the line   General term used to describe errors caused by external interferences such as impulse noise caused by lightning or man-made interference.

House cables   Conductors within a building used to connect communications equipment to outside lines.

HRC   Horizontal Redundancy Checking   A validity checking technique used for data transmission block checks where redundant information is included with the information to be checked.

Hybrid   See balancing network.

Hz   Hertz   (Cycles per second) The unit of analog frequency measurement.

IDF   Intermediate Distribution Frame   An equipment unit used to connect communications equipments by use of connection blocks.

Impedance   The total opposition offered by a component or circuit to the flow of an alternating or varying current; a combination or resistance capacitance and inductance.

Impulse noise   A type of interference on communication lines characterized by high amplitude and short duration. This type of interference may be caused by lightning, electrical sparking action, or by the make-break action of switching devices, etc.

Insertion loss   Signal power loss due to connecting communications equipment units with dissimilar impedance values.

Integrity of data   The status of information after being processed by software.

Interference   Refers to unwanted occurrences on communications channels which are a result of natural or man-made noises and signals, not properly a part of the signals being transmitted.

Intermodulation distortion   An analog line impairment where two frequencies create an erroneous frequency which in turn distorts the data signal representation.

I/O   The process of moving information between the central processing unit and peripheral devices. Also may refer to the particular peripheral hardware used.

ITDM   Intelligent TDM   A multiplexer device which assigns time slots on demand rather than a fixed subchannel scanning basis. Also called a statistical TDM.

Jitter   Type of analog communication line distortion caused by the variation of a signal from its reference timing positions which can cause data transmission errors, particularly at high speeds. This variation can be amplitude, time, frequency, or phase.

Jumbo group   The highest FDM carrier system multiplexing level containing 3600 voice frequency (VF) or telephone channels (6 master groups).

Kbps   Kilo bits per second   A data rate equal to 10^{+3} bps.

Leased line   Private line   Dedicated line   A communications line for voice and/or data leased from a communications carrier on a monthly basis.

Line protocol   A control program used to perform data communications functions over network lines. Consists of both handshaking and line-control functions which move the data between transmit and receive locations.

Local loop   The access line from either a user terminal or a computer port to the first telephone office along the line path.

Logging   The act of recording something for future reference such as error events or transactions.

Long line   A communications line spanning a long distance relative to the local loop.

Loopback   Directing signals back toward the source at some point along a communications path.

Loop current   A teletypewriter to line interface and operating technique without modems.

LSI   Large Scale Integration   A classification of electronic device comprising many logic elements in one very small package (integrated circuit) to be used for data handling, storage, and processing.

LTS   Line Test Set   Analog line test unit .001 AMP.

mA   Milliampere   Electric current measurement unit.

Master group   An assembly of 10 supergroups occupying adjacent bands in the transmission spectrum for the purposes of simultaneous modulation and demodulation.

Mbps   Mega bps   A data rate equal to 10^{+6} bps.

MDF   Main Distribution Frame   An equipment unit used to connect communications equipment to lines, by use of connecting blocks.

MHz   Megahertz   A unit of analog frequency equal to 10^{+6} hertz.

Message switching   Routing messages between three or more locations by either store-and-forward techniques in a computer, or circuit switching as in a dial telephone system.

MG Master Group   An FDM carrier multiplexing level containing 600 voice frequency channels.

Microcode   A set of software instructions which execute a macro instruction.

Microcomputer   A microprocessor with memory, I/O, and other support logic. It may or may not contain a power supply. The term is sometimes used interchangeably with microprocessor.

Microprocessor   A single or multiple chip set which makes up a CPU. Usually has a 4- or 8-bit word length. This text will use 8-bit words only.

Microwave   A radio carrier system using frequencies whose wave lengths are very short.

Midicomputer   Sometimes called a super mini. Has a 24- or 32-bit word size.

MIL-188   A military standard interface equivalent to RS232 between a modem and line controller.

Milliwatt   A power unit of measurement equal to 10^{-3} watts.

Minicomputer   A computer with a 16-bit word length.

Modem   (Data Set) An acronym taken from functions the unit performs by modulating and demodulating the digital information from a terminal or computer port into an analog carrier signal to be sent over an analog line.

Modulator   The sending function of a modem.

Monitor   A program or device used to observe an operation without interferring with the operation.

Multiplexed line   A data communications line equipped with multiplexers at the data line level.

Multipoint line   A communications line having several subsidiary controllers share time on the line under control of a central site.

Multiterminal controller   A terminal controller having more than one terminal device connected to it for subsequent access to the communication line.

Noise   A communications line impairment which is inherent in the line design or induced by transient bursts of energy.

Normal contacts   The circuit contacts of an access jack which are normally closed when a plug is not inserted into the jack and are interrupted by plug insertion.

On   line   A direct connection between a remote terminal and a central processing site.

Open   wire   Communications lines not insulated and formed into cables, but mounted on aerial cross arms on utilily poles.

OS   Operating System   The program which schedules tasks and allocates resources (memory, I/O, peripherals, etc.) in a computer.

OTC   Operating Telephone Company   The telephone company holding the local franchise to service a defined geographic area.

PAD   Packet Assembler/Disassembler   Equipment providing packet assembly and disassembly facilities.

Packet assembly unit   A user facility which permits non-packet-mode terminals to exchange data in the packet mode.

Packet disassembly unit   A user facility which enables packets destined for delivery to a non-packet-mode terminal to be delivered in the appropriate form, e.g., in character form at the applicable rate.

Packet mode terminal   A data terminal equipment which can control and format packets and transmit and receive packets.

Packet switched data transmission service   A service involving the transmission, and if necessary, the assembly and disassembly of data in the form of packets.

Packet switching   The transfer of data by means of addressed packets whereby a channel is only occupied for the duration of transmission of the packet. The channel is then available for the transfer of other packets. In contrast with circuit switching, the data network determines the routing during, rather than prior to, the transfer of a packet.

Parity error   An error which occurs in a particular entity of data where an extra or redundant quantity of bits is sent with the data based on a specific calculation made at the transmit end. The same calculation is performed at the receive end. If the results of both calculations do not agree then a parity error has occurred.

Pass band filters   Filters used in modem design to allow only the frequencies within the communications channel to pass while rejecting all frequencies outside the pass band.

Patching jacks   Series-access devices used to patch around faulty equipment using spare units.

PC   Phase Corrector   A function of synchronous modems which adjusts the local data clocking signal to match the incoming receive data, being sent by the remote clocking signal.

Peripheral device   A digital device which is connected to a computer to perform a unique function such as a disc unit used for data storage.

Phase jitter   An analog line impairment caused by power and communications equipment along the line, shifting the signal phase relationship back and forth.

PM   Phase Modulation   A method of combining digital type information on to a line-carrying signal by variation of the phase relationship of the signal.

Point to point   A communications line connected directly from one point to one other point as opposed to multipoint lines.

Polling   A control message sent from a master site to a slave site which serves as an invitation to transmit data to the master site.

Primary center   A class 3 telephone switching office, at the next level above toll center.

Privacy   The techniques used for limiting and/or preventing access to specific system information from otherwise authorized system users.

Propagation delay   The time necessary for a signal to travel from one point on the circuit to another.

Protocol   A formal set of conventions governing the format and control of inputs and outputs between the two communicating processes. Includes handshaking and line discipline.

Pulse modulation   The modulation of the characteristics of a series of pulses in one of several ways to represent the information-bearing signal. Typical methods involve modifying the amplitude (PAM), width or duration (PDM), or position (PPM). The most common pulse modulation technique in telephone work is pulse code modulation (PCM). In PCM, the information signals are sampled at regular intervals and a series of pulses in coded form are transmitted, representing the amplitude of the information signal at that time.

Quadrature distortion   Analog signal distortion frequently found in phase modulation modems.

Queuing   Operating a waiting line by some priority scheme such as first-come, first-served.

Reactance   Frequency sensitive communications line impairment causing loss of power and phase shifting.

Real time   The entry of information into a network from a terminal and immediate processing of the task.

Recovery   The necessary actions required to bring a system to a predefined level of operation after a degradation or failure.

Regional center   A class 1 telephone switching office, the top level in the DDD system.

Response time   The time measured from the depression of the "enter" key at a terminal, to the display of the first character of the response at that terminal site.

Reverse channel   An optional feature provided on some modems which provides simultaneous communication from the receiver to the transmitter on a two-wire channel. It may be used for circuit assurance, circuit breaking, and facilitating certain forms of error control and network diagnostics. Also called backward channel.

ROM   Read Only Memory   A nonvolatile memory storage device used to store fixed programs.

RTS   Request to Send   An RS232 control line between a modem and user digital equipment which initiates the data transmission sequence on a communications line.

Satellite microwave radio   Microwave or beam radio system using geosynchronously orbiting communications satellites.

Selector channel   A channel designed to operate with only one I/O device at a time. Once the I/O device is selected, a complete record is transferred one byte at a time. Contrast with block multiplexer channel.

SDLC   Synchronous Data Link Control   An IBM data communications message protocol.

Sectional center   A class 2 telephone switching office at the next level above a primary center.

Security   The techniques used for limiting and/or preventing physical access to information. May involve use of encryption techniques.

Super group   An FDM carrier multiplexing level containing 60 voice frequency channels.

Slicing level   A voltage or current level of a digital signal where a one or zero bit can be determined or not.

Slot   A unit of time in a TDM frame where a subchannel bit or character is carried to the other end of the circuit and extracted by the receiving TDM unit.

S/N   Signal-to-Noise Ratio   The relative power levels of a communications signal and noise on a data line, expressed in decibels.

SRC   Spiral Redundancy Checking   A validity-checking technique for transmission blocks where the redundant information sent with the block for receiver checking is accumulated in a spiral bit position fashion.

Store-and-Forward   A data communications technique which accepts messages or transactions, stores them until they are completely in the memory system, and then forwards them on to the next location as addressed in the message or transaction header.

Streaming   A condition of a modem when it is sending a carrier signal on a multidrop communication line when it has not been polled.

Supergroup   The assembly of five 12-channel groups occupying adjacent bands in the spectrum for the purpose of simultaneous modulation and demodulation. May be used as 60 voice grade channels, or five wideband channels, or combinations of both.

SYNC   (SYN) A bit or character used to synchronize a time frame in a TDM. Also a synchronizing sequence used by synchronous modems to perform bit synchronization and by the line controller for character synchronization.

Synchronous modem   A line termination unit which utilizes a clocking signal to perform bit synchronization with the incoming data.

Tariff   The published volume of rates, rules, and regulations concerning specific equipment and services provided by a communications common carrier.

TC   Telecommunications or Technical Control.

TDM   (See Time Division Multiplexing)

Telemetry   Transmission and collection of data obtained by sensing conditions in a real-time environment.

Text   That part of a message or transaction between the control information of the header and the control information of the trace section or tail that constitutes the information to be processed or delivered to the addressed location.

Thermal noise   A type of electromagnetic noise produced in conductors or in electronic circuitry which is proportional to temperature. Also see Gaussian noise.

Time Division Multiplexing   TDM   A technique for combining several channels into one facility or transmission path in which each channel is allotted a specific position in the signal stream based upon time. Thus, the information on each input channels is inter-leaved at higher speed on the main or multiplexed channel. At the receiving end, the signals are separated to reconstruct the individual input channels. The number of channels obtained in this manner is dependent on the speed and bandwidth of the channels to be multiplexed and the speed of the high-speed channel.

Time sharing   A processing technique where multiple users at their own remote terminals have the ability to share the computer resources at the same time.

Toll center   A class 2 telephone switching office at the next level up from the end or serving office named for the call billing apparatus found there.

T/P   Transaction Processing   A processing technique using on-line control programs and a remote terminal network so that inquiries and applications against a prestored data base can be performed at any processing site where the data is stored. Routing is performed based on the content of the message which contains the information to be processed.

Trailer or trace block   Control information which is transmitted after the body or text of a message or transaction. It is used for tracing error events, timing the communications through the network, and recovering misplaced blocks or transactions after system failures.

Turn-around time   The time required for a modem to reverse direction of transmission on a half-duplex line.

Uncontrolled terminal   A user terminal that is on line all the time and does not contain line control logic for polling and calling.

Validity checking   The techniques used to check the accuracy of data after transmission on data lines.

Validity of data   The status of information after being processed by a hardware component or communications equipment.

VF   Voice Frequency   A 4.2KHz/bandwidth telephone channel designed to carry the human voice from one telephone set to another.

VHF   Very High Frequency   A radio carrier frequency band used in emergency situations for telephone and data communications.

VRC   Vertical Redundancy Checking   A method of character parity checking.

WATS   Wide Area Telephone Service   A flat rate or measured bulk rate long distance telephone service provided on an incoming or outgoing basis. WATS permits a customer, by use of an access line, to make telephone calls to any dialable telephone number in a specific zone for a flat or bulk monthly rate. INWATS permits reception of calls from specific zones over an access line in like manner. The United States has been divided into five zones of increasingly greater coverage depending on the location of the customer.

White noise   See Gaussian noise and thermal noise.

Wideband   Data speeds requiring the equivalent of more than one VF channel for operation. Same as broadband.

Word   One or more contiguous bytes which, in most cases, can identify a class of computer.

INDEX